Poisonous People

Poisonous People

How to Resist Them and Improve Your Life

Leanne ten Brinke, PhD
with Seth Schulman

SIMON & SCHUSTER

London · New York · Amsterdam/Antwerp · Sydney/Melbourne · Toronto · New Delhi

First published in the United States by Simon & Schuster, LLC, 2026

First published in Great Britain by Simon & Schuster UK Ltd, 2026

Copyright © Leanne Marie ten Brinke, 2026

The right of Leanne Marie ten Brinke to be identified as the author of this work has been asserted in accordance with the Copyright, Designs and Patents Act, 1988.

1 3 5 7 9 10 8 6 4 2

Simon & Schuster UK Ltd
1st Floor
222 Gray's Inn Road
London WC1X 8HB

For more than 100 years, Simon & Schuster has championed authors and the stories they create. By respecting the copyright of an author's intellectual property, you enable Simon & Schuster and the author to continue publishing exceptional books for years to come. We thank you for supporting the author's copyright by purchasing an authorised edition of this book.

No amount of this book may be reproduced or stored in any format, nor may it be uploaded to any website, database, language-learning model, or other repository, retrieval, or artificial intelligence system without express permission. All rights reserved. Enquiries may be directed to Simon & Schuster, 222 Gray's Inn Road, London WC1X 8HB or RightsMailbox@simonandschuster.co.uk

Simon & Schuster strongly believes in freedom of expression and stands against censorship in all its forms. For more information, visit BooksBelong.com.

www.simonandschuster.co.uk
www.simonandschuster.com.au
www.simonandschuster.co.in

Simon & Schuster Australia, Sydney
Simon & Schuster India, New Delhi

The authorised representative in the EEA is Simon & Schuster Netherlands BV, Herculesplein 96, 3584 AA Utrecht, Netherlands. info@simonandschuster.nl

The author and publishers have made all reasonable efforts to contact copyright-holders for permission, and apologise for any omissions or errors in the form of credits given. Corrections may be made to future printings.

A CIP catalogue record for this book is available from the British Library

Hardback ISBN: 978-1-3985-3560-2
Trade Paperback ISBN: 978-1-3985-3561-9
eBook ISBN: 978-1-3985-3562-6

Interior design by Ruth Lee-Mui

Printed and Bound in the UK using 100% Renewable Electricity at CPI Group (UK) Ltd

A signed copy, for Dan.

Contents

Reader's Note   ix

    Introduction   1
1. Defining Dark Personalities   17
2. The Cost of a Malevolent Few   43
3. How the Poison Spreads   64
4. Spotting a Dark Personality in Ten Seconds or Less   85
5. Temporarily Terrible   110
6. Should I Stay or Should I Go?   130
7. Seven Rules for Managing Poisonous People   154
8. I'm the Problem, It's Me   179
    Epilogue: The Ultimate Arms Race   206

Acknowledgments   213
Notes   217
Index   267

Reader's Note

In this book, I recount the experiences of people who suffered harm as a result of interactions with dark personalities. For privacy and legal reasons, I've changed the names of the people involved as well as any identifying details. All stories, however, are real and based on phone and video interviews I conducted in 2023 and 2024.

Introduction

In 1959, a young Canadian named Clive Michael Boutilier was arrested in New York City for the alleged crime of sodomy with a seventeen-year-old. Boutilier had come to live in the United States four years earlier at the age of twenty-one. Although much about his life remains obscure, his motives for emigrating might have been economic: he grew up on a farm in Nova Scotia, and the living was apparently hard enough that he had to drop out of school as a teenager to provide for his family. Family dynamics also might have played a role. Boutilier's parents had divorced, and his mother and stepfather were living in the United States, as were other relatives. Whatever the case, Boutilier appears to have lived a quiet life following his arrival. He reportedly settled in Brooklyn with his male partner, working steadily as a maintenance man, attending church, and frequenting bowling alleys.[1]

The sodomy charges were reduced and eventually dropped, but they would change Boutilier's life. A few years later, in 1963, when he applied to become a US citizen, the subject of his prior arrest arose during an interview with an immigration official. An investigator with the Immigration and Naturalization Service (INS) followed up, interrogating Boutilier about the sexual encounter leading to his arrest as well as his broader sexual history. In an affidavit, Boutilier reported having engaged in sexual acts with both men and women starting at age fourteen, and he acknowledged having had an ongoing sexual relationship with a man he lived with in Brooklyn.

Based on this information, the government made what most Americans today would consider an outrageous decision. An agency called the Public Health Service formally proclaimed Boutilier a "psychopathic personality, sexual deviate," and the INS denied his citizenship request and began the process of deporting him. The agency relied on a law called the Immigration and Nationality Act of 1952, which made possession of a "psychopathic personality" a criterion for preventing someone's immigration into the United States. In its interpretation of the law, the INS determined that having had gay sex sufficed to qualify someone as a "psychopathic personality."

Boutilier appealed this decision all the way to the United States Supreme Court, but without success. In its 1967 decision *Boutilier v. Immigration and Naturalization Service*, the court upheld a lower court's decision by a 6–3 majority, affirming that those who engaged in gay sex qualified as psychopaths and could be deported for this reason.[2] Tragically, not long before the ruling, Boutilier was struck by a car and left with lasting brain damage, an incident that his family regarded as a suicide attempt. He was deported back to Canada in 1968. Family members cared for him for a while, and then he went to a group home, where he died in 2003.[3]

Although the court's majority proved unwilling to help Boutilier, one justice, William O. Douglas, did write a dissenting opinion, a seemingly noteworthy stance at a time when most of America was hostile toward gay people. Regarded as one of the most liberal jurists ever to sit on the high court, Douglas was a strong supporter of civil liberties, the right to privacy, free expression, and the environment, among other noble causes.[4] As the jurist Ronald Dworkin once wrote, Douglas "was probably more often on the right side than anyone else has been. His record in civil rights cases of all different sorts was particularly admirable."[5] Given this context, you might assume that Douglas's opinion in the Boutilier case would have reflected a concern for minority groups and stigmatized individuals. In fact, his disagreement was more semantic than compassionate. Douglas's position was that the concept of "psychopathic personality" was too opaque to justify a serious punishment like deportation. "The term 'psychopathic personality' is a treacherous one like 'communist' or in an earlier day, 'Bolshevik,'" he wrote. "A label of this kind, when freely used, may mean only an unpopular person. It is much too vague by constitutional standards for the imposition of penalties or punishment."[6]

The science of psychopathy has progressed a great deal since Douglas wrote these words. Researchers have learned more about what psychopathy is and isn't, what causes it, how it impacts people, how to test for it, and how best to treat it.* They understand better how the noxious mix of selfishness, callousness, deception, and recklessness associated with psychopathy intersects with other, so-called dark traits such as narcissism, Machiavellianism, and sadism. The science continues to evolve, and definitions of psychopathic personality traits remain notoriously complex. But based on how researchers presently think about and define these traits, there is widespread agreement that Justice Douglas was wrong: "psychopathic personality" isn't just a vague and insulting label, a stand-in

---

*Psychologists did have a clinical definition of psychopathy back in Douglas's day. The court's majority in *Boutilier* alluded to it, arguing that Congress used the phrase "psychopathic personality" as a "term of art" and not "in the clinical sense" when it wrote the Immigration and Nationality Act of 1952.

for "unpopular person." Psychopathy is real and measurable. And as psychological scientists today will also tell you, having gay sex is not a criterion for it.

There's a profound irony here, one that as a social and personality psychologist I was surprised to uncover. While there is no evidence that Boutilier would have met modern definitions of psychopathy, Justice Douglas very well could have. As we all know, people with lofty ideals don't always live up to them, and those who achieve professional greatness can behave monstrously toward those who know them best. Justice Douglas is a case in point. He was a serial philanderer who became the first justice ever to get divorced while on the bench. He was accused of abusing his wives, and he was cold and hostile toward his kids. They remembered him as "scary," and according to his daughter, he "would never apologize for anything, even if it was quite obvious that he was wrong."[7] He had trouble getting along with his peers, as evidenced by his long-running feud with Justice Felix Frankfurter.[8] And he was by many accounts a horrible person to work for, having once apparently proclaimed, "Law clerks are the lowest form of human life."[9]

Let's linger a bit on that last comment. Although some who worked for Justice Douglas have tried to rehabilitate his image, he was known among his peers for abusing his clerks. As former clerks and other witnesses remembered, he overworked his people. Berated them. Gave them the silent treatment. Belittled them.[10]

Sometimes, he went even further. At one point during the court's 1968 term, Douglas asked his young law clerk Peter Kay Westen to draft a memo about a matter pending before him that involved Eldridge Cleaver, the political activist and Black Panther member. Westen pored over previous opinions Douglas had issued on relevant topics before arriving at a recommendation on how Douglas should rule.[11]

One Friday after he had submitted the memo to his boss, a

buzzer on his desk went off, indicating that Douglas wanted to see him in his chambers. When Westen appeared, Douglas laid into him, denouncing the memo's argument as ridiculous and exclaiming, "Where did you go to law school, in the gutter?"[12]

In fact, Westen had gotten his degree at the University of California, Berkeley, where he'd been a top student.[13] And before that, he'd graduated from Harvard.

But Douglas wasn't content to yell at Westen and imply that he was stupid. He fired Westen on the spot. In an emotionless voice, he said, "By the way, I've got to leave for a speech and on Monday there will be a woman from the Labor Department in here. She will be my new law clerk, and I'd like you to prepare for her to take over."

Westen had heard that Douglas sometimes fired his law clerks only to rehire them. So Westen couldn't help but wonder whether Douglas really was serious about firing him. Douglas's secretary told him that while the justice was "eccentric" and fond of bullying, she'd "never seen anything quite like this."[14] Her assessment posed an especially stressful predicament for Westen. He was getting married that very weekend. The reception was taking place at the Supreme Court, with Douglas as an invited guest. If Westen was really being fired, could his wedding reception still take place as planned? And would Douglas show up? Would he make a scene?

Douglas's secretary advised Westen to proceed with the reception and see what happened. As it turned out, Douglas did show up, with his wife in tow. Douglas behaved as if nothing unusual had occurred, smiling and offering well-wishes. He played the role of the supportive boss, even though he was anything but. Douglas had *known* that Westen was getting married, and yet he'd deliberately led him to believe that he was being fired—which, it turned out, he wasn't. It's bad enough to bully a young employee day in and day out. But to fake-fire them just before their nuptials, letting them stress about whether the ouster was real on what was supposed to be the happiest day of their life? Who *does* that?

The Darkness in Our Midst

When we think of people with psychopathy, the most extreme and scary cases often come to mind: cult leaders like Charles Manson or serial killers like Aileen Wuornos, who murdered seven people in Florida during the late 1980s and early 1990s.[15] We don't stop to consider that a more populous group of lesser-but-still-dark personalities might walk among us, serving as our bosses, our romantic partners, our neighbors, our friends—even our Supreme Court justices.

Most people with dark traits aren't serial killers or rapists. These traits can crop up in the neighbor who delights in harassing us for no reason. In the colleague who boasts incessantly or sabotages us behind our back so that *they* can look good. In the romantic partner who cheats on us while also trying to control us and keep us trapped and subservient. In the relative who behaves recklessly and never takes responsibility for their actions. We might call these individuals manipulative, narcissistic, impulsive, antisocial, callous, or even sadistic, but that's not all they are. They're also a bit psychopathic. That's because psychologists define psychopathy to encompass a wide constellation of unsavory traits, making it an especially convenient concept for understanding the darker side of human nature.

I've been studying dark personalities—and, in particular, psychopathy—since the mid-2000s. As I discovered, dark personalities are not an incidental quirk of the human experience but rather an enduring aspect of it. Traits such as callousness, manipulativeness, impulsivity, and antisociality have been around as long as humans have, and they've also existed across cultures. We find antagonistic characters in the Old Testament and Greek mythology. There are words for "psychopath" in Inuit and among the Yoruba in Nigeria.[16] Psychopathic traits even show up in animals, including chimpanzees and house cats.[17]

My scientific research focused at first on human psychopaths who committed violent crimes. I wrote papers on how people with clinical levels of psychopathy who were locked up for sexual offenses were more likely to win release than those with fewer such traits, despite the good chance they'd reoffend.[18] I also spent countless hours reading criminal case files to identify the special characteristics of sexual homicides committed by people with psychopathic traits. The work was fascinating, all-consuming—and a genuine bummer. There was too much pain and suffering for me to bear, and I couldn't fathom spending the rest of my career inside prisons, juvenile detention centers, and probation offices.

I decided to take my scholarship in a different direction, exploring the impact of psychopathic traits in other, less depressing contexts. Pursuing postdoctoral work at the University of California, Berkeley's Haas School of Business, I began to investigate how psychopathy affects the ways people negotiate, invest, and lead in the workplace. One study found that there are about three times as many people with psychopathy per capita in senior management positions than in the general population.[19] As my research revealed, domination through fear was the psychopathic leader's preferred method of influence.[20] These aggressive, predatory individuals had a win-at-all-costs mentality, and while that could lead to personal success, it also caused tremendous pain for those around them.

In most cases, I didn't know whether these leaders were psychopathic as defined by the clinical tools often used in criminal justice settings. But in my observation of these leaders and their treatment of employees, it was clear that they possessed high levels of psychopathic traits and that their behavior brought an unending train of misery. In fact, everything that forensic psychologists had learned from studying psychopathy in criminal contexts seemed to translate to this setting. Business leaders with psychopathic traits tormented others around them, in many cases prompting them to leave.[21] But their impact was broader than this. They poisoned the culture of their workplaces, eroding ethical standards and sowing fear and mistrust. For a variety of reasons, they caused their colleagues to mimic their behavior and callously seek to dominate others as well.[22]

These leaders got away with it, too. Masters of manipulation, they lied prodigiously and could appear charming to their unsuspecting victims. They came across as confident, charismatic, and driven—the very kind of individuals we perceive as strong leaders.[23]

Having left the world of orange prison jumpsuits for one of $3,000 designer suits, I reflected on my research in both spheres and arrived at an intriguing insight: *people with psychopathic traits have a much greater and more negative impact than we think.* Although clinical psychopaths account for a tiny portion of the population—around 1 percent—they're responsible by some estimates for more than half of all serious crime.[24] Even at subclinical levels, people with more psychopathic traits cheat and abuse their spouses more than those with fewer of these traits, leaving a trail of depression and trauma in their wake.[25] Further, data confirms what Peter Westen experienced in Justice Douglas's chambers: in workplaces, they're more likely to abuse employees, leading to high levels of staff turnover.[26]

We also find a kind of proto-psychopathy in kids, namely those who score highly in what we call "callous-unemotional" (CU) traits. Children with these traits are more violent, impulsive, and insensitive than their peers.[27] I'm not talking about your garden variety bad behavior here. Youths with CU traits bully others, lead gangs, and engage in other antisocial behavior more frequently than kids without these traits.[28]

When we expand our view of psychopathy to include the larger slice of the population—perhaps 10 to 20 percent—who would score high on some traits related to psychopathy but not enough to be considered a "psychopath" by clinical standards, we find these people *everywhere*.[29] We all know someone who, although not a headline-making serial killer, consistently misbehaves. We see disgraced businessmen and politicians on television nightly. Closer to home, we might know people who habitually steal from their workplace or sexually harass subordinates. Some are worse than others, but the devastation they cause is enormous. Although most people don't realize it, psychopathic traits are a toxic influence on society, accounting for a disproportionate share of the pain and suffering we experience both individually and collectively.

The Good News About Bad Actors

This book analyzes that toxicity and its consequences, bringing it into clear view through data and stories. It does so not to scare or depress you, but to inspire you and leave you more hopeful. My research into psychopathy, which I've since extended to include both politicians and undergraduate students, has left me feeling *more* empowered, not less. If a tiny minority of people are very dark personalities and a bigger slice are shades of gray, that means the vast majority of us—80 or 90 percent—are not.[30] In our troubled era, with wars erupting, civil unrest simmering, and the planet warming, it might seem like human nature has become wholly degraded. My research and that of others in my field suggests it hasn't. A relatively small number of people are bringing the rest of us down.

For millennia, philosophers have scrutinized human nature, asking whether people are fundamentally good or evil. Pessimists—and there are plenty of them—assure us that human nature is bad. The philosopher Thomas Hobbes argued as much in his 1651 book

Leviathan, observing that humans left to their own devices would lead lives that were "nasty, brutish, and short."[31] He was far from the first to see humanity this way. The Chinese philosopher Xunzi wrote an essay bluntly entitled "Human Nature Is Bad" in the third century BCE. In Xunzi's estimation, humans "are born with feelings of hate and dislike. If they follow along with these, then cruelty and villainy will arise, and loyalty and trustworthiness will perish therein."[32] That's dark, even by forensic psychologist standards.

Others have argued for a sunnier view of human nature.[33] The Chinese philosopher Mencius held that we possess positive impulses, such as a desire for fairness and feelings of compassion for the suffering. The French philosopher Jean-Jacques Rousseau argued similarly that human nature is essentially good and that people can live in groups—peacefully and happily—without the government-imposed rules that Hobbes felt were necessary.

Modern science validates this latter view. Research has suggested that we underestimate people's tendency to behave ethically. In one series of studies, researchers gave participants five dollars to spend. If participants opted to hand that money over to an anonymous partner, the researchers would quadruple it to twenty dollars. Their partner then had a choice: they could return ten dollars—double the initial amount—to the participant or keep it all for themselves. Participants estimated that fewer than half of the anonymous recipients would return the money of their own accord. In fact, almost 80 percent did.[34] It's tempting to expect the worst when dealing with strangers. But we're wrong to be so distrustful.

As evolutionary psychologists have observed, altruistic, cooperative behaviors are embedded in us and serve to support humans' pronounced sociability.[35] We help others even when it costs us because we want to protect our kin, we hope for something in return, we want to maintain a positive reputation, or we seek to avoid punishment.[36] We learn to be kind by observing others doing the same, and we possess the building blocks of morality—such as an altruistic bent or an ability to empathize with others—from a very young age. As studies have found, children at the age of two already begin to help others whom they perceive to be in pain.[37] Even infants who can't yet speak seem sensitive to the kindness of others and gravitate toward these people.[38]

All of us become aggressive at times, tell lies, and behave in ways that hurt others. In moments of stress or when we've had too much to drink, we might lash out. But most of us—the vast majority—don't *usually* act like this. When we do, we apologize, make amends, and try to improve. The more we probe the personalities of those who consistently behave maliciously, and the more we recognize that these people comprise a minority in society, the better we can feel about humanity in general. Only a relative few of us seem to be missing the cognitive and emotional building blocks of morality.

Seeing Poisonous People Clearly

This sunnier view of human nature supported by psychopathy research has important implications. If only a few people cause most of the harm, we have an edge in trying to reduce that damage. The answer isn't so simple as changing the personalities of these malevolent few. As research has suggested, it's extremely difficult to rehabilitate people with psychopathy.[39] But even if we can't imagine a future without dark personalities, studying these individuals yields insights and practical techniques for *containing* their antisociality and preventing them from wreaking havoc.

Mobilizing the latest science about people with psychopathic traits, we can learn to spot poisonous people and take evasive action before they target us. If we're already in relationships with them, we can learn how to exit them safely, or if we choose to stay, we can learn how to manage our interactions to minimize the damage we sustain. If we recognize certain dark traits in ourselves, we can learn to moderate them to protect other people and improve our own well-being. And we can learn how to prevent dark personalities from occupying positions of authority in organizations and society as a whole.

We have more power to protect ourselves than we think. One bad apple can indeed ruin the barrel, as the saying goes, but we shouldn't lay the blame solely at the feet of these people. We give dark personalities power—over ourselves, our companies, our governments—because they behave as we think good leaders should. We admire "strong" leaders—confident, charismatic, competitive personalities who enjoy wielding power and appear willing and able to do what's necessary to "win."[40]

Although these values might seem innocuous, they leave us vulnerable to selecting people with dark traits to lead. Once they assume power, they ruin life for the rest of us, enshrining brutality, callousness, and a winner-take-all mentality as norms. They create chaos and then convince us that only they can fix it. Containing this harm will require more than simply locking up all the mass murderers, serial rapists, and corporate schemers. It will mean shifting our own values, making different choices when we vote, select a boss, choose a romantic partner, or follow someone on social media.

Departing from our traditional beliefs about powerful people might feel uncomfortable. In times of fear and uncertainty, when nothing feels safe and everyone seems out to get us, we're more inclined to gravitate toward leaders who appear strong.[41] But if we can break our infatuation with dark personalities, the payoff will be huge. Based on everything I've learned as a psychological scientist, I believe we can significantly reduce the amount of harm and suffering in our own lives and in society by identifying the darkness among us and learning to perceive them differently. Perhaps we don't need big, structural changes to reduce crime and improve our workplaces. We just need to elect, follow, respect, and listen to people who actually care about others.

About This Book

In the pages that follow, I'll reveal surprising truths about poisonous people and the damage they do, how they maneuver their way into powerful positions, and, most important, what can be done about it. The first part of this book illuminates the current scientific understanding of dark personalities, the damage they cause, and how they manage to cause so much harm. In chapter 1, I delve into how scientists think about malevolent traits. Most people think of psychopathy as a caricature of evil—a person who is so different from us that they might as well be a different species. In reality, individuals with dark traits just have more extreme versions of qualities that we might find in ourselves.

That's not to say these less extreme versions aren't harmful—as we'll see in chapter 2, they are, much more so than we think. Dark traits don't always seem that bad at a glance. Some of them—low emotionality, aggression, and fearlessness, for instance—even appear desirable, especially in competitive environments such as business or the military. I used to assume that antagonistic traits, although harmful to some, could give leaders a valuable edge. But then I did the research. My conclusion: any success that dark personalities achieve is probably selfish and short-lived, and easily eclipsed by the extraordinary financial, emotional, and moral damage they inflict on others. The wake of destruction one person can leave behind can be truly astounding.

An important question—addressed in chapter 3—is how dark traits cause so much harm. As I'll suggest, there are three important pathways by which bad apples can spoil the barrel. Poisonous people wield the dark arts of deception. They also target individuals who are most likely to submit to them. Finally, they cause damage because of their extraordinary ability to influence the rest of us to misbehave.

As dire as all of this sounds, the compassionate and trustworthy majority can fight back. In the second part of this book, I'll give you powerful, science-based tools for mitigating the harm poisonous people do in a range of everyday contexts. I'll start in chapter 4 by showing you how to identify a dark personality before you end up marrying, working for, befriending, or voting for one. I'll describe in detail how to spot them from a "thin slice" of their behavior—just a few seconds of observation.

In addition to looking out for poisonous people, we must stay alert to situations that bring antisocial behavior to the fore—a topic I cover in chapter 5. Those of us without strong psychopathic traits can still be deceptive, callous, or impulsive under the right (or wrong) conditions. An awareness of the role played by our environment cautions us against rushing to label others around us as dark personalities: the context might be causing them to act poorly, not their ingrained personality. It also helps us look out for dicey situations and respond effectively when we encounter them. I'll show you how to prevent others and ourselves from behaving badly, and I'll offer advice for getting out of rotten situations unscathed.

If you're already in a relationship with a poisonous person, you might wonder whether you should stay in hopes that your partner, boss, or friend will change, or whether it's better to cut your losses. As I'll reveal in chapter 6, people with dark traits might be able to modify some specific behaviors through therapy and hard work, but they're highly unlikely to change who they are at their core. A critical factor in determining whether they can adjust their behavior is their motivation to try, so you'll want to take that into account when making your decision. I'll lead you through a set of hard truths that can help you weigh the benefits of the relationship against the effort required to work with these individuals and the risk that they won't change.

If you decide to stay, or if you find yourself in a personal or professional situation where ending a relationship isn't an option, you can learn to handle poisonous people so that they inflict less damage. Mustering research and the experiences of people who found ways to cope with the dark personality in their life, chapter 7 offers a playbook you can refer to in everyday situations.

All of us land somewhere on the psychopathy continuum, and we can use this insight to identify opportunities for improvement. Drawing on metrics that psychologists use to quantify psychopathic traits, chapter 8 gives you a behavioral checklist you can consult to spot malevolent traits of your own. I'll suggest some simple behavior shifts you can adopt to smooth out these traits. Further, I'll issue a challenge: to make it our personal mission to rein in poisonous people in the wider world. If influence is power, we can make the world more harmonious by deciding to whom we should give our time, attention, and loyalty. We must reevaluate what we really need in our partners, coworkers, and leaders as well as the best way to pick them. Finally, we can limit darkness in the world by deciding to extend our empathy and compassion even to people with psychopathy. Although they mistreat others, they can benefit greatly from feeling understood, observing kindness, and being rewarded for behaving better.

I'll end the book with an epilogue that takes a broader view, explaining why we must get serious about containing dark personalities. The benevolent majority is in an epic arms race with those who harbor psychopathic traits. We can learn to detect and avoid these individuals, but our advantage will prove temporary: over the long term, dark personalities will evolve methods of skirting our strategies and exerting their dominance. In ways that I'll explain, this survival-of-the-fittest process leaves society vulnerable. To future-proof society, we must strive not only to prevail in the arms race but to end it entirely. Embracing certain strategies described in this book at scale might allow us to do precisely that.

The world today feels dark—and like it's getting darker. But we know more about poisonous people than ever, and we have more tools that we can use to neutralize their toxicity. If we learn to identify psychopathic personalities, steer clear of them when necessary, and empathize with them when possible, we can start to reduce conflict and chaos, creating a future that is kinder, more trusting, and more prosperous.

1

Defining Dark Personalities

Some of us discover our life's work at an early age. Others follow a more circuitous path. Tricia Hunter falls into this second group. A biology major in college, she planned to get an advanced degree and become a researcher but was turned off by the prospect of conducting animal experiments. By chance, a teaching assistant at her university told her of her plans to go to pharmacy school. Tricia had never thought about becoming a pharmacist, but the idea of helping people in a healthcare setting appealed to her. She applied and was thrilled to be admitted.

Tricia's program was stressful, but she studied hard and did well. Working part-time in pharmacies to earn extra money as a student, she enjoyed her experiences building personal relationships with customers. As I sensed when interviewing her, she was well suited to pharmacy work. She was not only intelligent but empathetic and diligent, the kind of person who would triple-check her work because she cared deeply about patients and their safety.

Upon graduating, Tricia landed a well-paying job in a Midwestern city working as a pharmacist for a large national chain. Her job was to float around and fill in for days or weeks at a time at stores that needed extra staff. It wasn't ideal since she didn't get a chance to put down professional roots and build specialized skills, but she was willing to pay her dues. After about three years, she heard that a permanent position had become available at a nearby pharmacy that catered to nursing homes. Tricia was nervous: serving this population would require her to learn a whole new system for processing prescriptions. But she was also excited. Since the pharmacy wasn't open to the public, the work would be more focused and predictable than at a retail pharmacy. Her job would also be more stable, since there would always be strong demand for prescriptions from area nursing homes.

At first, her new job seemed great. The location's manager, Kelly, appeared to be effervescent, energetic, and friendly. The technician and other pharmacist who rounded out the team were welcoming, too. But within the first week or so, Tricia noticed some strange behavior. Her two other colleagues were talkative and at ease when Kelly wasn't around, but they clammed up in her presence, becoming "meek little mice," as Tricia put it. Kelly was pretty and blond and took great care with her appearance—she always came to work with perfect hair and makeup. But she had an intensity about her—a tightness in her jaw, a look in her eye—that jarred Tricia. "I'm usually pretty good at reading the room and getting along with lots of different people, but I couldn't really read her."

It soon became clear that Kelly wasn't the nice, friendly person she first seemed to be. She verbally abused her team members, yelling at them for minor mistakes, calling them names, and ridiculing their perceived shortcomings. She behaved normally for a time and then flew into a rage without warning. Everything Tricia and her colleagues did seemed to be wrong. Tricia might be doing her work, typing at her keyboard, and Kelly would snap, "I can't listen to your goddamn typing all day long!" She seemed to enjoy watching team members struggle to perform tasks after she had failed to train them or share vital information. When they tearfully asked for help, she tore into them for their supposed ignorance.

As the weeks passed, Tricia noticed that Kelly had an inexplicable need to remain in control at all times and dominate others. Her refusal to share information was a case in point: Kelly liked feeling superior and indispensable. Her controlling nature came through in other ways as well.

One day, Tricia came into work early to organize a box of vital medications for a nursing home that had joined as a customer. She knew the nursing home would need these medications, and she wanted the team to be able to deliver them with a minimum of stress. Since she had a key to the office, she let herself in. When Kelly arrived, she screamed at Tricia for arriving early without asking permission. It didn't matter that Tricia was doing something for the team's benefit or that she was authorized to come and go as she pleased.

Kelly knew that she'd stepped over a line by blowing up at Tricia, and she was worried that Tricia would tell others about it. So she went to bizarre and irrational lengths to cover up her misbehavior. Tricia was scheduled that morning to visit some of the nursing homes her location served. When she arrived at the first one, she found that Kelly had called and warned the staff that Tricia might arrive upset. Kelly invented a scenario to explain Tricia's emotional turmoil, one that had nothing to do with her own bad behavior. Since Tricia didn't want to upset her boss any further, she didn't dare reveal to their customers what had actually happened.

Kelly frequently engaged in such subterfuge, and it made an already difficult situation harder to bear. She would rant at Tricia and Shelly, the technician, until the two were in tears. Then, if a corporate boss or some other visitor came by, she would shift, appearing perky and endearing and greeting them warmly. "It was as if she were on an extreme sugar high," Tricia says. "Just so excited to see everyone. So smiley. So happy. So excited to show them around. Over the top." Not once did Kelly apologize for her bad behavior. "There was a complete lack of empathy. There was no real emotional connection at all. I've worked with difficult people before, but this was so beyond that."

Kelly's need to control and belittle others led her to take actions that Tricia felt certain were endangering the nursing home residents served by the pharmacy. On one occasion, an influenza outbreak struck, putting patients at extreme risk. Standard practice was to treat them proactively with an antiviral medication, which lowered the chances that they would become severely ill or die. It was vital to deliver the medication as soon as the authorities declared an outbreak. True to form, Kelly never bothered to tell Tricia how to distribute the medication properly. When authorities declared an outbreak, Kelly happened to be on vacation. Tricia called her, frantic to know what to do. Kelly refused to help, telling Tricia to figure it out herself. This was a crisis, and Kelly knew that any delays could prove fatal for patients. Her response was not only unprofessional; as Tricia notes, it was reckless and "completely unhinged."

Tricia and her colleagues weren't alone in regarding Kelly as the boss from hell. At one point, Tricia met a couple of staffers who used to work for Kelly. "They basically came up to me, grabbed my hands, and said, 'Are you okay?'" Another pharmacist referred to Kelly as "Satan" on account of her wicked behavior. Still others confirmed that she had a history in previous jobs of treating others poorly. In fact, Tricia learned that the company had moved Kelly from a bigger, more central location to this one precisely to minimize her contact with staff and the public. If only Tricia had discovered this when first interviewing for her position, she could have saved herself a world of stress and torment. But she hadn't.

Understanding Poisonous People

When most of us encounter someone like Kelly, we don't soon forget it, even if our encounters are much more fleeting than Tricia's was. Just a few minutes with a dark personality can make a strong and lasting impression.

In 2006, while I was a senior in college, I volunteered at a local parole office in Halifax, Nova Scotia. My job included attending a weekly group therapy session for men who had committed sex crimes. Not the most wholesome experience for a naive twenty-one-year-old woman, I know, but I had dreams of becoming a clinical psychologist, and this seemed like a good way to learn what the work was really like—not the Hollywood version of forensic psychology but the actual, day-to-day grind.

We held the sessions in the evenings. To reach the government building where the sessions were held, I had to walk from my apartment in downtown Halifax past a spooky graveyard called the Old Burying Ground. The city always seemed darker and more ominous on therapy nights than at any other time. I quickened my pace, huddled against the cold wind coming off the Halifax harbor, half expecting that someone would jump out and grab me.

Inside, the two psychologists running the session, myself, and around twenty men sat on dilapidated chairs hastily arranged in a circle in the middle of a large, drab office—a million shades of dirty beige under flickering fluorescent lighting. Some of the men were convicted of child molestation, while others had been found guilty of rape or other violent offenses. There was a clear distinction, even to my novice eye. The men convicted of molestation were timid and nervous; they avoided eye contact and spoke in hushed tones. Those convicted of rape seemed much more threatening to me—dominant, alpha-male types.[1]

One evening, we talked about the impacts that sex-related crimes had on victims. Most of the men seemed to understand that they had harmed people, and they expressed real remorse. But not everyone. I noticed that one of the parolees was glancing my way from time to time. He was clean-shaven with slicked-back hair, wearing faded jeans and a flannel over a faded Nirvana T-shirt. His wardrobe was a perfect time capsule of the prior decade—before he had entered prison.

Everyone was supposed to share; we went around the circle and the men took turns speaking. At one point perhaps twenty minutes into the discussion, the group's attention turned to this man as he began describing the rape for which he had been sent to prison. He spoke coldly and matter-of-factly, seeming to relish the memory, all while downplaying the impact on his victim and even blaming her for the assault.

He went on to describe his young victim's physical appearance—her height, weight, body shape, eye color. Grinning ever so slightly, he stared at me. "Actually," he said, a devious glint in his eye, "she looked a lot like you. Tall, thin, similar face, too. Yeah, you kinda look like my type, you know."

Everyone turned to me. The man's comment amounted to a veiled threat—if he had the chance, he implied, I might be next on his list of victims. I felt vulnerable, exposed, and frightened, which I suspect was exactly how he wanted me to feel. He seemed to revel in my discomfort, smiling as I squirmed and sank awkwardly into my chair. This man had psychopathy. He was prone to callousness, manipulation, impulsivity, and aggression. And he got a rush out of frightening me. He was a predator, and in his eyes, I was prey.

As you probably know, people with psychopathy include serial murderers such as John Wayne Gacy, serial rapists such as Ted Bundy (who also murdered his victims), and perhaps even genocidal despots like Hitler.[2] These individuals don't experience the same empathy, compassion, or moral qualms the rest of us do. They think about murder with the cold calculation that others might bring to a math problem.[3] But they're skilled and devious enough to cover up that reality. They can make you *think* they're normal, feeling humans like the rest of us, donning a "mask of sanity," as one early scholar of psychopathy put it.[4] This and a strong dash of superficial charm allow them to lure in unsuspecting victims, whose lives they promptly wreck—or end.

These people might seem to have little in common with the boss who haunted Tricia at her pharmacy or the dark personalities you've encountered. As callously and viciously as Kelly behaved, she didn't commit a serious crime or physically harm anyone, at least as far as Tricia knew. Kelly's behavior might have put elderly patients at risk, and it definitely hurt others around her, but it was still a far cry from that of a serial criminal.

Or was it? If you analyze Kelly's behavioral patterns, you find that she and Ted Bundy had quite a bit in common. Both were superficially charming, manipulative, callous, and aggressive; Kelly just exhibited these traits to a lesser extent. In fact, *we can often understand our own personal villains as people who possess elevated levels of so-called dark personality traits, especially those related to psychopathy.* These levels aren't so extreme that these people would rack up a high score on the Psychopathy Checklist-Revised (PCL-R), a test psychologists use to assess clinical psychopathy among criminals, or the Psychopathy Checklist-Screening Version (PCL:SV), which is designed for use in noncriminal populations.[5] But they're higher than normal, often leading people to cause grave harm to others around them. Some bad apples are rotten to the core, others less so. But even the latter can leave a bad taste in your mouth.

The Cholesterol Theory of Psychopathy

To understand psychopathy's impact on our lives, we must shift how we think about personality disorders. We're used to conceiving of them as discrete conditions akin to medical illnesses. If you have chills and a fever, you can take a quick test to determine whether you have genetic material from the COVID virus in your body. If this single condition holds true—if that genetic material is present—then you have COVID.

Personality disorders are commonly portrayed in this way, as a distinct thing we either do or don't have. Researchers and clinicians define these disorders as abnormal patterns of thoughts, feelings, and behaviors that occur consistently across a person's life (at work, at home, and so on), don't change much as a person ages, and affect them negatively in some way. They assess the presence or absence of seven to nine specific personality traits (for example, one feature of narcissistic personality disorder is having a greatly inflated perception of one's own importance). A person need not exhibit every one of these patterns to qualify as possessing a disorder. But if about five of them are present, then usually a psychologist or psychiatrist can make the diagnosis.[6]

Defining personality disorders categorically—something that either does or doesn't describe a given person—is useful because it provides a simple criterion for determining whether to provide treatment. If a doctor diagnoses someone as having a disorder because five or more criteria are present, then they should receive treatment. Otherwise, they shouldn't. In recent years, however, some scholars have questioned such a simplistic, black-and-white system of classification.[7] If four criteria are met, should we just proclaim "No problem here!" and go on blissfully with our lives? Probably not. Anyone who has experienced anxiety or depression knows that *degrees* of distress exist and that addressing those feelings can save us a world of pain, even if these feelings aren't severe enough to lead to a diagnosis.

Something similar holds true for psychopathy. Psychologists and the legal system regard scores of thirty or above on the PCL-R as evidence of "having psychopathy." But someone who scores a twenty-eight or twenty-nine isn't much different.[8] Indeed, psychologists increasingly regard psychopathy and other personality disorders not as exotic conditions that have nothing to do with a normal personality but rather as reflecting extreme levels of otherwise normal personality traits.[9] These disorders are a matter of degree rather than kind—less like a virus and more like cholesterol. You might not have so much of those harmful lipids in your blood that you're on the verge of a heart attack, but you do have at least some of them coursing through your veins.

Dissecting Psychopathy

Let's delve more deeply into how psychologists define psychopathy. One influential model of the disorder pioneered by Dr. Robert Hare and his colleagues defines it in terms of four groups or, as I like to call them, buckets of traits, covering how people relate to others, experience emotions, take risks, and handle social rules and conventions.[10] Given a PCL-R assessment, someone with clinical levels of psychopathy would likely score highly across multiple buckets. The notorious criminals Charles Manson and Ted Bundy are said to have had total scores of thirty-six and thirty-four out of forty, respectively.[11] But if we consider each of these dimensions in more detail, it becomes clear that the dark personalities we encounter in our own lives exhibit these traits as well, albeit unevenly and at lower intensities. Since each of these individual traits exists on a continuum, your personal villain might score high on some but low on others.

Bucket 1: How They Relate to Others

People with psychopathy are selfish and manipulative. Rather than trying to connect with others, they look at others as a means to an end. They might come across as charming, but that's by design. They'll say *anything* to get you to see them in a positive light or to do what they want, lying far more than the average person does.[12] They have an inflated sense of self and need you to think highly of them, too.

Justice Douglas is a case in point. He wrote several memoirs about his lowly upbringing and rise to judicial power, but as his biographer Bruce Allen Murphy discovered, these were only loosely based in reality. He didn't have polio as a child or live in a tent during college, as he claimed. He also exaggerated his military service. Although he claimed to have served in the US Army during World War I, and even had a small flag emblem placed next to his name in the Yakima City Directory indicating his status as a veteran, he didn't come close to seeing real action. Rather, he participated in the Whitman College Students Army Training Corps for ten weeks in 1918 and never laid hands on a gun.[13]

Kelly also engaged in manipulative behavior. She mistreated others around her and then went to considerable lengths to cover it up. She switched from demon mode to a saccharine smile, turning on the superficial charm for clients. But that's nothing compared with the web of lies that other poisonous people might spin.

Not long ago, I went to a bachelorette party attended by a bunch of ladies. Most of us were in our thirties, so it was a relatively tame affair. The personal chef we hired did a great job with the food: there was a decadent charcuterie board, watermelon mint salad, bruschetta with truffle oil. But he served up something else with all those tasty nibbles: a buffet of lies.

Trying to charm us, he talked about himself for a full ninety minutes, boasting about all the high-end restaurants at which he'd worked. In addition to his illustrious culinary career, he'd been a professional drummer in five bands and had recently released an album. Oh, and he'd run one of the largest cannabis operations in Canada. In that capacity, he said, he'd driven his Harley down the Pacific Coast, surfing "every break between California and Nicaragua," and had also visited Red Rocks Amphitheatre in Montana.

I asked him how he'd managed to carry a surfboard with him on his bike. He mumbled something about having modified his Harley and quickly changed the subject. But in fact, nothing he said added up—it was either vague, implausible, or obviously deceptive. Having lived in the Denver area for several years, I knew that Red Rocks Amphitheatre wasn't in Montana but in Colorado. None of the businesses he mentioned turned up in our subsequent web searches. The band he claimed to have been in didn't exist, either. This guy was working the room, and he was willing to say anything to keep our attention and get us to think he was a total stud. Did he harbor clinical levels of psychopathic traits? I can't say. But I suspect he would have scored higher in this set of interpersonal traits than the average person.

Bucket 2: How They Experience Emotions

People with psychopathy have severe emotional deficits. While they can *simulate* emotions, passing themselves off as warm, loving, and affectionate, in truth they are cold, unfeeling, and unempathetic. When they do wrong, they don't experience remorse or accept responsibility, although they might sometimes act like they do if they perceive it to be in their interest. As one pair of researchers once wrote, a person with psychopathic traits "knows the words but not the music" of emotion.[14]

One woman I interviewed—I'll call her Maya—was twenty-three years old when she encountered a dark personality named Kevin. He was a colleague of hers, and after seeing her several times in work contexts, he cozied up to her and tried to start a relationship. Once they had gone on a date and become just a little bit more than friends, he ramped up the emotion, telling Maya that he loved her and always did. For days on end he texted her, telling her how badly he wanted to have a relationship with her. Some of his proclamations were quite intense: "We may not have a relationship now," he said, "but I'm sure that when I die, you will be [the last] person that I want to talk to."

Naive and vulnerable, Maya felt appreciated and special. Believing that Kevin was head over heels for her, she slept with him. The next day, he ghosted her, refusing to respond to her phone calls and texts. A couple of weeks later, he resurfaced, making excuses for his absence. He resumed his professions of love and also seemed to open himself emotionally to her, telling her about his vexed relationship with his parents. Once again, Maya slept with him, and once again he disappeared.

Maya didn't know what to make of this pattern, which happened repeatedly. She tried to convince herself that Kevin loved her and that she should believe his excuses. Before long, she realized that everything he said was a lie. She discovered that he was cheating on her during his absences, playing the same games with another woman, who reached out to Maya to tell her to "back off." In retrospect, Maya reflects that she never saw Kevin cry, even when he was discussing intense subjects. He seemed to shift his emotions—one minute he seemed sad, and the next moment, inexplicably, he was chipper. When he was angry at her, he became cold and devoid of emotion, as if she were a total stranger. He never seemed sorry for stringing her along or lying to her. Eventually, frustrated at his incapacity to feel normal human feelings and tired of the drama, she cut off her relationship with him for good.

Based on Maya's description of his behaviors, it appears Kevin experienced emotions only superficially, if at all. Instead of feeling deeply, he *feigned* emotions, expressing what he thought others around him expected to see, depending on the situation. Because his emotions weren't real, he could seemingly turn them on or off in an instant. He might not have harbored clinical levels of psychopathy, but he displayed a marked callousness and lack of remorse. Similarly, Kelly, Tricia's boss from hell, might not have harbored clinical levels of psychopathy, but she didn't care that she was putting elderly patients at risk, nor did she have any qualms about hurting her colleagues. She tried to come across as a normal, feeling person, but in reality, she was stone cold. Justice Douglas, too, was, as his former law clerk Lucas Powe told me, "indifferent" to other people.[15]

Bucket 3: How They Weigh Risks

The third bucket has to do with a penchant for sensation-seeking and risk-taking. People with psychopathy are prone to boredom and constantly seek that next rush. They don't think through their actions and hence behave irresponsibly. You know those people who plan for the future and diligently work toward their goals? That's *not* psychopathic behavior. These people don't have realistic long-term goals. They're addicted to the fast life—sex, drugs, gambling, power. Because they're such reckless, short-term thinkers, they tend to leech off others to get by. Of course, people might become addicted to vices for all sorts of reasons—you shouldn't presume that everyone who abuses alcohol, for example, has psychopathy. People who score high on this cluster of traits exhibit recklessness and a taste for risk-taking *generally*, across multiple areas of their lives.[16]

Fictional characters such as James Bond or Ethan Hunt from the *Mission Impossible* movies exhibit fearlessness and excessive risk-taking. While we like to perceive such characters as heroic, this bucket of traits can cause serious damage, especially when combined with the first two buckets. This is true even at the subclinical level, when these traits are present but not so severe as to produce a PCL-R score above thirty. It might seem hard to believe, but according to some accounts Justice Douglas always seemed restless—even bored—with his work on the Supreme Court.[17] His opinions were often short and hastily written—far from the judicial masterpieces that other justices have published.[18] More than anything, he looked forward to leaving the court each summer to explore the remote Cascade Mountains, riding his horse, as one observer noted, "like he rode his car, with his foot down on the accelerator."[19]

One woman I interviewed, Ginny, told me of a fast-rising employee, Tim, whom she met while working at a technology company. Tim was a larger-than-life, vivacious man whom everyone wanted to be around. But he had a darker side. At work, he manipulated rules to his advantage and stole computers. During his off hours, he broke the trust of many people in his and Ginny's circle of friends—lying to them, cheating them, failing to repay loans, and so on, without any remorse. This behavior coincided with considerable risk-taking. Tim would take drugs or drink and then get behind the wheel, not remembering it the next day because he'd blacked out. He would gamble with money he didn't have, borrowing from his friends in order to pay up when he lost. And, ominously, he had a fascination with guns. His abusive behavior coupled with his risk-taking became so concerning that many of their common friends severed ties with him.

People with psychopathy often find that their recklessness leaves them in trouble with the law. Stella recounted how her ex-husband, Marty, seemed daring and charming at first when she met him at an Australian ski resort. That day, he showed off his ability to do backflips and gutsy jumps on his snowboard. Once they were married, though, Marty's risk-taking started to seem much more worrisome. He spent their money extravagantly, and as a result Stella always felt that they were living on the edge. He also took his work as a massage therapist in dangerous directions. When working with female clients, he touched them inappropriately while making benign small talk. He would take minor risks at first, letting his hands wander seemingly accidentally, and then make bolder advances. Eventually, this risk-taking caught up to him: he was convicted of sexually assaulting eight women. Acting without concern for consequences caused incalculable harm to his victims, family, and friends.

Bucket 4: How They Handle Social Rules and Conventions

Marty's misdeeds also fall into our final bucket, which has to do with antisociality. People with psychopathy are prone to breaking rules, often in creative ways. You know that kid who acted out in class during elementary school, shoplifted in middle and high school, and then went on to commit felonies as an adult? A trajectory like that isn't uncommon. Some researchers argue that antisocial, often criminal behavior isn't a defining quality of psychopathy, but rather a consequence of being manipulative, callous, and impulsive.[20] There might be something to that. As Marty's story illustrates, it's not hard to imagine that if you have any one of these traits, let alone several, you might end up behaving in ways that put you afoul of the law.

As I've noted, criminal behavior didn't feature in the story Tricia told me about Kelly. Generally speaking, Kelly played by the written rules but broke the unwritten rules of workplace conduct. Justice Douglas did the same, treating his law clerks in ways that "went too far" for his colleagues to accept.[21] He broke other unwritten rules of normal conduct, too. I mentioned earlier that he was the first justice to get divorced while on the bench. In fact, he would divorce three times during his tenure on the Supreme Court, cheating on each wife with her eventual successor. He also took a salary from a charitable foundation with "underworld connections" while on the bench, raising questions about his impartiality that led to an (unsuccessful) impeachment attempt.[22]

Throughout this book, we'll meet individuals like Marty the Masseur who *do* show stronger antisocial tendencies. A good example is President Donald Trump. Although I don't know how he would score on the PCL:SV, even a cursory review of his known behavior suggests that he is likely elevated on traits across the first three buckets.[23] *The Washington Post* estimates that he told thirty thousand lies over his four years in office (bucket 1: how they relate to others).[24] He was widely criticized for his inability to show empathy for victims of COVID, and he mocked a disabled reporter early in his first presidential campaign (bucket 2: how they experience emotions).[25] Even the Russian government assessed him as being an "impulsive, mentally unstable and unbalanced individual" (bucket 3: how they weigh risks).[26] And remember that time he looked directly at the sun during an eclipse?[27]

But Donald Trump also fills bucket 4. During his first term, he demonstrated a striking lack of regard for social norms and conventions. In fact, that's why many of his supporters love him so much: because they want to see him tear down norms that they associate with a corrupt system and the ruling elite. The innumerable examples of Trump's deviation from established social and political norms include his unwillingness to release tax documents; his disparagement of military families; his failure to condemn the white supremacists who marched in 2017 in Charlottesville, Virginia; his frequent, off-the-cuff rants on social media; his deportation of migrants with little concern for due process; and his sudden implementation of tariffs on longtime trading partners.[28]

Some of Trump's actions, such as his efforts to subvert the 2020 election, may have veered into the criminal realm. Prior to Trump, an American president had never been formally accused of potentially criminal wrongdoing. As of this writing, Trump has been found guilty of thirty-four felony counts; dozens of other charges were dropped when he regained the White House.[29]

Regardless of your politics, you probably recognize some of the traits I've described in this chapter when considering Trump's behavior. In one study, researchers asked Americans across the political spectrum how strongly Trump exhibited dark personality traits. Left-leaning participants perceived him as more psychopathic than did right-leaning folks, but both groups gave him an average score above the midpoint on the scale. People across the political landscape place Donald Trump fairly high on the psychopathy spectrum.[30]

Most of us know people who routinely lie and manipulate, are callous and grandiose, take reckless risks, and flout social norms. Maybe it's the boss who delights in embarrassing us in public. Or the spouse who cheats on us and abuses us emotionally. Or the colleague who lies to our face and undercuts us in meetings. Or the seemingly friendly neighbor who steals something from our home. Or the middle schooler who mercilessly bullies other kids on the playground without remorse.

In fact, the more closely we analyze psychopathic traits, the more ordinary they appear. Scholars have observed strong links between psychopathic traits and some of the less pleasant parts of normal personality. One dominant model of human character boils each person down to a score on five basic categories of traits.[31] People who score very low in one of these categories, "agreeableness," are what psychologists call antagonistic: they place a low value on social harmony and prefer to pursue their self-interest instead. As one scholarly paper put it, antagonism "references traits related to immorality, combativeness, grandiosity, callousness, and distrustfulness."[32] But wait: that sounds like the kinds of personalities captured by the four buckets of traits related to psychopathy. As these researchers found, antagonistic traits and definitions of psychopathy largely overlap. Antagonism lies at the heart of dark personalities. Again, normal personality traits and psychopathic traits really aren't so different after all.

The Extent of the Darkness

Psychologists have estimated that 1 percent of the population show clinical levels of psychopathy (scoring at or above thirty on the PCL-R).[33] Estimates range higher for people with nonclinical but still elevated expressions of these traits, but thankfully this group still appears to comprise a relatively small segment of the population.

Some of the best data we have about the prevalence of psychopathic traits come from studies in which hundreds or thousands of people complete a questionnaire testing for these traits and researchers plot everyone's scores on a graph. One group of scholars had 638 people in Eugene, Oregon, answer sixty-four questions that measured the interpersonal, emotional, risk-taking, and antisocial dimensions of psychopathy.[34] They also had university students in Texas and Belgium and prison inmates in Wisconsin complete the survey. No surprise—inmates scored highest. The fine folks of Eugene scored the lowest, on average. But even there, there were shades of gray. The scores among these people were distributed in a pattern that scholars would describe as a "positive skew." Similar to the distribution in figure 1, relatively few people scored at the high end of the scale (those with the highest levels of this dark trait), and more people clustered at the lower end of the scale.

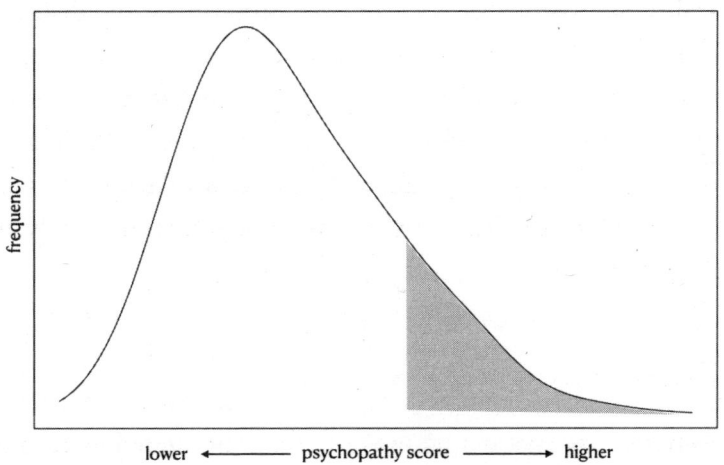

Figure 1: A positively skewed distribution approximating self-report psychopathy scores in a community sample. The shaded "tail" on the right indicates relatively few cases of "elevated" scores. Copyright © 2016 Multi-Health Systems Inc. All rights reserved. Reproduced with permission from MHS.

This chart confirms that psychopathic traits exist on a continuum. If psychopathy were a discrete phenomenon that you either had or didn't, we'd expect to see two humps, one representing those who scored high and *are psychopaths* and one corresponding to all those who scored low or near zero and *aren't psychopaths*. Instead, we see just one hump representing people who scored low followed by a gradual downward slope. Many people scored relatively low—but not zero. Relatively few people scored highly.

Crunching the numbers, researchers found that about 18 percent of people had scores that were either "elevated" or "extremely elevated"—what we might regard as dark territory.[35] Two other studies by my colleague Dr. Craig Neumann of the University of North Texas involved more than thirty-six thousand participants and put the segment of people with dark personalities at about 7 and 26 percent, respectively.[36] All told, we can assume that roughly 20 percent of the population has a dark personality profile—a number that can rise or fall depending on the specific group you're studying. If you surveyed people who donated blood to the Red Cross or volunteered at homeless shelters, that number might be lower. By contrast, in the survey of prison inmates mentioned above, 92 percent of respondents had scores that would rank as "elevated" or "extremely elevated" by Eugene, Oregon, standards.

Evidence suggests that psychopathy stems from a fairly even combination of nature and nurture.[37] There is a genetic component, but adverse childhood experiences such as parental rejection or abuse are also related to the emergence of these traits.[38] In one study of identical twins, researchers found that the twin who received harsher parenting and less parental warmth developed more callous and unemotional traits.[39] Like our family environment, the enduring culture and context in which we live can also affect our personality development. Recent research by my colleagues and I found that people who live under more authoritarian governments report more psychopathic traits than those in democratic countries.[40] And others have found that the extent to which countries and US states exhibit corruption, inequality, poverty, and violence is linked to greater dark traits among residents, measured twenty years later.[41]

In addition to people with elevated psychopathic personality traits, the approximately 80 percent of us who are genuinely kind, empathetic, and truthful can sometimes behave like situational psychopaths, as I call them. The psychologist Kurt Lewin famously theorized that environment as well as personality helps to determine people's behavior.[42] You might have noticed in your own life that you behave differently in some environments than others. Plop yourself into a coffee shop, say, and you might suddenly relax and become more gregarious, whimsical, and open-minded. Back in a high-pressure, fast-paced office environment, however, you're all business—you remain quiet and work in a disciplined way, staying focused on what you're doing.

Likewise, some environments can cause otherwise good folks to behave in harmful ways. Perhaps you feel stressed, or you've had too much to drink, and you lash out. You can probably think of a time when you didn't feel remorse for doing something wrong, or when you acted a bit impulsively. You wouldn't score high on measures of psychopathic traits unless this behavior was persistent—a core component of who you are. But a minority of people do harbor psychopathic traits that are latent; their personality leads them to behave badly across time and context. These are the people we need to worry about. The rest of us can take steps to become more alert to our environments and prevent ourselves or others from caving to situational pressures.

The Dark Tetrad

The notion of dark personality traits helps us understand a wide range of bad behavior we encounter in everyday life. Psychopathy is one-quarter of what personality psychologists call the "Dark Tetrad." The other three components are narcissism, marked by a tendency toward inflated self-regard; Machiavellianism, marked by a tendency to manipulate and exploit others; and sadism, marked by a tendency to take pleasure in others' pain. These personalities are all malevolent, and they overlap with one another.[43] Some scholars conceive of psychopathy as the umbrella under which malignant elements of narcissism and Machiavellianism fall.[44] Others consider them to be related but distinct constructs that share a "dark core." That core aligns closely with bucket 1: how they relate to others and bucket 2: how they experience emotions. You might think of each component of the Dark Tetrad as having a unique flavor but sharing with the others a basic set of ingredients: a propensity for manipulation and callousness.[45]

Consider Niccolò Machiavelli, who had one of these dark personalities named after him. His classic book, *The Prince*, offered guidance on how to obtain power by force or by fraud. He argued that a powerful person should *appear* virtuous, but that to actually be good or kind would be their undoing.[46] He advised that other people are a means to an end, pawns to be used to gather power. Someone who constantly pursues dominance over others through these tactics will tick the interpersonal and emotional boxes of psychopathy, but they may not be very impulsive. In fact, this kind of calculated manipulation might require considerable restraint.

Someone who scores high in narcissism might also experience little empathy for others and exaggerate their personal abilities on account of their relentless self-focus. Frank Lloyd Wright, the American architect of the Guggenheim museum and Fallingwater fame, was well known for his overblown ego. Once asked about his vanity, he famously replied, "Early in life I had to choose between honest arrogance and hypocritical humility; I chose honest arrogance." This arrogance limited his empathy for others. As one apprentice remarked, "He is devoid of consideration and has a blind spot regarding others' qualities."[47] He also showed little concern for his clients when the homes he created for them quickly crumbled. One customer, Dr. Ludd Spivey, called to complain about a leaky roof that left his desk soaked. Wright's response: "Move your desk."[48]

Similarly, sadism is related to a callous disregard for others' welfare.[49] Regardless of whether we think of psychopathy as an overarching prototype for human darkness, or as one of a series of overlapping circles in a Venn diagram, it's clear that the Dark Tetrad personalities have a lot in common. And when a person is characterized by any one of them, problems will likely follow.

Beyond the Dark Tetrad, we find that psychopathy also overlaps conceptually with several personality disorders. People suffering from antisocial personality disorder, for instance, can cause enormous suffering. They display, as the American Psychiatric Association puts it, "a pervasive pattern of disregard for and violation of the rights of others," with behavior that includes "criminal activity, deceitfulness, impulsivity, recklessness, aggressiveness, callousness, disinhibition, and irresponsibility."[50] Likewise, interactions with someone who has borderline personality disorder will probably be tumultuous. These individuals can cause all kinds of harm to others thanks to their impulsivity, explosive emotions, and unstable relationships.[51]

Just because a person is diagnosed with another personality disorder doesn't mean they can't also exhibit psychopathic traits. In particular, psychopathy bears close relationships to several of the so-called Cluster B personality disorders, which include antisocial, narcissistic, and borderline personality disorders. Individuals who score most highly on the interpersonal and emotional aspects of psychopathy (buckets 1 and 2) are more likely than others to meet criteria for narcissistic personality disorder, while those who score most highly on impulsive and antisocial traits (buckets 3 and 4, respectively) are more likely to meet criteria for antisocial personality disorder. [52]

The swirl of terms, traits, and diagnoses that describe the darker side of human nature is confusing even to many scientists.[53] To navigate a path through the intellectual whirlpool, it can help to identify a single "big tent" concept that covers a broad set of traits leading to interpersonal strife. No concept is perfect, but the Dark Tetrad—and psychopathic traits in particular—seems like the best candidate. By focusing on this continuum, we can cover a wide range of dark personalities that any of us are likely to encounter.

Tyranny of the Minority

All this talk of psychopathic personality traits might be hard to process emotionally. After all, one out of every five of us is predisposed to do serious damage to others—that's pretty bleak. But maybe it isn't. Turning that data point around, we find that four out of five of us *aren't* predisposed to malevolence. As unpleasant as dark personalities are, they still represent a small minority of the population. Most of us are kind, decent, compassionate people.

Some scholars believe that psychopathy evolved as an alternative life strategy precisely because the majority of us are good. As the theory has it, by taking risks and seeking self-interested, short-term gains at the expense of longer-term stability, people with psychopathic traits gain an adaptive edge. For example, they can better pass on their genes because they have sex earlier, more often, and have more children with multiple partners.[54] But taking risks and living for today have their disadvantages. Because people with higher levels of psychopathic traits expose themselves to more danger, they have shorter lifespans.[55] Critically, scholars believe that psychopathy as an alternative life strategy only works because it is adopted by a small minority of the population. If too many of us were moving through life using deception and manipulation as our primary strategy, suspicion would set in—there would be too few kind souls vulnerable to such shenanigans. So, psychopathy remains relatively rare.[56]

In furthering that optimistic interpretation, by no means do I wish to diminish the harm that dark personalities cause. Although a small minority, people with these traits really can tyrannize and traumatize the rest of us. Take Tricia, the pharmacist. Her boss Kelly's bad behavior took a terrible toll on everyone who encountered her. Tricia learned that several staffers at the pharmacy had left over a two-year period before she arrived, including her direct predecessor. During the better part of a year when Tricia was working for Kelly, several technicians came and went, unable to handle the toxic environment. Tricia was tempted to follow, but her diligence and compassion for patients made her stay. She did her best to hang on, trying to explain away Kelly's behavior, "meet her where she was," and manage her own emotions. When that proved untenable, Tricia lodged a formal complaint against Kelly with human resources. They told her to document Kelly's bad behavior, which she did. In the end, though, human resources failed to take action. Other team members were too frightened to back up Tricia's complaints, and human resources claimed that Tricia couldn't prove Kelly's misdeeds—it was her word against Kelly's.

Eventually, Tricia buckled under the extreme stress of dealing with Kelly. It was painful to see Kelly hurt others and to feel powerless to do anything about it, and disheartening as well to see the organization take no action. Tricia had experienced anxiety before, but as she remembers, the agitation she was now experiencing "was next level. I was not functioning. I was really unwell." When she sought professional help, her therapist told her that she could no longer be around Kelly and had to take an immediate medical leave.

Tricia wound up needing four months off to recover. When she finally felt well enough to go back to work, she was astonished to find that the company reassigned her to the same job, sitting right next to Kelly. Tricia refused to work with Kelly again, and the company agreed to send her to a different location. At this point, Tricia lost track of Kelly. She later learned that Kelly had left the company and started her own independent pharmacy business.

Today, some ten years later, Tricia still works as a pharmacist and is satisfied with her job. But she remains traumatized by those months she spent working for Kelly. She continues to take medication and attend therapy for her anxiety. She remains terrified that she'll see Kelly at a professional conference or when running errands, a response she regards as akin to PTSD. "I don't think I can ever forget how I felt [while working for Kelly]," Tricia says. "I'm always afraid there could be someone else who comes into my life that does something like that to me or to a person I care about. Certain people just shouldn't manage other people. They shouldn't have that power."

As badly hurt as victims like Tricia are, our society usually doesn't register the damage. On the contrary, we valorize dark traits and minimize the harm they cause. We might fear the criminal psychopaths of this world, but we fall under the spell of dark personalities who occupy leadership roles. We admire the ruthlessness and callousness of people such as Steve Jobs or former General Electric CEO Jack Welch, regarding these traits as assets in a world that seems hypercompetitive and zero-sum. We wouldn't necessarily want to work for these people, but we attribute their outsized success to their urge to dominate, their willingness to do whatever it takes to win, and their disregard for people's feelings. Further, we find leaders who behave brashly, impetuously, and without regard for others to be perversely likable, perhaps because their antics are entertaining.

Our embrace of these poisonous people is misguided. By passing quickly over the harms suffered by people like Tricia and rationalizing them as collateral damage, we compromise our own standards, allowing the immorality of dark personalities to infect our thinking and our institutions. Even if we take a purely pragmatic stance, we find that dark personalities bring more pain than gain. Although they might deliver results in the short term or for themselves, their victories come at enormous cost to everyone else. Just as dark traits are much more common than we think, so too are the harms these traits engender. As we'll see, they hurt teams, organizations, families, schools, and society as a whole, in ways we can't even fully quantify.

2

The Cost of a Malevolent Few

In late 2013, my postdoctoral advisor at UC Berkeley, Dacher Keltner, approached me with an opportunity to step into a world some might perceive as a haven for psychopaths: finance. A San Francisco investment advisory firm he knew of helped large institutional investors—corporate pension funds, mostly—decide which hedge funds they should trust with their money. The firm's CEO, David, invested in hedge funds based partly on the character of the managers running them. As a rule, he sought to invest with managers he found trustworthy, but he had a hunch that ran counter to this strategy. He liked to keep half an eye on managers with psychopathic—in his words, "killer"—traits because he suspected they might have a competitive edge. These investment managers had a "win at all costs" mentality, were willing to act ruthlessly, and took risks that others couldn't stomach. Given the right incentives, they could deliver bigger returns for his clients. Or so David thought.

David wondered whether Dacher and I could validate his intuition, and at first, I thought we could. Psychologists have remarked on "successful psychopaths" whose traits allow them to avoid prison and perform well in highly competitive or dangerous fields. In a corporate setting, for instance, it might be that the dark personality's charisma, risk-taking, and dominance would allow them to negotiate better deals, win over more customers, or do a better job of inspiring team members.[1]

After studying psychopaths in the criminal justice system, I was well aware of how aggressive and brutally self-interested people with dark traits could be. Nevertheless, I thought vocations probably existed in which their unsavory qualities would give them a boost. I knew nothing about high finance, but I googled "What is a hedge fund?" and quickly felt certain that this ultracompetitive field was a place where dark personalities could thrive. Dacher disagreed. He thought these traits would prove destructive regardless of the setting. In his idealistic view, collaborative team-builders would outpace heartless, alpha-dog leaders every time.

Eager to resolve this question, we headed across the San Francisco Bay to collect data.[2] David's company had access to a unique video library. It didn't include major Hollywood films, informative YouTube cooking videos, funny TikToks, or, frankly, anything else that most people would ever want to see. Rather, it contained hundreds of ten- to fifteen-minute-long clips of interviews with hedge fund managers talking about their investment strategies, their firm's recent performance, and their sense of the "investment landscape." Watching these videos of sober-looking men in suits (and yes, they were all men), directors at David's firm could begin to evaluate whether they'd be interested in investing their funds with new hedge fund managers and get updates on the firms that were already managing their clients' money.

For Dacher and me, this library was like catnip, offering a unique opportunity to study the personalities of hedge fund managers. Our research team sifted through the videos, drawing out a subset of 101 managers whose firms had been in business for the past decade and had financial results during those years that we could access. All told, the managers in our sample worked for firms that managed on average over $4 billion in assets.

To determine which of these managers were dark personalities and which weren't, we analyzed their videos, conducting what we call a "coding" exercise. For each video, we took a "thin slice" of two minutes around the middle of the interview. Observing what managers said during these two minutes, how they said it, and their nonverbal movements, we looked for classic behaviors that related to one or more dark traits. For instance, when we saw a manager who was trying to come across positively by flattering the interviewer, we coded that as a sign of the superficial charm that falls into bucket 1. I watched thin slices from all the videos in our set, tracking how many cues I spotted for each of the dark traits. On this basis, I gave each manager a psychopathy, Machiavellianism, and narcissism score on a scale of one to seven.

Next, we reviewed these scores alongside measures of the financial performance these managers delivered. The companies they led each oversaw multiple funds for investors. We focused on the financial performance over a ten-year period of the "flagship" fund for which each manager was responsible, reasoning that these funds were usually the largest and those on which managers had built their reputations. Recognizing that investment strategies, firm size, and the number of years a firm has been in business can impact returns, we controlled for these factors.

Then came the moment of truth. Statistically analyzing the relationships between dark trait ratings and actual performance, we discovered that I was wrong, and Dacher the idealist was right. Managers who displayed more psychopathic traits delivered *worse* returns than those who were kinder and more compassionate. The most malicious and cunning managers generated returns 30 percent lower than the average manager over a ten-year period. If you want to make *less* money as an investor, you would do well to find the meanest, most cutthroat predator to manage your wealth. The smart money looks for compassionate, kind hedge fund managers and invests in them. In finance, at least, nice guys finish first, not last.

This study didn't pinpoint *why* these managers have poorer investment returns, but I suspected that it had something to do with the workplace climate they created.[3] When your boss routinely lies and manipulates and behaves in other ways characteristic of dark personalities, it stands to reason that you and others around you will pay a hefty price. You won't be as motivated to perform as you would otherwise. You'll probably tune out at work and call in sick on account of stress. Eventually, you'll head for the exit. The directors at David's firm were always concerned with employee turnover at hedge funds—for good reason.

Ample evidence suggests that bad behavior at work exacts enormous economic costs. One estimate from 2006 found that "abusive supervision" by managers—including disrespectful comments, wrongly touting a subordinate's work as your own, embarrassing employees in front of their peers, and so on—saddled US companies with nearly $24 billion in annual costs related to attrition, poor performance, and more.[4] A more recent study of employees at a nonprofit found that their bosses' psychopathic tendencies figured mightily in their desire to leave. With all the reasons people have for quitting jobs, ranging from a need for better pay to a shorter commute to a desire to advance one's career, it's striking that study participants based so much of what was ultimately a life-changing decision on their bosses' personalities.[5] Researchers have found that toxic cultures are "10.4 times more powerful than compensation in predicting a company's attrition rate compared with its industry."[6] Of course, such a finding can't fully capture the value that evaporates when poisonous people alienate clients or potential business partners, create infighting on the teams they lead, cause stress for colleagues, or erode cultural norms.[7]

If we delve further into the character of people with dark traits, we can understand better how their personalities might affect performance. Research suggests that some psychopathic traits such as fearlessness, boldness, and a drive to dominate can support success in certain situations, especially those that are dangerous or risky.[8] A police officer with these traits might be more inclined to charge valiantly into hazardous situations without much hesitation or self-doubt. And a cold or callous disposition might insulate police officers from experiencing negative mental health effects because of on-the-job traumas they experience. Previous research with incarcerated men has found that those with greater PCL-R scores (especially the interpersonal and emotional traits found in buckets 1 and 2) experienced less post-traumatic stress.[9]

But other core psychopathic traits such as recklessness, egotism, and self-aggrandizement might cause police officers to harm others on the job by breaking ethical rules, behaving selfishly, manipulating others, and lashing out at authority figures. One set of case studies detailing the personality of two police officers with high levels of psychopathic traits suggests that the *absolute and relative strengths* of these traits can influence whether the officers behave antisocially or not. One officer in these studies who was fearless and dominant was a decorated officer who had risen in the ranks. Another who had these traits but was *also* self-centered and reckless faced disciplinary action for on-the-job infractions and found that his career was stagnating.[10] These findings suggest that having lower overall levels of the impulsive and egotistic aspects of psychopathy might allow for some personal success in this setting, even if a person has higher levels of other psychopathic traits.

Other research with first responders has suggested that the same dark traits can lead to both good and bad behavior. In one study, researchers compared groups of first responders and civilians with one another. They suspected that first responders would behave more altruistically and courageously than the civilians, and they were right. First responders also scored higher on psychopathic traits than their civilian counterparts. Among this group, researchers found a link between heroism and traits such as boldness and narcissism. But they were also surprised to find that the more heroic first responders acted out more, broke workplace rules, and had disciplinary problems. The authors observed that "at least some prosocial behaviors, especially those linked to heroism, appear to be cut from some of the same cloth as antisocial behaviors."[11] The very psychopathic traits that might confer benefits also entail costs.[12]

To help settle the question of whether psychopaths are ever truly "successful," we must consider more carefully what we mean by that word, weighing the benefits of these traits against the harms. In calculating benefits and harms, we must consider not just dark personalities but also the people around them. In some situations, psychopathic traits might help people achieve some level of status. But in the process, they often cause tremendous pain and hardship for everyone else.

Accounting for Darkness

Many people associate dark traits with criminality, and indeed this realm offers us a clear view of the horrendous costs these personalities inflict on society. By the time of his arrest in 2008, the disgraced financier Bernie Madoff had executed the largest investment scam ever perpetrated in the United States, defrauding tens of thousands of clients of approximately $65 billion. It was such an egregious crime that a judge saw fit to sentence Madoff to 150 years in prison.[13] But as large a number as $65 billion is, there's a lot it *doesn't* cover, such as all the hours spent by attorneys and judges involved in his case or what it cost society to keep Madoff in prison. More significant, it doesn't begin to cover the pain and suffering experienced by his tens of thousands of victims as well as members of his own family.

Madoff was a charismatic guy who developed a persona as a reputable investment guru. He was selfish, egotistical, and unable to show remorse for his misdeeds. Certainly he was a liar, eventually owning up to his untruths once he was caught. And he was a domineering man who inspired fear in others. In short, he harbored many of the traits that define psychopathic personalities. Although we don't know whether a PCL-R was ever administered to Madoff or if so, how he scored, one scholarly analysis suggests that he met many of the criteria for psychopathy, with the exception of traits related to impulsivity.[14]

Madoff is a sensational example, but this pattern of outsized negative harms isn't unique. Although people with clinical psychopathy comprise about 20 percent of the criminal population, they perpetrate more than half of all serious crimes.[15] Moreover, the vast majority of criminal psychopaths—about 80 percent—will reoffend.[16] And these crimes cost society *a lot*.

One 2021 estimate calculated all the "costs that would not exist if all US laws were obeyed," taking into account not just direct monetary losses and all that governments and businesses spend on police, fences, and other forms of protection, but also the losses suffered when perpetrators and victims miss work, are physically injured or killed, and so on. The total bill to society: $5 trillion each year.[17] If we take just 20 percent of that number, we can say that criminal psychopaths at a minimum cost society $1 trillion annually. But remember, incarcerated people with psychopathy have committed more crimes than their non-psychopathic cellmates. If these individuals account for maybe 40 or 50 percent of crimes committed, the estimated costs balloon to $1.5–$2.5 trillion. We're talking here about criminals who possess clinical levels of psychopathy. If we were to factor in crimes committed by dark personalities who have nonclinical but still elevated levels of these traits, the costs would soar higher still.

Even these costs don't capture all the harm poisonous people do to us. In 2017, I was working at the University of Denver, and my husband and I had recently brought home a golden retriever puppy named Fischer.[18] One day, I parked at the university and jumped out of my car, swinging the door closed behind me with my keys still inside. My heart sank as I heard the *beep* and *click* of the locks engaging and saw Fischer gazing at me expectantly through the back window, unaware that he was now trapped. Although intended as a convenient crime deterrent, the automatic locks had become a most *inconvenient* feature. Since my phone was also locked in the car, I had to walk to the nearby campus gym to call the car company's roadside assistance. Bad news: it would take them hours to help me. When I told them my dog was in the car, they said I should call 911 and request a rescue.

So, that's what I did. Forty-five minutes later, a massive ladder truck pulled up, and six burly men hopped out. I was mortified to think that I was asking these firefighters to take a pause on saving lives so that they could help a hapless professor. It took them all of thirty seconds to jimmy the door.

Afterward, I reflected on how distracted I'd been and promised myself that I'd be more attentive. But as I thought about it, I realized that this episode pointed to the myriad ways that crime in our society affects us, even when we're not direct victims. If people weren't breaking into cars, we wouldn't need to make locking doors a regular part of our lives, and we probably wouldn't expect cars to automatically lock when we park them. I wouldn't have had to take up the valuable time of six firefighters.

We all know that crime can be devastating and even life-changing for its victims. But think, too, of all the time you've spent *worrying* about being a victim of crime. Think of the time you've wasted scouring your credit card bills each month and reporting suspicious charges. Think of the stress you've experienced putting things right after having your identity stolen or your website hacked.

Think, too, of the times you've locked yourself out of your car or house or set off your burglar alarm accidentally. Think of the times you passed someone on the street and stared at the ground rather than saying hello because you were afraid of them. Think of the times you declined to let your kids enjoy activities unsupervised because you feared kidnappers or abusers. Crime degrades our lives, subtly but comprehensively. It erodes trust and fellow feeling in our communities. And because people with psychopathic traits commit an outsized slice of crime, we can pin a great deal of that damage on them.

Oops, There Goes Democracy

To grasp the vast toll poisonous people take on our lives, we must go beyond criminality to consider how they shape public life. Politics is a breeding ground for people with psychopathic traits. Research has found that individuals scoring high on dark traits take more interest in becoming politically active and may also stand a greater chance of *winning* elections.[19] That's not just true in the United States: one study of candidates in dozens of countries (among them Donald Trump, Hillary Clinton, Emmanuel Macron of France, Jair Bolsonaro of Brazil, Angela Merkel of Germany, and Vladimir Putin of Russia) found a weak correlation between psychopathic traits and an ability to win over voters.[20] Likewise, studies fielded by myself and my colleagues revealed that US senators whose behavior evoked the dark traits lasted longer in office and won more elections.[21]

Unfortunately, the same psychopathic traits that get poisonous people elected wind up impeding their performance once they're in office. In 2014, my colleague Dacher and I collected random clips of 151 politicians speaking on the Senate floor during their time in office, taking the first minute of each clip as a thin slice.[22] Just like when we studied the hedge fund managers, we watched these videos and tracked behaviors related to psychopathy, narcissism, and Machiavellianism. Other members of our team had already tallied how many colleagues each senator could get to cosponsor bills with them, so we worked together to assess how effective senators with these traits were at the essence of their job: wielding influence. We reasoned that senators who could muster a lot of their peers to sign on would eventually get more bills passed into law.

As we found, senators who displayed the most psychopathic behaviors saw their influence *decline* when they ascended to a powerful committee chair position. Their inclination to manipulate and dominate others and to regard politics as a zero-sum, "survival of the fittest" competition didn't garner them more sway. Quite the opposite. Zooming out, these findings suggest that empowering dark personalities reduces the amount of collaboration in our democratic institutions, likely contributing to the polarization and dysfunction that has been endemic as of late.

Politicians with dark traits corrupt the democratic process in other ways, too. Dark personalities like to win, and they aren't hamstrung by ethical concerns. No surprise that they often communicate nastily, hurling character attacks at their opponents or using scare campaigns that appeal to voters' baser emotions and impulses.[23] The 2018 US Senate midterm elections were particularly negative, with around 70 percent of ads levying attacks. Subsequent analysis of that election found that candidates rated by experts as having high levels of dark traits campaigned more negatively.[24]

There's also a link between dark character traits and the populist demagoguery that in recent years has threatened democracies worldwide. Rabble-rousers such as Donald Trump, Viktor Orbán of Hungary, or Recep Tayyip Erdoğan of Turkey score more highly in psychopathic traits than do more mainstream, nonpopulist leaders.[25] Relatedly, right-wing autocrats (including Jair Bolsonaro, Benjamin Netanyahu, Narendra Modi, and Vladimir Putin) score higher on dark traits than both right- and left-wing nonautocratic leaders.[26]

The degradation of democratic norms by poisonous politicians is by no means new. These destructive leaders have always been there, coarsening and diminishing public life for the rest of us. If you look back at US presidents from George Washington to the modern era, you find a result similar to that which we saw earlier with first responders. Psychopathic traits—specifically, those linked to the desire to win and boldly dominate others—correspond with some metrics of better performance, including the ability to communicate and persuade the public. People with these traits also come across as more capable in times of crisis. But politicians with other dark traits—those linked to impulsive, antisocial behavior and grandiose narcissism—are impeached more often, allow more ethical shenanigans in their administrations, and abuse power themselves.[27]

The poison can spread by digital means, too. One study found that 80 percent of all fake news shared on Twitter came from just 0.1 percent of accounts.[28] Despite the small number of (often anonymous) people creating this content, the damage it can cause is enormous, not least because of algorithms that prioritize this attention-grabbing content and serve it up to millions of eyeballs.[29] Not surprisingly, online trolls possess high levels of dark traits. The online troll, as one study puts it, "is callous, enjoys both watching and causing harm to others, is able to effectively predict what will emotionally hurt others without sharing the emotional experience, and is motivated by causing this social mayhem."[30] By now, you'll recognize these traits as the hallmarks of the psychopathic personality.

Darkness at Home

Poisonous people aren't always anonymous predators but sometimes turn out to be the people we know best. Staci, a mother of two in her thirties, had an extended run-in with a dark personality starting when she was in eighth grade. Craig was a few years older than her, and he could charm anyone; everyone in their town loved him. What they didn't know—and what Staci would soon discover—was that Craig harbored a darkness that would follow her for decades. He would behave recklessly—shoplifting, driving erratically, taking drugs, having Staci over alone when he wasn't supposed to—and then lie to his parents and other authority figures to cover it up. He tried to control Staci's every move, making threats or punishing her anytime she tried to assert her autonomy.

Early in their relationship, Staci realized she was in a bad situation and wanted out. When she tried to break up with Craig, he threatened her life. They were driving in his car and he floored the accelerator, heading straight toward a pier and telling her he'd rather kill both of them than release his grip on her. To calm him, she frantically recanted, telling him she hadn't meant what she'd said and wanted to stay together. Afterward, he told her that if she told anyone what happened, he'd kill himself, and everyone would think it was her fault.

What followed was several years of torment and chaos that continued even after Craig and Staci graduated high school and left for college. Craig arranged for Staci to have a cell phone on his calling plan so that he could monitor whom she called. Once, when she tried to stick up for herself, he drove her to an isolated spot outside of town and left her there—in the dark, surrounded by dense forest—to fend for herself. Another time, he refused to let her leave his apartment. On still another occasion, he kept her locked for hours in the dingy basement of his house while he went to the movies.

Staci routinely missed classes and exams because of Craig. She was smart, but her grades suffered. She found herself lying to cover for him, an experience that left her feeling helpless, alone, and degraded. For years, she suffered from headaches and digestive problems, which she attributes to the constant stress Craig put on her.

Staci tried in subtle ways to alert others to what was going on, but she got nowhere. She was too ashamed and scared to tell anyone directly how Craig treated her, and he did such a good job cultivating a likable image that nobody in their town suspected him of being so manipulative and abusive. When she was nineteen, she tried to get away from him by jumping into a new relationship with a much older man who said he would protect her. Soon, she was practically living at this new guy's apartment. After a period of time with no contact, Craig called her with an ominous message: he'd leave her alone for now, but if she ever got married, he'd come to kill her husband and her kids. Staci was freaked out. After the abuse, manipulation, and callousness she had experienced, she had every reason to believe that Craig was serious.

Fortunately, Staci's relationship with Craig ended right then. For reasons she doesn't understand, she never saw him again. Good riddance! Nevertheless, when I interviewed Staci during the summer of 2023, it was clear that Craig remained a noxious presence in her life. She married in 2011 and went on to have two kids. Craig's threat to kill her family continued to haunt her. She would stay up until dawn watching the front door while her family was asleep, fearing he would come. "It just really spiraled," she said. "I was very paranoid all the time that he was just going to come and do something." Intensive therapy has helped, but she looks back with sadness on her time with Craig and the effect it had on her. "I wonder who I would be if I wasn't ever with him," she tells me all these years later. "I do wonder how much that changed me as a person. Clearly a lot."

People with psychopathic traits don't make for loving, compassionate romantic partners. They torment and victimize by behaving callously, manipulatively, and sometimes violently. Studies have found that people with dark personalities are more likely than others to be unfaithful to their partners and experience breakups.[31] Other research links psychopathy with a range of abusive behavior.

In one study of hundreds of people in relationships with psychopathic personalities, 50 percent of respondents reported being physically assaulted, 80 percent experienced controlling behavior regarding their finances, 96 percent said they'd been lied to, and 98 percent reported emotional abuse.[32] The more dark traits their partners displayed, the more damaging their treatment was. And such abuse left horrible destruction in its wake. Victims struggled with a range of negative emotions as well as symptoms of PTSD. They experienced physical symptoms, like high blood pressure and migraines, behavioral issues such as addiction or insomnia, and difficulty in subsequent relationships due to an inability to trust others.[33]

What the Parenting Books Don't Prepare You For

Parenting an emerging dark personality can be just as devastating as dating a fully formed one. One case study described Luke, a five-year-old who was acting out so acutely that he'd been sent to a psychiatrist.[34] Although Luke had been diagnosed with other conditions, a widely used test revealed that he also was high in callous-unemotional traits (CU), a potential precursor to adult psychopathy.[35] According to the boy's mother, he had trouble experiencing emotion and showing empathy, and he would veer quickly between emotions, screaming one moment and going stone-cold calm the next. He behaved recklessly, seemingly heedless of the consequences, and he often lied. He expressed little contrition for his misdeeds, sometimes finding his malicious behavior funny.

Luke's behavior terrified others around him. This wasn't your typical "difficult" child who didn't clean up his room or had trouble listening. This kid pointed an air gun at his parents, poured gasoline on his older sister, and lit a fire in his house. When his mom asked why he behaved in these ways, he responded, "I'm trying to scare you." On one occasion when he didn't get a toy he wanted, he punished his mother by peeing on the furniture.

Kids like Luke often cause a world of stress for their parents. "The physical abuse from my son was terrible," one mother of a child with these traits posted anonymously. "I had a constant stream of injuries from my child. He was also manipulative. He gaslit like he was trying to evangelize for the return of, well, gas lights. Nothing in the parenting books prepared me for a child that manipulated people and tried to make them think they were crazy."[36]

Research has confirmed a link between kids manifesting CU traits and "parental distress," a deceptively innocuous academic term if ever there was one. It's not simply these kids' poor behavior that bothers parents; the callousness and lack of remorse these kids show compound the pain. What do you do with a kid who not only is destroying everything in their path but seems to *like* to see others around them suffer? Parents respond by withdrawing emotionally, which can perpetuate a psychologically unhealthy dynamic.[37] "As horrible as this is to say, as a mom, the truth is that you put up a wall," one mother told the *New York Times*. "It's like being in the army, facing a barrage of fire every day. You have to steel yourself against the outbursts and the hate."[38]

Nobody in the home remains unscathed when a kid with CU traits is running amok. Evidence suggests that CU kids physically abuse their siblings more than typical kids do, and they may recruit their younger siblings to behave in antisocial ways, too.[39] One child with CU traits caused a toddler to fall into a swimming pool just so that they could witness a drowning.[40] Another, a six-year-old, tried to choke her two-year-old brother to death and told her mother, "I want to kill all of you."[41] Family pets aren't safe: in another ghastly instance, a child sliced off portions of a cat's tail out of curiosity about the cat's reaction.[42]

"Psychopathy is clearly a familial disorder and a disorder of the family," the psychiatrist Dr. Liane Leedom writes. "Dysfunctional family relationships both worsen and are worsened by psychopathy."[43] But the suffering doesn't stop with the family. It continues everywhere these budding bad apples go. Youth displaying CU traits stand a greater chance of joining gangs and masterminding crimes that their gangs conduct.[44] At school, they behave more aggressively than other children, bullying and victimizing their peers.[45] Even if they're not bullies themselves, we often find kids with CU traits supporting bullies rather than standing up for the targeted child.[46] And CU kids are less apt than others to behave in kind, helpful ways that allow teachers to maintain positive learning environments.[47]

One study asked teachers to describe their experiences with callous-unemotional traits in the classroom. As one reported, these kids "constantly wind other pupils up . . . insult them quietly, below teachers' hearing, or lying about things others have apparently said or done. They are far more violent and manipulative outside of class . . . sometimes causing a fight between two others rather than fighting themselves."[48] Another teacher noted that these kids were "totally uncaring, about the way they treat others and the way they are treated." Teachers often didn't know how to handle these kids, as standard forms of discipline didn't work.

Unfortunately, the small minority of children with callous-unemotional traits has a widespread negative impact. One study of more than a thousand children found that either teachers or parents rated about 5 percent of them as having a conduct disorder (marked by disruptive or aggressive behavior) and also being unconcerned with others' feelings. Another 7 percent showed marked callousness but didn't have a conduct disorder. Take a class of twenty-five kids and you're probably going to find at least one who has a conduct disorder or CU traits or both.[49]

The Man on Talisman Drive

One reason we underestimate the devastation dark personalities cause is because suffering defies an easy accounting. We can quantify some of it, but the harm is so great and diffuse that it becomes hard to identify and track. In individual cases, we often can't observe the damage directly, much less process it. And yet, when we stop to ponder it a bit, we find that it's there, like a kind of dark energy running through the heart of society.

Residents of Talisman Drive in the Virginia suburb of Vienna during the 1990s probably wouldn't have paid much attention to one of their neighbors, Robert. He seemed like a traditional family man. Lived in a typical split-level home. Worked a government job. Drove a Ford Taurus. Went to church on Sundays. Sent his six kids to private school. Seemed to love his wife. He wasn't the friendliest person, and he lived a little above his means. But he appeared normal enough.[50]

What his neighbors and colleagues didn't know—because Robert hid it well—was that he was spying for the Soviet Union and had been doing so for years. "Robert" is Robert Hanssen, one of history's most notorious spies. An FBI agent with access to highly sensitive government information, he had an arrangement in place with the Russians whereby he passed along documents, dead-dropping them in public areas for them to recover, and they paid him. While the international espionage made headlines, Hanssen's history is littered with other antisocial acts: sexual and emotional manipulation of his wife, a long string of tawdry affairs, a physical altercation with a colleague, two instances of breaking and entering university administration to "improve" his student records, and reckless driving.[51]

Let's compare Hanssen's behaviors to our model of psychopathy. First, he behaved in ways associated with lying, selfishness, manipulation, superficial charm, and a heightened sense of self (bucket 1—interpersonal). He left an earlier position at the Chicago Police Department because he was angry that his talents didn't receive enough recognition. At the FBI, according to his biographer David Vise, he "felt his brilliance was being overlooked. And he felt much smarter than the people around him."[52] And he maintained a double life for decades. Hanssen offered to sell secrets to the Soviet government in 1979 and continued to feed them information until his apprehension in 2001. A few years into his illicit gig, when his wife caught on to what he was doing, he downplayed his transgressions, promising to stop and donate the money he'd received from the Soviets to charity. This was another of his lies. To distract her from his continued espionage, he manipulated her fragile emotional state, fueling her anxieties and paranoia about evil forces out to get her. He also maintained an apparently convincing facade of normality for his neighbors' benefit.

As for bucket 2, Hanssen was callous and unemotional. An empathetic person doesn't abuse his wife the way Hanssen did, and he didn't express much remorse for his misdeeds upon being sent to prison. Although he did say that he was sorry for what he'd done to his family, he showed no remorse to the FBI, his country, or the people whose lives he put in danger—or ended.[53]

In addition, Hanssen showed a pattern of thrill-seeking (bucket 3—risk-taking). He drove recklessly as a youth, found excitement in the spy business, and engaged in risky sexual behavior. His adventurousness around sex sometimes verged into illegality, as when he shared a video feed of his and his wife's bedroom with a friend without his wife's consent.[54] As for the fourth bucket (antisocial), his prolonged criminality tells us what we need to know. This guy didn't abide by social norms or laws and committed a wide range of antisocial acts throughout his life.

Once again, we find ourselves in the presence of an individual with elevated psychopathic traits. And once again, we find that he did extraordinary harm. Because of Hanssen, the Russians got their hands on some six thousand documents, an intelligence haul that led them to execute at least three people on their side who, as they discovered, were helping US intelligence.[55] The Russians also learned other important details, including how the United States was spying on them, the identities of all Russian and Soviet spies working for the United States, and the US government's contingency scenarios in case World War Three broke out.[56] Interviewed for an obituary of Hanssen in the *New York Times*, the government prosecutor who handled his case remarked, "The magnitude of Hanssen's crimes cannot be overstated. They will long be remembered as being among the most egregious betrayals of trust in U.S. history."[57]

We can catalog some additional damage Hanssen did. Geopolitical relationships suffered: in the wake of his capture, dozens of diplomats were expelled by both the United States and Russia.[58] Also, trust inside the FBI and other national security agencies took a big hit. If you worked in that field, how could you be sure your colleagues weren't spying?

In general, though, when it comes to taking stock of Hanssen's negative impact, what we *can't* quantify seems much greater than what we can. Even in a case as well documented and highly publicized as his, so much of the harm remains invisible to us, although we can be certain it was there. As journalists noted during the early 2000s, the US government couldn't pin down the true extent of the information Hanssen gave away. Although Hanssen pleaded guilty to more than a dozen counts of espionage, he didn't receive the death penalty: the government wanted the option of interviewing him again if it needed to. Elaine Shannon, *Time* magazine's national security correspondent, said in 2002, "His interrogations did not go particularly well. The polygraphers weren't very happy with him, the Justice Department and CIA weren't happy. He was very forgetful for a man of his intelligence. This is pretty suspicious...."[59]

Members of the public can only guess what was in those roughly six thousand documents the government *did* know about, to say nothing of what else he might have divulged. We also have little idea of the damage such a vast amount of stolen information might have done to diplomatic relations and national security. Hanssen's crimes cost our society not just in the ways we can track, but in deep and diverse ways we can scarcely imagine.

Something similar holds true for any poisonous person. We might know about some of the harms that, say, a boss with psychopathic traits caused, but there are likely countless, daily acts of malice large and small they committed throughout their lives that we *don't* know about. As a result, we can't begin to understand the damage such a boss caused over years or decades to parents, friends, colleagues, and strangers, nor the spiraling, outward impacts of this damage. Given such unfathomable costs, it seems misguided to valorize dark personalities by admiring their personal success. The benefits of psychopathic traits are truly minuscule when stacked against all the known and possible harms.

We make another mistake when it comes to poisonous people. We assume that we're powerless in the face of their charm, manipulation, and abuse. That it's a psychopath's world, and we're just living in it. The problem with that line of thinking is that it limits our agency. When we scrutinize how dark personalities cause so much harm, we discover that much of the damage occurs because we *let* them harm us. Surprisingly vulnerable to their charms, we welcome them as romantic partners, promote them in our businesses, and vote them into office. To reduce the cost in our own lives and across society, we can take back control, becoming more aware of poisonous people and taking steps to contain their toxicity.

3

How the Poison Spreads

Imagine you're assigned a partner, a person you don't know and will never meet. The two of you play a game and amass points. Now imagine that the game's organizers pull you aside and announce they're going to let you determine how this game will end. You have three choices. You could end up winning 500 points and your partner only 100. You could both end up winning 500 points. Or you could end up winning 550 points and your partner only 300.

In the first option, you receive way more points than your partner—you utterly dominate them. In the second option, you both receive an equal number of points, and also quite a high number: 500 each. And in the third option, you receive the most points available in any of these options, but the spread between you and your partner is less than in the first option. You beat them, but they don't fare too badly either.

Which option would you choose?

This scenario is a test psychologists use to measure so-called social value orientations (SVOs), or how inclined you are to share what you have with others.[1] Most people choose the second option, in which both partners receive 500 points. Why not? It's the fair choice and the one that maximizes the number of points shared by you and your partner. It's a win-win outcome, leaving everyone happy.

Dark personalities choose differently. They tend to go with the first option, in which they receive 500 points and their opponent only 100. Even though they might have received more points with option three, they would rather sacrifice that extra margin to increase how much they dominate their partner in relative terms.[2] These choices reveal people's underlying interests. What people who score higher in psychopathic traits care about isn't maximizing everyone's well-being, including their own. They'd prefer to dominate others.

Stepping outside the laboratory, we find that psychopathic personalities do indeed seek to dominate those around them, an important way they cause so much harm. They crave power, prestige, and wealth. They're more inclined than others to think that acquiring material possessions makes for a good life.[3] And they cut others down, because what matters most to them is their *relative* position.

The impulse to dominate can manifest in multiple ways: as a tendency to abuse or humiliate other people, talk over and silence them, or control their lives. As we saw in chapter 1, the political philosopher Machiavelli argued that leaders should do whatever is required to obtain power: lie, cheat, manipulate, threaten—or worse. "It is much safer to be feared than loved, if one has to lack one of the two," he wrote.[4] Dark personalities love that kind of approach. They can initially seem charming, attentive, and compassionate (what some in the context of romantic relationships have called "love bombing"), but once they've reeled in their unsuspecting victims, they turn on the abuse, forcing others to submit.[5] As we've seen, dark personalities dominate their romantic partners through an array of behaviors, including physical violence, emotional abuse, financial abuse (controlling their access to money), and more.

Poisonous people are adept at domination in part because they're more predatorial than the rest of us—more attuned to weaknesses that they can exploit. As research shows, dark personalities have a knack for sniffing out vulnerable people with whom to form relationships.[6] They might also have a superior memory for potential victims once they've noticed them, filing that information away for future use.[7] People with psychopathy are like lions on the hunt; as they scan the horizon, their finely tuned instincts allow them to zoom in on the weakest gazelle. But this isn't the whole picture. It turns out that we, too, play an important role in their ability to gain power. Without realizing it, we *give* it to them. And we do this even when we're seemingly well-equipped to spot poisonous people and stop them from dominating us.

Paul, a retired midlevel officer with a national police force, is the last person you'd think would ever help a dark personality attain a position of authority. A committed public servant, he cares deeply about ethical standards. He truly is one of the good guys. Moreover, as a veteran police interrogator, he is an expert judge of bad actors and knows every psychological trick they can throw at him. He's adept at reading people, teasing out lies, and inducing reluctant interview subjects to divulge important information. And yet, even he got snookered by a dark personality, facilitating that person's rise to power inside his organization. In the end, it brought shame to his police force and cost Paul his job.

Paul first met this dark personality, an undercover operative at his agency named Dirk, about twenty years ago. The two chatted about interrogation techniques, and Paul found Dirk to be "an absolutely brilliant human being, so articulate, so positive," not to mention charismatic and affable. Paul was so keen on Dirk that he urged his boss and others at the agency to promote Dirk and transfer him to their interrogation team.

As a close colleague, Dirk proved every bit as smart as Paul had thought he was. He also turned out to be a callous and unprincipled self-promoter. Bent on moving his career forward, he cozied up to their boss, Kent, while subtly marginalizing Paul. He looked down on other officers when they expressed sympathy or remorse. He projected empathy, but it was a facade. If you looked closely, you found that, as Paul says, "he didn't care about anyone." Worst of all, Dirk was unethical and reckless in his approach to his work. He was willing to bend the law if it would help him solve a case and bolster his reputation.

For a while Paul sought to avoid conflict, but eventually his ethics and determination to honor suspects' legal rights led him to challenge Dirk. It happened one day when Paul was about to interview a young murder suspect. He was waiting for legal counsel to arrive, but Dirk, feeling that they had waited long enough, told Paul to just start the interview. Paul knew that doing so would cross a red line, and that he wouldn't be able to defend this decision at trial in front of a judge, so he refused and accused Dirk of unethical behavior in front of their whole unit. From that point on, Dirk saw Paul as an enemy and worked to sabotage his career by turning Kent and others against him. "The knives came out, and I saw a huge difference in how he acted. He wanted me gone," Paul says.

Dirk convinced others to doubt Paul's abilities and to sideline him professionally. Whereas previously Paul had received important assignments, now he was given the grunt work. Disheartened and stressed by Dirk's attacks, Paul began drinking too much, which provided an even bigger opening for Dirk. Following Dirk's suggestion, Kent took Paul off the team and forced him to go to rehab, a move that clearly was intended as a punishment. "There was no empathy involved," Paul recalls. "It was devastating." As another officer made clear to Paul, he was effectively off the team for good. When he finished rehab, he'd have to find another assignment within the agency. Dirk had maneuvered him out of a job.

Paul managed to find a new assignment in a different department. Over the decade that followed, he watched as Dirk got himself promoted multiple times and also found ways from a distance to cut into Paul's authority inside the organization. Frustrated at the power Dirk had been able to achieve, Paul eventually decided to leave the police force, taking early retirement. To this day, his memories of working with Dirk are painful. "Every time I hear about him, I still cringe."

Others do, too. Dirk never stopped misbehaving; he actually grew bolder. At one point, his outrageous and blatantly illegal behavior led to a scandal and talk of lawsuits against the agency. But rather than publicly disavow Dirk and remove him from power, higher-ups in the organization promoted Dirk and transferred him to an obscure location in an attempt to cover up his misdoings and the organization's complicity in it.

Dirk attained power and wreaked havoc *because other people let him*. There was Paul, who unwittingly invited this dark personality into his midst. There was Paul's boss and colleagues, who likewise were taken in by Dirk and didn't stop him from amassing power. And eventually, there were the organization's top leaders, who found it more convenient to sweep Dirk and his problem behavior out of sight rather than take him down. All of these individuals had some ability to prevent a poisonous person from rising up the ranks and corrupting the organization, but they failed to act.

Our Manspreading Problem

Dark personalities can cast a spell over us, and in recent years scientists have advanced some intriguing theories as to why that might be. One leading explanation of our vulnerability has to do, in part, with how humans react to dominance. When you're on the subway and the guy sitting next to you manspreads, stretching and positioning his limbs so that he encroaches on the common space between you, how do you respond? Do you manspread yourself, claiming your share of precious space? Or do you recoil, shrinking back in your seat and taking up less room?

Psychologists who study nonverbal behavior have found that expanding our body communicates dominance, while constricting it sends the opposite message.[8] Whether consciously or not, that manspreader is making a subtle power grab. But what's even more interesting is our reaction. One study paired participants with another person who purported to be a fellow participant but actually was a member of the research team. When those imposter participants adopted an expansive posture that took up more physical space, most participants *didn't* respond in kind. They became submissive, constricting their bodies. Researchers found that this wasn't a reasoned response. Participants didn't decide that it was worthwhile to shrink so that they could reach their destination without provoking a conflict. Rather, as the authors noted, "people seem to be unaware of these effects."[9]

We humans are attuned to social hierarchy, and in a peculiar way. Confronted with a display of dominance, most of us accede to it. Animals do this as well. The next time you visit a zoo, spend a few moments hanging out with the chimps. You might notice one who looks much larger than the rest—hair a bit on end, standing tall, walking slow and heavy, like a fighter entering the ring. You'll probably see the other chimps become cowed, making themselves small, literally bowing to the dominant chimpanzee. Scientists speculate that such behavior allows for more peace and harmony in the chimpanzee world. When chimps don't submit in the face of a dominance display, conflict usually erupts, and it isn't pretty.[10]

Shifting from the literal zoo to the figurative one that is the corporate boardroom, we can now understand why a disproportionate number of business leaders have clinical levels of psychopathy.[11]

These personalities are louder and brasher than others around them. They interrupt more. They're less concerned with social niceties. They're unafraid to threaten or harm others to obtain power. In organizations, they seek out managerial roles where they can boss people around. And we often defer to them. Instead of resisting, we clear a path for the dark personalities in our midst to seize and keep power.

We are also easily persuaded that these power-hungry people are competent. In one study, researchers divided a hundred college students into groups of four and had them work on math problems. They asked students to rate how competent and influential they felt their group mates were. They also had students fill out questionnaires that allowed the researchers to measure their personality traits. As researchers found, the students rated by their peers as most influential also were more likely to have dominant personalities. These alpha dogs were usually the first ones in the group to answer math problems, although their answers weren't more accurate. Their quick, confident responses prompted others to see them as stronger intellectually.[12]

Much as we might bristle at the interpersonal style of dark personalities, seeing them as overbearing and obnoxious, we also admire their leadership qualities. They conform to ingrained assumptions we have about how leaders are supposed to behave: as dominant, brash, self-confident, coldhearted personalities. In fact, these stereotypes are so ingrained that many of us regard bad behavior on a leader's part as a sign of their power. One study showed participants two videos of an average guy sitting in a café. In one of them, he acts like a jerk, letting ash from his cigarette fall to the ground, resting his feet disrespectfully on a nearby chair, barking an order at the waiter. In another, he acts in more agreeable ways, flicking ash into an ashtray, refraining from putting his feet up on the furniture, and politely asking his waiter for his food. Incredibly, participants were more inclined to see the jerk as powerful.[13] We not only overlook bad behavior in handing people power. We perceive them as powerful *because* they act badly.

In truth, dark traits are *terrible* for teams. Empathetic leaders perform better than cold, domineering ones do, as they have an easier time inspiring respect from team members and building strong, trusting relationships.[14] Leaders who are prone to feeling guilt also have an edge over the coldhearted. A capacity for guilt signals a sense of responsibility to others, which likewise arouses affection from subordinates.[15] These are the leaders who'll sacrifice themselves for others' benefit and who'll work harder to understand how their team members are feeling. Guilt-prone people also appear better at comprehending others' points of view and at arriving at helpful solutions when handling interpersonal conflicts.[16]

Leaders with dark traits underperform in all kinds of ways we seldom appreciate. Research suggests that people in work groups regard narcissistic leaders as more effective, but that in truth the personalities of these leaders lead to subpar decision-making.[17] This is because narcissistic leaders hog the limelight, preventing team members from sharing valuable information. Likewise, studies suggest that superstar athletes with big egos can inhibit their teams' success, despite their own prowess at putting points on the board. Athletes with higher levels of narcissism exhibit worse teamwork and are less likely to win.[18]

The baseball great Barry Bonds was notorious for being selfish, egotistical, and an all-around bad teammate. According to Jeff Pearlman, a seasoned sportswriter, Bonds not only shouted obscenities at kids asking for autographs, he "held a franchise hostage and refused to help teammates in need" while also flouting league rules by taking performance-enhancing drugs.[19] Even Bonds admitted that he "wasn't the best clubhouse guy."[20] He was a standout performer on the field, especially with some chemical assistance. But he wasn't a leader capable of bringing out the best in others and inspiring superior team performance. No accident, perhaps, that despite all the accolades Bonds won for his personal performance, including seven Most Valuable Player awards, his teams never won the World Series.[21]

Unfortunately, most of us overlook the noxious impacts of narcissistic, egotistical leaders. We regard overconfident people as good leaders even *after* we've been told that their egos outweigh their abilities.[22] But that's not the only reason poisonous people manage to insinuate themselves into organizations and then stay entrenched. Another dynamic that dark personalities set in motion, wittingly or not, plays an equally important role.

Faced with perceived threats to their power, dark personalities respond in ways that create open conflict. When they encounter a dominant person, backing down isn't their first instinct.[23] Pit a person with psychopathic traits against someone who is also seeking to dominate, and you'll often wind up with a "pissing contest" as each tries to one-up the other. Poisonous people also respond to perceived threats by sowing division. It's a classic strategy that we encounter on reality TV show competitions, which are rife with backbiting and other attempts to prevent rivals from forming alliances. Among chimpanzees as well, a dominant male will often become animated and attack two less dominant males who appear to be becoming friends.[24] In organizations, domineering leaders try to isolate talented subordinates who they believe threaten their status, preventing them from communicating with others and building friendships, even to the detriment of team performance.[25] We see a similar dynamic in families, too. In one study of women who reported having been in a relationship with a highly psychopathic partner, 75 percent said they were prevented from communicating with or seeing other family or friends, or were forcibly isolated from the outside world.[26]

Both pissing contests and divisive politicking unleash chaos, which makes us more inclined to defer to darkness. We see this with special clarity in politics. It's no coincidence that authoritarian strongmen in countries such as the United States, Brazil, Turkey, and India have all won elections over the past decade. Combining election results and economic data, researchers have found that support for dominant leaders increases as people experience more economic uncertainty.[27] When our world feels chaotic, we seek leaders who exude strength and control, presuming that they'll be able to set things right. In truth, these leaders are precisely the ones who sow instability thanks to their aggressive, impulsive, and self-serving behavior.

Dark personalities dominate. We submit. They create chaos and uncertainty as they defend and expand their power. We feel even *more* drawn to these leaders as the chaos mounts. Round and round we go. The next thing you know, we have officials who prefer to pursue win-lose solutions rather than win-win outcomes or compromises. We have democracies eroding and authoritarian regimes taking charge, driven by dark personalities.

Cursed by Credulity

Our susceptibility to dominance isn't the only way poisonous people harm us. Our natural benevolence also plays a role. We humans generally trust others.[28] We expect them to deal fairly with us. And we do so for good reason: most people are in fact trustworthy. But this "truth-default," as psychologists call it, leaves us vulnerable to dark personalities. We're terrible at spotting lies, even when we expect them.[29] We become unknowingly complicit in the harm poisonous people cause because we believe their many lies.

Evidence of our gullibility is everywhere: Anna "Delvey" Sorokin conning wealthy New York socialites into picking up her tab; Billy McFarland convincing concertgoers to drop huge sums of money on tickets to the Fyre Festival; Simon Leviev conning women out of millions of dollars after meeting them on Tinder and sweeping them off their feet; Donald Trump convincing millions of voters that he, not Joe Biden, won the 2020 US presidential election. Then there are the memoirs we buy that turn out to be at least partially fraudulent—James Frey's *A Million Little Pieces* (2003) and Greg Mortenson's *Three Cups of Tea* (2006) come to mind as examples.[30] And think of the multitude of phishing attacks that convince unsuspecting victims to click on a link, leaving them or their organizations open to theft and fraud.

Research I've conducted has confirmed just how bad we are at spotting lies. Chances are you've seen a relative of a missing person on TV begging for their safe return. My former doctoral student Chris Gunderson led a study in which he showed participants videos of these pleas for help. We asked participants to watch each video and then indicate how much sympathy they had for the pleader. We also asked them how much they would hypothetically donate to a GoFundMe campaign to help find the missing person. In total, each participant watched a dozen of these emotional appeals for help.

After our study, we asked participants if they noticed anything suspicious. Only about 6 percent of them (nineteen out of almost three hundred) wondered whether some of the pleaders might have been lying. In fact, *every* participant saw six videos in which the people pleading for help had actually killed the very person they were aiming to find. These participants watched lie after lie—and had no clue![31]

People with psychopathic traits exploit the good-natured gullibility that most of us exhibit. Research has found that people who score higher on dark personality traits are more inclined to lie.[32] These folks aren't bothered by the pangs of guilt that deter most people from deceiving others. They seem to *enjoy* deceiving others more than the rest of us. Such "duping delight," as psychologists call it, might serve as a kind of internal reward for deception, reinforcing that behavior and increasing the odds that psychopathic personalities will continue to lie.[33]

We shouldn't presume that people with psychopathy are necessarily better at lying than the rest of us. Research is mixed on this point. Some studies suggest that people with psychopathy are *less* believable than most people because they tell less coherent stories and appear to be thinking hard when lying.[34] Others assert that they are more successful than most people at manipulating others, especially in the context of dating. The sexual exploitation hypothesis, for example, holds that psychopathic traits could allow men to embody what women typically find attractive and desirable, and to do it by lying about their true feelings, experiences, and traits.[35]

One woman, Jodi, experienced the sexual exploitation hypothesis firsthand in 2018 when she dipped her toe back into the dating pool. She received a message from a man named Andy. As she told Courtney Shea in an interview for *Chatelaine* magazine, she fell for him hard: "Everything he said was exactly what I wanted to hear."[36] Andy was affectionate, they had similar experiences and interests, and he was taking a break from a lucrative run as an engineer. He was financially successful, although his funds were temporarily tied up in gold bars. At first, his requests for money were small; he needed to borrow $500 to take a recertification test required for a new job. He needed some cash to pay his subcontractors and for accommodations near his new jobsite, but he promised to pay her back.

Andy—who turned out to be the noted Canadian con artist Marcel Andre Vautour—vanished with almost $50,000 of Jodi's money. Vautour was finally arrested in October 2022. While we don't know how he would score on a personality test, his behavior is broadly consistent with psychopathic traits, particularly those related to deception, superficial charm, and a parasitic lifestyle.[37] In the office, these same traits might show up as a conniving colleague who claims to be your best friend but bad-mouths you to your boss to get ahead. In politics, it might show up as a politician who claims to pray for victims and feel their pain but then, paid off by a wealthy donor, betrays the victims by voting against legislation that would have protected them.

Whether or not people with psychopathy are more effective liars, they're going to wreak havoc simply because they lie so much and the rest of us are too trusting to catch all their falsehoods. In other words, they exploit our "truth-default." Understanding this dynamic, we might feel tempted to cast ourselves as innocent victims whose only sin is our good-natured naivete. The reality is more complicated—and less flattering. We don't just believe the lies poisonous people tell us. We start to *act* like them. That old saying turns out to be true: a rotten apple really *can* spoil the whole barrel.

The Machiavellian Mom

Diana, a stay-at-home mom living in an upper-crust East Coast suburb, can attest to that maxim. Some years ago, she enrolled her five-year-old daughter in one of the country's most prestigious and highly rated private schools. During her initial encounters with other parents, she noticed that one of the moms seemed to be the school's "queen bee." Kendra had movie-star looks and a husband from a wealthy, socially prominent family. At every event, she held court, with legions of moms fawning over her. She seemed warm and welcoming, but something about her friendliness rang false to Diana—"I just had a very bad vibe," she says. Nevertheless, everyone else was enamored with Kendra, so Diana kept her "bad vibe" to herself and began to second-guess her own judgment.

Diana's instincts about Kendra turned out to be correct. Over the next several years, she watched as Kendra behaved maliciously to maintain her dominant position in the school's pecking order. She backstabbed other moms, seeming warm and friendly to their faces but speaking horribly about them behind their backs. She was also a master at sowing discord, making small, seemingly innocuous comments that made other moms resentful and distrusting of one another.

In episodes straight out of the Machiavellian playbook, Kendra punished and ostracized moms she didn't like or perceived as a threat to her position. When her husband was organizing a basketball team, she had him leave out one of her best friend's daughters (apparently, Kendra nursed a grudge toward her), making it seem that the league's organizer, not her husband, was preventing the girl from participating. On another occasion, when a well-liked mom was pushing into her territory at the posh country club where many of the moms played tennis, Kendra penned an anonymous letter to the club's leaders requesting that this popular mom's application to join the club be denied. The letter's claim? The popular mom "grunted" in unseemly ways while hitting the ball. Although the popular mom ultimately became a full member of the club, the letter succeeded in humiliating her.

Kendra's malice spread. One mom who was insecure and eager for Kendra's friendship became her "minion," Diana says, spreading nasty gossip at her direction. Likewise, while working to ostracize her competitor at the country club, Kendra exerted pressure by convincing another mom to deny her time on the tennis court. Kendra was "very clever about how she makes it look like it wasn't her fault by using someone else," Diana says. "And all these people would do her dirty work, and they would be the ones that looked bad, and everybody thought that they were mean." As an outsider lingering at the edges of Kendra's group, Diana was appalled. "It was so frustrating watching these people getting abused almost like right in front of my face, and no one would pick up on it. A couple of times I would try to hint to people to see it, and they'd be like, 'Oh, Kendra's the nicest person.' "

Over time, Kendra's social set became thoroughly corrupted, with the moms around her at school and the country club constantly fighting with one another, often over the pettiest of slights. It was "like they're in middle school," Diana says, true reality-show material. Nobody seemed bothered enough to either stand up to Kendra or leave the group—such rancor had become normalized in their eyes.

The discord was especially striking given that relationships among other groups of moms at the school were much more harmonious. Likewise, during periods when Kendra didn't participate socially with other parents in her kids' classes, the tone of their gatherings markedly improved. Kendra's gaggle of moms had been "acting fake because she was there" in hopes of gaining her acceptance. Now, with her gone, they became kinder. Everyone got along better and forged new friendships.

A few dark personalities can cause harm at scale because they create conditions that give the devil on our shoulder a megaphone, increasing the likelihood that we'll cheat, steal, lie, bully, and in general act badly. Before we know it, we're deviating from our own moral codes and allowing their values to inform our behavior. Ever notice that many people who behave poorly in public subsequently apologize by proclaiming some variation of "This is not who I am" or "I know I'm better than that"? Perhaps they really *are* better but have unwittingly allowed themselves to fall under the spell of a dark personality.

Cultures of Rot

In the business world, poisonous people can corrupt entire teams and organizations—all the more so if they occupy positions of authority. Science sheds light on exactly how this happens. We've all seen or heard about kids who appear to mirror the bad behavior of their parents. In a set of famous experiments, the psychologist Albert Bandura provided experimental evidence of this pattern, finding that kids who saw adults receive rewards for hitting a Bobo doll were more likely to bat around the doll as well.[38]

Informed by this study, the Drexel University psychologist Dr. Mary Bardes Mawritz and her colleagues found that the same "monkey see, monkey do" phenomenon exists between bosses and employees, too. Surveying people in 288 work groups, including employees and their immediate supervisors, the researchers found that supervisors were more inclined to behave abusively toward others when *their* managers were abusive. In turn, employees with abusive supervisors were more likely to act rudely toward, publicly embarrass, or curse at others at work. If the climate at work was already toxic, the likelihood of trickle-down abuse became even greater.[39]

Kind and empathic people are prone to infection by dark personalities in at least three ways. First, people with psychopathic traits distort norms for acceptable behavior, especially when they occupy positions of power. The Hollywood producer Scott Rudin, regarded as "an absolute monster" to work for, created a corporate culture that, according to an exposé in *The Hollywood Reporter*, was "a new level of unhinged."[40] But it wasn't just the big boss who behaved poorly. The same senior leaders whom he abused meted out similar behavior to others. A former employee recounted how one of his senior leaders threw objects off a desk during tantrums alongside Rudin. And a junior creative executive told *New York Magazine* that the team members who stuck around were those who tended to "share some sort of adversarial spirit and lock horns with him."[41]

When Rudin threw a laptop or a glass bowl across the room in anger, or when he shouted insults at subordinates, he implicitly or explicitly encouraged others to adopt those same standards.

Employees came to regard his behavior as normal, expecting it or not fully registering it when he behaved aggressively or violently. At least one former assistant remembered Rudin training them, in essence, to behave like he did. "He would try to get me to yell at people on the phone," this employee said. "I remember once I was talking to the office, relaying some piece of information he didn't like. And he was like, 'You tell him this!' I would say it in a more human way, and he would start screaming at me to say what he'd said: 'Tell him he has the IQ of a plate or a baked potato,' or 'Tell him he's brain-dead,' trying to get me to channel his anger more."[42]

Norms powerfully constrain our worst tendencies; we adhere to them even when they seem to defy reason.[43] When norms of decorum, prosociality, and honesty become degraded, bad behavior spreads.[44] I witnessed this phenomenon during the early 2010s while I was living in the San Francisco Bay Area. A start-up incubator invited me to speak to an audience of entrepreneurs and venture capitalists about how to detect when people lie. I gave them some practical tips, including some I'll describe later in this book. I hoped to help idealistic entrepreneurs spot lies so that they could steer clear of bad actors.

Some in the room had ulterior motives. One approached me and asked whether I could teach them how to pass a lie detector test. "I could," I said, "but I won't." Here was an authority figure who seemed to condone lying so long as you knew you could get away with it. With people like this setting the tone in the rarefied world of high-tech start-up funding, it wouldn't be surprising to see many others adopting that same behavior. And indeed, the *Forbes* 30 Under 30 list is littered with cheaters, including the disgraced crypto wunderkind Sam Bankman-Fried, the biotech fraudster Elizabeth Holmes, and the notorious pharma bro Martin Shkreli.[45]

Human psychology gives bad actors an assist in distorting norms. Thanks to evolution, we notice negative information more than we do positive.⁴⁶ The negative stuff can cause us harm, and chances of survival are better if we're aware of it and can prepare. But focusing on the negative distorts our view of the world. In an organizational setting, it becomes easier for us to spot a few instances of bad behavior and presume that it's the norm, lowering the bar for our own behavior. As we and others begin behaving badly, the norms erode. In the wider world, the media amplifies this effect, highlighting negative stories over positive ones, which drum up less engagement.⁴⁷

Poisonous people also corrupt cultures by sparking emotional reactions from those they hurt. When people inside an organization are abused by dark personalities, they become angry and stressed, and these feelings can propagate bad behavior. Consider the classic example of an employee berated by their boss who comes home and kicks the family dog. Similarly, scholars have found that people with more psychopathic bosses report increased work-family conflict, meaning their work causes problems at home.⁴⁸ Research also suggests that anger can incline us toward risk-taking. When we feel wronged by a dark personality, we can take on some of their characteristic impulsivity.⁴⁹

Since emotions can be contagious, our anger spreads, causing others to behave aggressively, recklessly, or unethically.⁵⁰ And remember the dominating behavior described earlier? The fear that this causes spreads, too. Former Uber CEO Travis Kalanick is known for his aggressive, manipulative, insensitive behavior, and for creating a broader culture in which dark personalities could thrive.⁵¹ As employees told the *New York Times*, ruthlessness and a "Hobbesian environment" reigned inside the company: to get ahead, it was okay to trample and abuse others.⁵² The poor treatment people received stayed with them. In one instance, a leader sent an email to thousands of team members berating an engineer for making a mistake. Years later, the memory of this incident was still fresh, instilling a sense of fear in employees.[53] The presence of legions of fearful employees further entrenches and encourages dominating behavior on the part of some.

A third way dark personalities spread their poison is by ingraining a harshly competitive mindset. Domineering leaders instill a zero-sum logic in their subordinates.[54] We come to think that we can only achieve our goals if others lose in the process, so we become more antisocial. Everything becomes a fierce competition. Instead of celebrating other people's successes, we take them as a personal slight and rein in our natural desires to share resources and help others. When we're working in a competitive environment alongside people who lie, cheat, and steal, we might well lose out if we stick to our principles. To get ahead, we must behave poorly, too—as all too many of us do.

Across society, we find dark personalities spreading harmful behavior. Parents with psychopathic traits can pass on their bad behavior to their children, especially those genetically predisposed to it.[55] In politics, candidates with dark personalities are more likely to use dirty campaign tactics, leading their opponents to respond in kind. False, polarizing, and rage-inducing posts on social media spread more quickly than accurate, less polarizing posts.[56] This owes to our psychology (the tendency, as noted earlier, to pay attention to negativity), but it also occurs because the algorithms of social media platforms prioritize posts that capture our attention—and extreme sentiment does just that. Since social media companies sell ads based on the number of eyeballs they attract, their algorithms are primed to deliver those eyeballs, giving poisonous people a megaphone for spreading vitriol. Meanwhile, toxic comments inspire other people to respond in kind, further coarsening public discourse.[57]

More often than we'd like to admit, we allow our own behavior and values to become corrupted. The good guys stand by as norms erode. We grow angry and fearful, lashing out at others, or willingly submit to dominance. We say "the hell with it" and do whatever it takes to win, adopting the zero-sum logic as our own. In each of these ways, we become vectors of bad behavior ourselves.

Lifting the Veil

We may be only dimly aware of the wide-reaching consequences of ceding power to poisonous people. Think back to Kendra. Most of the other moms were oblivious to what she was doing—for years. They didn't perceive that she was causing discord between them, nor did those who behaved poorly at her behest understand that she was manipulating them. According to Diana, some of the moms didn't want to see Kendra's true colors even after she had mistreated them.

If the unseen damage caused by one mom can be so far-reaching, the consequences are likely to cut even wider and deeper when a dark personality takes charge of an entire country. People often pin the events of January 6 on Donald Trump, faulting him for calling on his supporters to march on the US Capitol. In fact, his corrosive effect on democracy has been far broader. One study found that Trump supporters who read his false tweets about election interference and media corruption (versus relatively benign tweets from his account) later reported less support for democratic ideals. They were less likely to agree with statements such as "The more people participate in politics and elections, the better" and "The government should never treat members of one religion differently than members of any other religion."[58] Even if you don't support a national leader who is a dark personality, your faith in democracy might still dwindle. Researchers found that corruption by the highest-level politicians in seventeen Latin American countries was associated with more violent protests, less trust for politicians and neighbors, and decreased voter turnout.[59]

And yet, these malevolent leaders aren't really bulletproof, nor are the everyday dark personalities we encounter. In Kendra's case, the other moms did eventually catch on. An important turning point, Diana suggests, was when Kendra wrote that anonymous letter bad-mouthing another mom who was applying to join the country club. The mom in question was known by many to be a kind person, making the contentions in the letter seem particularly undeserved. When others discovered that Kendra was behind the letter, she lost a great deal of her credibility and social cachet at the club. Something similar happened at the school, where the director took her aside and told her to stop causing trouble. "It finally just all collapsed," Diana says, "but it took years." And in the meantime, enormous damage had been done.

As psychological science teaches us, we have the power to stop the rot *before* it spreads. Because we give poisonous people so much of their power, we can decide not to do so. The first step takes place in our minds: we must recognize the motivations and tactics of dark personalities. By understanding malevolent types and how easily we let them gain a foothold in our lives, and by clarifying how we want people in our lives (including ourselves) to behave, we'll go a long way toward inoculating ourselves against their toxicity.

Another important, preventative move we can make is to develop a mental radar system for detecting individual dark personalities. We know the general patterns that characterize psychopathic traits, but if we can learn to recognize the subtler behaviors that these traits entail, we can rebuff the advances of poisonous people or even avoid them entirely. As we'll see in the next chapter, by becoming just a bit more knowledgeable, we can begin to contain the darkness while still allowing our innate optimism, generosity, and kindness to prevail.

4

Spotting a Dark Personality in Ten Seconds or Less

In 2008, when I was in graduate school in Halifax, Nova Scotia, a twelve-year-old girl named Karissa Boudreau was reported missing in Bridgewater, a town about an hour down the road. According to Karissa's mother, Penny, she and her daughter had stopped at a local grocery store and Penny had gotten out of her car, leaving Karissa to wait while she picked up some food. When she returned, Karissa was gone.

Penny appeared terrified for her daughter: it was January, and when last seen Karissa was wearing only jeans, a hoodie, a vest, and some Crocs—nothing close to what she'd need to survive in the elements.[1] Two days after Karissa's disappearance, Penny appeared at a press conference and made an emotional appeal for her safe return. Dabbing her face with a tissue, she explained that she and her daughter had been squabbling, but not about an issue so significant that it would have prompted her to run away. "Karissa, we love you," she said, addressing her daughter. "Your grandparents are looking for you. All of us are. I don't know where you are, but just come home or call or something. Please."[2]

At the time of the press conference, police said they had no evidence that a crime had been committed. A week and a half later, however, Karissa's body was found nearby on a snowy stretch of riverbank. She hadn't just run away; she'd been murdered. The community was devastated. Locals couldn't fathom that a crime like this could happen in their peaceful little town.[3]

The year before, I had started studying deception, and in particular what people do with their faces when they tell lies. To identify and analyze these cues to deception, I brought in undergraduate students and showed them images known to evoke emotions (happiness, sadness, disgust, and so on). I asked them either to express their genuine emotions or to simulate or suppress their true feelings. I was looking for subtle differences on the face when they faked certain emotions—and indeed we found some.[4] But this was an artificial experiment in a lab. Would brief facial movements betray people when they were lying in a high-stakes, real-life situation, such as a government background check, or when being interviewed as a witness in a legal case?

I wasn't sure at first how to go about answering that question. Few researchers had studied the facial expressions of liars in the real world, and for good reason: outside of the lab, it's hard to know for sure who's lying and who isn't.

Then I came upon a 2001 study by Drs. Aldert Vrij and Samantha Mann of the University of Portsmouth in the United Kingdom.[5] Seeking to determine how adept police officers were at detecting lies, the two had shown a group of police officers some clips from press conferences featuring people like Penny Boudreau who were asking the public to help locate missing loved ones. In the specific cases Vrij and Mann selected, courts already had found that the individuals making the public pleas were guilty—they had actually been the murderers and their emotional pleas were high-stakes lies. This paper was exactly the inspiration I'd been looking for. I, too, could use video of convicted killers who had made public pleas for their relatives' safe returns, this time focusing not on our skills at lie detection but rather on liars' behavior itself.

Vrij and Mann kindly shared their videos with me, and I collected other clips of people from around the world who had gone on television and asked for help finding a missing loved one. Some of these people had lied to the public—they had actually been involved in their loved one's disappearance. Others were genuinely distraught—they had no idea where their relative had gone and desperately wanted them home. In these cases, another person was convicted of the homicide, or the missing person was found alive. By comparing facial expressions across the two groups, I thought I could perhaps spot patterns that betrayed lying.

I was midway through this research, painstakingly documenting facial actions, when I happened to see Penny Boudreau's press conference on TV. Immediately, I knew something was off. As was the case with other, documented liars I was studying, the expression on her face didn't quite match the emotions she was purporting to convey. When we're sad, we generally pull the corners of our lips down in a pout while pulling our inner eyebrows upward and together, creating a characteristic furrowed brow.[6] That motion of the eyebrows is critical, since it's a hard movement to produce voluntarily. I didn't see it in Penny.[7] Instead, she was raising both of her eyebrows entirely, as one would do when they are surprised. This action is easy to fake. Try it yourself, and then try to simulate sadness. Feel the difference?

I conducted a thorough, frame-by-frame analysis of Penny's first press conference. Penny's face looked like prototypical sadness on only 140 of 2,000 frames, and these expressions only involved muscles in the lower portion of her face, where it's easier physically to simulate emotions.[8] At no point did her entire face evoke sadness. I couldn't help but wonder: was Penny really as sad about her daughter's disappearance as she claimed? My analysis also picked up disgust in her upper face and fear and anger in her lower face—emotions that a distressed parent probably wouldn't show while begging for their child's return. I concluded that Penny was likely lying, and that she might have played a role in her daughter's disappearance.

I jotted down my findings in an email and shot it off to my supervisor.[9] He was also suspicious, but neither of us thought we had rock-solid proof that Penny was lying. We didn't have much experience yet working with this kind of data, nor did we have a wealth of other scientific findings to draw on. Ours was basically a hunch, albeit an educated one.[10] Still, I wasn't surprised some months later when the police arrested Penny and charged her with her daughter's murder. She later admitted to the killing, pleaded guilty, and received a life sentence.[11]

Researchers have uncovered a number of science-based techniques in recent years that help us spot deception. That's good news for anyone seeking to avoid harm at the hands of poisonous people, since lying is one of psychopathy's defining behaviors. Of course, Penny wasn't necessarily high in psychopathic traits—some people commit heinous crimes yet score low on the PCL-R.[12] But many prolific liars do possess dark personalities. If we can quickly spot their lying ways, we can steer clear of them *before* they can ensnare and manipulate us. Even if we don't manage to spot lies during a given interaction, research has revealed other techniques that can allow us to cue into dark personality traits with just seconds of shrewd observation.

How to Spot a Liar

US president Harry S. Truman famously called Richard Nixon "a shifty-eyed goddamn liar."[13] To many people, shifty eyes are the most reliable sign someone is lying. We presume that if someone can't look us in the eye, they're trying to hide something and fear being found out. One study asked more than two thousand people from dozens of countries to name the behaviors they associate with lying. Two-thirds claimed that liars averted their gaze—by far the most popular response.[14]

Truman was right about Nixon's deceit, but wrong about shifty eyes being a reliable cue.[15] One meta-analysis of more than thirty studies that measured eye contact or gaze found that people sometimes averted their eyes both when they were lying or telling the truth—there was no difference.[16] Likewise, some researchers have proposed that liars glance up and to the right more often than truth-tellers do.[17] Analyzing the televised pleas of people such as Penny Boudreau, several colleagues and I found that this behavior didn't distinguish liars either.[18]

Another widespread belief—that liars fidget nervously—also fails to pan out. In one study, researchers asked ninety-nine British police officers to watch videos of suspects being interrogated and to flag truthful and false statements. All the videos contained portions of testimony that were truthful and others that weren't. Officers who reported paying more attention to fidgeting were *less* skilled at detecting lies. The more that officers paid attention to nonverbal cues in general, the worse they did.[19] Although departments traditionally have trained police officers to rely on these cues, researchers have found that they can't sniff out lies any better than if they were making judgments at random—despite what seasoned officers might think.[20]

It would be nice if there were some obvious sign like Pinocchio's nose that we could rely on to help us spot lies quickly and reliably, but there isn't. This makes sense: if lying were so easy and straightforward to detect, there would be little point in doing it. Fortunately, we can tease out when someone is fibbing by attending to *verbal* cues—the words people use when communicating. Specifically, I recommend listening for two kinds of verbal cues: how detailed a person's statements are, and whether those statements contradict one another or a person's nonverbal behavior.

One study by Dr. Bruno Verschuere of the University of Amsterdam assessed what happened when participants set aside the multitude of potential behavioral cues and instead just paid attention to how *detailed* a person's communication was and whether they could verify those details. Some people tell stories that go heavy on the specifics, such as what color a person's car was, the way they styled their hair, or the precise time they picked up the phone. Others are vague in their storytelling. Likewise, some people provide details we can verify, for instance by checking in with someone else who witnessed the events in question or by checking footage from a security camera. As Dr. Verschuere and his colleagues found, paying attention to these cues allowed people to boost their accuracy at detecting lies from about 50 percent—in other words, about as good as flipping a coin—to about 65 to 70 percent. That's not perfect, but it's significantly better, just by focusing on one aspect of our speech.[21]

In applying this method, be sure to ask open-ended questions. Posing yes-or-no questions pretty much guarantees that you won't get much detail, regardless of whether the person is lying or telling the truth. If someone offers a short answer to an open-ended question, politely encourage them to say more. Truth-tellers won't have difficulty with simple requests for additional detail, but liars will be challenged to come up with more. Even better—ask unexpected questions.[22] People who hope to lie their way through a first date, job interview, or political campaign often prepare their answers in advance. By asking questions that surprise them, you can thwart their stock answers.

Let's say you doubt whether a job candidate really has five years of experience working at the Apple Store in Berkeley, California, as they claim on their résumé. They will probably be expecting a question such as "Tell me about your role at the Apple Store in Berkeley." They probably *won't* expect "I'm wondering, what was your favorite place to grab lunch when you were working at the Apple Store in Berkeley?" Someone who worked there for five years would have no problem handling this random question. If they never worked there, they'd likely struggle to generate a detailed and verifiable response. That difficulty might lead to other signals that liars are maxing out their brain power. They might speak very slowly, stumble over their words, or generally appear to be thinking hard.[23]

If you happened to catch the cyclist Lance Armstrong's supposedly "tell-all" interview with Oprah Winfrey in 2013, you would have spotted such cues in abundance. Armstrong is famous for overcoming cancer to win seven consecutive Tour de France titles. Unfortunately, he cheated his way to those titles by using performance-enhancing drugs. Despite denying cheating for many years, he came on Winfrey's show expecting to admit to his doping habit. What he might not have expected was a question about whether he'd pressured others on his team to dope, too.

When Oprah asked him about allegations from a former teammate, Christian Vande Velde, that Armstrong threatened to kick him off the team if he didn't partake in doping, Armstrong's response wasn't so smooth. "That's . . . that's not true. There was a, uh, a level of expectation. We expected guys to be fit to be able to compete."[24] He appeared to be thinking hard, taking his time to formulate his response, which was littered with pauses and speech hesitations. None of these behaviors necessarily meant that he was lying, but they certainly should have raised some red flags. And in fact, an official anti-doping agency report later found that he had "enforced and reenforced" doping among his teammates, threatening to kick them off if they didn't comply.[25]

On rare occasions, questioners pose an unanticipated query so adeptly that you can almost see the gears turning inside someone's head as they realize that they are well and truly screwed. In 2016, the publication of the Panama Papers revealed the identities of wealthy individuals and public officials who were holding money offshore to avoid domestic taxes. One of those implicated was Sigmundur Davíð Gunnlaugsson, who then served as Iceland's prime minister. When asked in an interview whether he had any connection to offshore companies, he gave a vague response and noted, "That's an unusual question for an Icelandic politician to get."[26] The interviewer, Sven Bergman of the Swedish television station SVT, followed up about Gunnlaugsson's connection to a specific offshore company called Wintris, prompting Gunnlaugsson to stutter and stammer over the course of an excruciating thirty-second nonanswer. His exact words: "Well . . . Um, it's a company . . . if I recall correctly . . . which is associated with one of the companies that I was on the board of, and ah . . . it was ah . . . had an account which as I, as I, mentioned has been ah with the tax ah, ah, on the tax account since it was established." Upon entering parliament in 2009, Gunnlaugsson had failed to disclose his ownership of Wintris, an omission that violated ethics rules and created an undisclosed conflict of interest. After protests, Gunnlaugsson resigned from his post as prime minister.[27]

A second feature of speech that can cue us into potential lies is the *consistency* of what we hear.[28] If we listen closely to what others tell us, we might notice that the data doesn't all align. A coworker might claim to have graduated from a certain university, yet when we ask about the small town where that university is located, they appear not to have ever heard of it. A parent at your kid's soccer game might have claimed to have been away on vacation the previous week, yet a few minutes later they casually mention having eaten at a local restaurant during that week. If you're already feeling suspicious about a person's honesty, you can approach your conversations strategically. If a friend said they saw your new beau in town when you thought they were traveling to a work conference, you might ask them, "How was your workweek?" instead of "Why did Sandra see you in Starbucks on Monday if your conference was across the country?" Instead of revealing what you already know in your question, listen to their answer first. That way, you can see whether your friend's sighting has a simple explanation (for instance, their outbound flight was delayed by a day) or whether their answer directly contradicts what your friend witnessed.[29] If you reveal your suspicions in your question, an adept liar can create an answer that accounts for the information you already have. If you hold your cards a little closer to your chest, a liar will more likely provide an answer that's inconsistent with known facts.

Inconsistencies can also arise between what people are saying and the emotions they're expressing. At one point when Penny Boudreau was facing the cameras, someone asked her how it had been for her as a mother to see her daughter Karissa go missing. "Plain and simple hell, to put it in plain English," Boudreau said. "Not knowing where your kids are is horrible. She didn't go anywhere without me taking her, so I always knew where she was."[30] You might expect someone uttering these words to be sad, angry, or fearful, but Penny's face didn't seem to express any of those feelings. Rather, she appeared surprised, with her eyebrows raised rather than furrowed, as in sadness. This look of surprise might not have indicated actual emotion but rather a failed effort on her part to simulate sadness.

In addition to these cues, we should consider how useful the lie might be from the liar's point of view. Most people seldom lie, and when they do, they usually tell white lies intended to spare people's feelings, not big, self-aggrandizing lies.[31] By contrast, people high in psychopathic traits not only tell many lies, they often do so to achieve specific goals: establishing themselves as the alpha dog, avoiding punishment for outrageous behavior, or convincing others to have sex with them.[32] We might supplement our attention to verbal cues by asking ourselves: "What does this person stand to gain by convincing me of a lie in this situation?" If it seems plausible that the person could pursue the dark personality's typical goals by getting us to believe what they're saying, then we should handle their statements more skeptically.

The next time you meet someone new, concentrate on what they're saying, keeping detail and consistency foremost in mind. If you're getting vague statements, details you can't verify, and inconsistencies within the statements, or between the statements and the emotions people are expressing, you might want to deploy your new investigative interviewing skills. By asking unanticipated questions and using your knowledge strategically, you can make the cues to deception more obvious and improve your odds of identifying lies accurately. Consider it a red flag if their lies are plentiful and seem likely to deliver the kind of self-serving benefits that poisonous people crave.

First Impressions

Besides prolific deception, other telltale signs can signal that a person might possess dark traits, both when you're meeting them for the first time and when you know them from a distance or on a casual basis. Let's first consider the situation where you're encountering a total stranger. Even before you come face-to-face with a new person, you would be wise to consider the context in which you're meeting. For example, someone you meet at a Habitat for Humanity volunteering event might have greater empathy and compassion than the average person. However, you might expect a player who boasts about their kill count in violent video game chat logs to show darker traits, such as callousness or sadism.[33]

If you're looking to find a new romantic or business partner, you'll also want to be mindful of the message *you're* sending. In an early study on psychopathic traits, Dr. Cathy Widom at Harvard University posted ads in a "counterculture" Boston newspaper, requesting "charming, aggressive, carefree people who are impulsively irresponsible but who are good at handling people and looking after number one."[34] She found that her ads attracted a select group of people—namely, those with seriously dark traits. One respondent actually asked her, "Are you looking for hookers or trying to make a list of all the sociopaths in Boston?"

Similarly, recent research finds that job postings that recruit for people who are "tactical" communicators, who think "outside the box," and who are "results-oriented" attract more narcissistic applicants than postings for the same position that emphasize "straightforward" communication, collaboration, and a "process-orientation."[35] If you are genuinely looking for a bold, charming, carefree romantic partner or employee, you'll want to be aware that these words can be used as euphemisms for dark traits and that they may come with other, less attractive qualities. You may want to reconsider your wording, or be on guard for more dark traits than you had bargained for.

Fortunately, research has shown that novices can identify strangers with dark traits—particularly those linked to psychopathy—in mere seconds with just a bit of guidance. In a study published in 2009, researchers from Emory University and the University of Minnesota asked psychology students at the undergraduate and graduate levels to watch video clips of inmates at a Florida prison being interviewed as part of a scientific assessment for psychopathy (the PCL-R). The clips were short: five-, ten-, or twenty-second "thin slices" of behavior. The scientists asked the students to rate how strongly the inmates displayed psychopathic traits.[36]

As part of the rating process, students read brief summaries of what to look for. For instance, they read the following explanation: "Psychopaths tend to be charming and engaging on the surface, but often manipulate, lie to, and exploit others to get what they want, without guilt or empathy. They tend to be irresponsible and to lack impulse control." Students were also given descriptions of specific psychopathic traits described in chapter 1, one that emphasized the interpersonal and affective buckets of traits, and the other marked primarily by descriptions of impulsivity and antisocial behavior. Specifically, students learned that psychopaths "have an inflated sense of self-importance," are unempathetic, "rarely accept responsibility for the things they do wrong," and "are impulsive, frequently seek stimulation because of boredom, lack realistic long-term goals of their own, and often find ways to live off the support of parents, friends, and sexual partners."

As it turned out, the judgments by untrained students corresponded pretty well with the inmates' actual PCL-R scores—they were "reasonably reliable and valid," the researchers found. Bear in mind, the PCL-R scores were measured by a trained psychologist who conducted an hours-long interview and reviewed the inmates' correctional files. When it comes to picking up on psychopathy, our quick first impressions shaped by just a bit of knowledge allow us to do well relative to a seasoned pro.

I wondered how people managed to detect psychopathic traits from such small snippets of video, so I performed follow-up research with the scientists behind this study. A member of our team went through the videos, analyzing the inmates' verbal and nonverbal behaviors. We compared this data with the ratings that the students had given in the previous studies. Did inmates high in psychopathic traits behave differently from those who presented fewer of these traits? If so, were people in the earlier study picking up on these behaviors to detect psychopathy?

People with more psychopathic traits did behave in telltale ways. They displayed more genuine-looking smiles, the kind that combine upturned lip corners with the crinkle of skin in the corners of your eyes—what scientists call "Duchenne smiles," named after the French neurologist who first described them.[37] Those with more psychopathic traits also used more angry language than did other inmates, and they used more hand gestures in expressing themselves. It might seem puzzling that these individuals would smile more while also expressing more anger, but this probably owes to the efforts these people make to deceive others and manage how they come across. It might also reflect the delight that people with psychopathic traits often take in deceiving others.[38]

When we statistically analyzed students' first impressions, comparing them with the data about inmates' behavior, we found that the students were using these verbal and nonverbal cues to form judgments about the presence of psychopathic traits. But interestingly, the students were also taking into account behaviors that *didn't* accurately signal psychopathic traits. They were noticing whether the inmates were able to avoid pauses in conversation, taking that as evidence that inmates were charismatic "smooth talkers" and therefore high in psychopathy. It might seem valid to make such a connection, but the data didn't support this relationship. If students hadn't been looking for signs of smooth-talking, they might have identified people with psychopathy even more accurately.

The upshot: you might be better equipped than you think to spot malevolent personalities in your life, but you'll do best if you take a structured approach, one that seeks those cues that really do reflect dark traits.[39] In fact, the 2009 study mentioned previously also suggests how important it is to pay attention to select cues. Not only had researchers asked students to provide rough ratings of psychopathic traits, they also had them fill out a questionnaire that screens for psychopathy, what is known as the Interpersonal Measure of Psychopathy, or IM-P.[40] Although the PCL-R test is much more thorough, the IM-P can help a psychologist detect psychopathic traits by having them scan for twenty-one specific behaviors. When untrained students used the IM-P to evaluate what they saw in the thin-slice videos of inmates, their judgments were more on target.

Drawing on elements of the IM-P test, I've developed a set of questions you can use to spot when someone possesses psychopathic traits. I've combined these questions with additional ones that can help you spot traits associated with the other three elements of the Dark Tetrad: Machiavellianism, narcissism, and sadism. Familiarize yourself with the questionnaire in advance, and keep it in mind as you interact socially. After a first date or an interview with a potential new boss, spend a few minutes running through the questions, recalling the behaviors you encountered. If you find yourself answering "yes" to more than a few of these questions, you might have had a brush with a poisonous person.

Detecting a Dark Personality:
Verbal and Nonverbal Cues

1. Do they interrupt you often but refuse to tolerate it when you interrupt?
2. Do they consistently ignore personal or professional boundaries?
3. Do they ramble a lot, veering off on strange or random tangents?
4. Do they seem weirdly calm?
5. Do they give off an air of being "holier than thou"?

6. Do they seem to be an authority on every subject?
7. Do they seem unusually angry?
8. Do they offer impulsive, off-the-cuff responses to your questions?
9. Do they seem to come across as tough, combative, or cruel?
10. Do they make intense eye contact with you, seeming to peer into your soul?
11. Do they seem to lack emotions related to self-awareness, such as embarrassment or shame? For instance, do you *not* see them blushing or looking down at their feet when expected?
12. Do they assert an air of dominance, for instance by holding their chin up or glaring down at you?
13. Do they seem to be showing off, for instance by dressing scantily or in eye-catching ways?
14. Do they seem to be flirting with you in a way that is inappropriate given the context?
15. Do they spend a lot of time talking about themselves and show much less interest in learning about you?
16. Do they speak rudely or put others down?
17. Do they smile or laugh when others experience pain or failure?
18. When others are struggling, do they find it enjoyable, annoying, or boring?

Nonexperts aren't just able to detect psychopathic traits. Research shows that they can detect other aspects of personality—the so-called Big Five traits of openness, conscientiousness, extraversion, agreeableness, and neuroticism.[41] But as this research also showed, our first impressions aren't perfect. Nonexperts who watched five-seconds-long video clips of opposite-sex pairs of college students getting to know each other had *some* ability to identify whether individuals in the clips strongly expressed these Big Five traits. When they had a chance to watch longer clips of people, their ability to detect traits improved. First impressions give us a kernel of truth, but we shouldn't expect to walk away from a quick conversation fully understanding the people we meet.

Use these questions to spot potential dark personalities, but don't rush to judgment. Personality is a *pattern* of behavior, so even the sharpest observer can only tell so much about another person in ten seconds or less. If we wrap up our assessments too quickly, we risk becoming too judgmental and depriving ourselves of social opportunities that might be beneficial. The wisest approach is to treat insights gleaned from your new, science-informed radar as a running *theory* about another person, updating your understanding of others as you go. That said, if you must make a quick decision about whether to accept a first date or recommend a job candidate for a second interview, pay attention to these potential red flags. Although incomplete, ten seconds of structured observation is better than nothing.

Evaluating Casual Acquaintances

In many situations when we're not meeting someone for the first time but know them casually, we *do* have a chance to gather data about their personality over an extended period. Perhaps this person is a neighbor, someone we regularly encounter at the gym, a colleague from a different department, or a friend of a friend whom we see occasionally at parties. Before deciding whether to take our relationship to the next level, we can deploy our personality radar to assess their behavior patterns and determine whether they might harbor dark traits. Here again, we do best if we take a structured approach validated by science.

In a 2020 paper, Delroy L. Paulhus of the University of British Columbia and his colleagues demonstrated the value of a short, question-based tool for assessing dark personality traits called the Short Dark Tetrad (SD4).[42] Based on this tool, I've amassed a list of behavioral patterns to look for when interacting with acquaintances in everyday life. Some of these patterns might seem obvious, which means you already have some sense of how psychologists define dark personalities. But we often fail to acknowledge these patterns to ourselves when we encounter them. We put a positive spin on them, not wanting to speak poorly of others.[43] Use the following Dark Behavior Scanner to spot worrisome patterns of behavior and the kind of language we might use to justify them to ourselves and others.

The Dark Behavior Scanner

Psychopathy

1. Are they "brave," or: Do they like to take risks for the rush of it? For example, do they drive fast cars, drink heavily or take drugs, have a lot of promiscuous sex, and have a "go big or go home" attitude on the job?
2. Are they "independent," or: Do they have antagonistic relationships with the powers that be, including bosses, parents, or the police?
3. Are they "driven," or: Will they do anything, including lie or manipulate others, to get something they desire?
4. Are they "competitive," or: Do they take a zero-sum approach to life, behaving selfishly and not caring about the welfare of others?
5. Are they "principled," or: Do they express desires or take action to "get even" with others who they believe wronged them? And do they experience no guilt or remorse for their actions?

Machiavellianism

6. Are they "savvy," or: Do they consistently "manage up," trying to get on the good side of bosses or others in positions of power?

7. Are they "shrewd," or: Are they crafty and self-interested when engaging with others, remembering indiscretions by others so that they can use them against them in the future, forming strategic relationships with others who they perceive can be useful to them and ignoring those who they think can't help them?
8. Are they "strategic," or: Do they carefully plan social situations in order to manipulate the thoughts and feelings of those involved?
9. Are they "persuasive," or: Do they often presume that people can be convinced, under the right conditions, to do their bidding?

Narcissism

10. Are they "entertaining," or: Do they often put themselves in situations where all eyes are on them? Do they pride themselves on being the life of the party and get upset when others try to grab the spotlight?
11. Are they "assertive," or: Do they always seem to have to be the one in charge?
12. Are they "self-assured," or: Do they love it when others compliment them and yet refrain from lavishing compliments on others unless doing so somehow benefits them?
13. Are they "confident," or: Do they see themselves as "the best," a "born leader," "exceptional," a "genius," or "special"? Do they become upset when others don't see them that way?

Sadism

14. Are they "tough," or: Do they bully others or otherwise treat them poorly? Do they have a taste for movies, sports, and video games showing graphic violence?
15. Are they a "prankster," or: Do they find it funny when other people get hurt or fail? Do they enjoy watching other people suffer?

> 16. Are they "outspoken," or: Do they know how to hurt someone with their words and enjoy watching the fallout? Do they say cruel or hurtful things on social media for the fun of it?

A questionnaire like this one has its limits. We can't pose these questions to someone in our orbit and say for sure based on the answers that they have a dark personality, especially one that would meet the clinical criteria for psychopathy or narcissistic personality disorder. We need tests administered by trained professionals for that. We also must remain mindful of our biases, which might be significant. Research shows, for instance, that we often think the worst of anyone who hurts a close friend, that our memories of ex-lovers are more negative in retrospect than our feelings at the time, and that opposing-party politicians seem more malicious than our preferred political leaders.[44] Also, since social contexts can affect our behavior, we'll want to be sure that any worrisome patterns really are enduring personality traits and not just situational. We might interact with a given person in other settings and find that they behave differently. Still, the Dark Behavior Scanner can offer valuable clues about a person's character that we would be foolish to ignore.

If patients of a British doctor named Ian Paterson had the Dark Behavior Scanner in hand, perhaps they would have spared themselves considerable heartache and suffering. Paterson displayed several seemingly attractive personality traits and abilities. He was the busiest surgeon at his healthcare system, completing two or three breast cancer operations in the time it took his peers to do one. He developed an innovative "cleavage-sparing" variant on the mastectomy and convinced his bosses that the procedure was safe. He was charming and charismatic, and his unwavering confidence was reassuring to the anxious patients referred to his care. "He was God to us," one patient remembered.[45]

Despite appearances, Dr. Paterson's behavior was more sinister than saintly. His innovative new surgery actually left patients with too much tissue, increasing the chances that their cancer would recur. Paterson also manipulated patients into receiving unnecessary, invasive surgical treatments by exaggerating their risk of developing cancer. The speed he showed in the operating room was the result of cutting corners, which also put patients in harm's way.

Paterson got away with it in large part because vulnerable patients saw his dark traits in a positive light. Impressed by his confident demeanor and swayed by his authority as a surgeon, patients believed his lies and signed up for his dubious treatments. Between his work for Britain's National Health Service and independent sector, he operated on at least five thousand patients, disfiguring hundreds and causing untold physical and mental anguish.

Eventually, his harmful acts caught up with him. The authorities brought criminal charges, and a jury convicted him of seventeen counts of wounding with intent, and three counts of unlawful wounding. As the judge said at his sentencing, "I have no doubt, as those who support you have attested, that you can be both a charming and charismatic individual; although, it is to be regretted that these are the same characteristics which you deliberately misused in this case . . . to manipulate your patients into believing what you were advising them."[46]

We can't be certain that having a methodical way of assessing Paterson's behavior would have helped patients see through his veneer of charisma. But more critical awareness of dark traits might have given them a fighting chance.

When to Listen to Your Scanner

Before treating someone as a poisonous person, take steps to ensure that the behavior you've uncovered is indeed a true pattern. First, look for information about them in a variety of social contexts. Let's say you're a middle manager at a company, and the acquaintance in question is another manager from a different department. Do their dark behavior patterns persist, albeit perhaps in slightly different ways, when they're engaging with senior leaders, not just peers, or when they're out in the field schmoozing with customers? What about when they are at home with family or out with friends? We all act out of character on occasion, but personality traits are consistent across time and place.

A great way to answer these questions is to consult others who know the individual. Gossip gets a bad rap and can harm innocent targets, but it can also protect social groups by helping to sideline individuals who shouldn't gain status or power. One study of sorority sisters found that gossipers targeted individuals who really were more likely to behave in harmful, antisocial ways.[47] Likewise, whisper networks inside organizations often serve positive social functions, warning women about the existence of predatory men.[48] I'm not suggesting that we take rumors as fact, passing them on without giving it a second thought. We owe it to ourselves and others to think critically about what we hear and to avoid hurting others by gossiping idly about them. But if we notice disturbing behavior, staying alert to gossip can validate our impressions and encourage us to protect ourselves. We also might have a duty to alert others so they can avoid harm.

Another source of information can help us assess others: our own emotions. If you observe patterns that might suggest someone harbors psychopathic personality traits, ask yourself how you *feel* about the person. Do you become nervous or on edge in their presence? Do you dislike them and doubt what they're telling you? Do their actions leave you feeling muddled and confused? These reactions are valuable data in their own right. In research with the experts who conduct PCL-R interviews, scholars found that the interviewers were more likely to harbor negative feelings such as these about people who scored higher on psychopathic traits.[49] These personalities wig us out a little—we can *sense* something isn't right. If we find ourselves responding negatively *and* rumors are swirling *and* we can point to habitual behaviors that connect back to dark traits, the case becomes strong indeed.

> ### When to Steer Clear of a Colleague or Acquaintance
>
> ✓ You apply the Dark Behavior Scanner to an acquaintance and notice worrisome behavior patterns. You also might observe behavior cues indicating dark traits when first meeting someone.
> ✓ You can verify these patterns, looking across social contexts and consulting others around you.
> ✓ You interrogate your own feelings and find that you experience some serious bad vibes.

Updating Our First Impressions

Applying the three criteria above, you might still find yourself doubting your conclusion. Are you *really* seeing what you think you're seeing? Or are you being too harsh in your judgment, perhaps because of your biases? Given your own desire to treat others kindly and with respect, shouldn't you give this person the benefit of the doubt? It's worth asking these questions, but we shouldn't just be wary of negative biases that make us too quick to identify bad apples. In some situations, we can be biased in the opposite direction.

At a glance, Paul Bernardo and Karla Homolka would have seemed incapable of brutally raping and killing young girls. During the early 1990s, they were a blond and attractive young couple, the picture of youthful innocence. And yet, the "Ken and Barbie Killers," as they were known, not only committed violent acts but made videos of themselves doing it.[50] We believe that what is beautiful is good, but that logic can lead to a faulty first impression, inclining us to see attractive people as more honest, trustworthy, forgiving, principled, selfless, or responsible than they really are.[51]

Similarly, people like the excessive self-confidence that narcissists often display when it comes in small doses. In one study of student study groups, students with narcissistic personality traits came across initially as more competent, agreeable, well-adjusted, and likable. After seven weeks of meetings, though, their peers felt differently about them, perceiving the most narcissistic members as hostile, defensive, and arrogant.[52] Former romantic partners of people with psychopathic personalities report that they too came on strong and seemingly perfect at first, only to reveal their true selves over time.[53] When the red flags keep popping up and yet we find ourselves wavering, we should question whether lies and strategic self-presentation might have contributed to any positive first impressions that we had. Like good scientists, we should be willing to update our beliefs when confronted with strong data.

Having trusted confidants by our side can help us. "Cecilia," a woman I interviewed, suffered mightily growing up with a stepdad who possessed dark traits. More recently, as an attractive woman on the dating scene, she has had her share of brushes with malevolent men. But she has a secret weapon that prevents her from getting into trouble: the platonic male friends in her life. As she reports, they've "been super helpful for seeing clearly [sic] and not putting up with any manipulative nonsense." Since they've seen and heard other men talking openly about their treatment of women, she felt they could provide better guidance than her female friends.

In one instance, Cecilia reconnected with a former colleague whom she had long found attractive and had considered the "ultimate man." Although he was married, he surprised her by trying to talk her into sleeping with him. She declined his overtures, uninterested as a matter of principle in a one-night stand. But she stayed in touch with this Mr. Wrong, thinking she might be able to take it slower with him and build a relationship once he separated from his wife. He seemed unhappy in his relationship and on the verge of divorce—a position she had found herself in not too long before. She suspected that he might be a dark personality, but she still felt drawn to him.

Knowing that she needed to check her judgment, she asked two male friends what they thought about her pursuing a relationship with her former colleague. Her friends both told her that she should avoid him. One of these friends "helped me see that this guy was actually operating in a predatory way and explained the playbook to me."

Cecilia wound up keeping a healthy distance between herself and her former colleague. As more time passed and she had a chance to study his behavior more closely, she realized that all he really wanted from her was sex. Moreover, if the "ultimate man" was kind, considerate, and generous, he turned out to be the opposite—egotistical and self-absorbed. When arranging time together, he refused to accommodate her schedule, perceiving himself to be too busy and important to work around her commitments. He also saw his own judgment as superior to hers, deriding her as naive and overly idealistic. "Dodging any involvement despite my feelings about him was a really good thing," she said. Her advisors had come through for her. They were "really good reality checks when I was dazzled [and] confused."

The wisdom of the crowd often exceeds that of individuals when it comes to predicting future events such as political elections.[54] And collective wisdom works in interpersonal situations as well. Groups of people do better at spotting lies than individuals operating alone.[55] They also do better at assessing an individual's personality.[56] As powerful as the science-backed tools described in this chapter can be, they aren't perfect, in part because *we're* not perfect. Our friends can help us see what we can't, making it easier for us to trust what our radar seems to be telling us.

Leaning into our relationships with others can help protect us, as can sharpening our own social skills and instincts. The radar system I've presented entails nothing more than leveraging our ability to identify others' thoughts, feelings, motivations, and perspectives. Psychopathic personalities seek to exploit our kind, trusting natures for dark purposes, but our best defense is a kind of jujitsu move in which we fall back on our prosocial natures, mobilizing our ability to understand and connect with others as a source of strength.

Detecting poisonous people can help keep us out of harm's way, but it won't protect us entirely. Since contextual factors shape our behavior, we also must guard against social settings that make people behave badly, even if their personalities are largely good. As I've suggested, the kindest among us can become *situational* psychopaths when dropped into the right—or wrong—situations. We'll discuss later in this book how we can smooth out the parts of our own natures that might lead us to misbehave more than we'd like. For now, let's consider how to avoid common situations that might cause other, normally good-hearted people to harm us.

5

Temporarily Terrible

My friend Martin has a job that's straight out of a Hollywood thriller. Working for an elite law enforcement agency, he takes down major drug rings, terrorist groups, and pedophile networks by recruiting informants and overseeing agents working deep undercover. Martin's a good guy operating in a seedy underworld populated by very bad actors. He's spent decades studying these malevolent personalities so that he can outmaneuver them and keep the rest of us safe.

I interviewed Martin for this book hoping to learn about dark personalities he recruited or brought to justice. Martin complied, and as a bonus he shared some interesting insights into his agency and how it develops young talent. Recruits who get the job must be smart, psychologically stable, and exceptionally skilled at what they do. But as Martin told me, they must also be principled. The best agents have a strong moral sense and a commitment to playing by the rules. Even in high-pressure, life-and-death situations, they aren't easily swayed into betraying their consciences or flipping their loyalties.

To make sure it has found these people, Martin's agency puts recent hires through elaborate psychological tests during their training. Every interaction is a chance to gain insight into these new recruits. One morning, trainers might put a new agent under stress, assigning him an urgent project to complete by day's end. The agent might be told that to get the job done, he must work closely with a junior staff member. If the junior staffer doesn't perform some vital tasks on the new agent's behalf, he'll fail to complete the project. That afternoon, a couple of hours before the project is due, trainers will get the agent to come into a break room, where he'll find himself alone with the staffer. As trainers watch via hidden cameras and microphones, the staffer will inform the new agent that she's sorry—she didn't get around to completing the tasks he requested. She had gone out to lunch with friends, lost track of time, and returned late to the office. As a result, she only finished two of the three items he had requested; she wasn't told how important they were to him.

    This news will thrust the new agent into an emotionally charged situation. He was counting on the staffer, who has let him down. Thinking that nobody else is watching, will he become angry, abusive, and overbearing, threatening the staffer to "get the task done now or else"? Or will he behave more compassionately—say, by acknowledging that the staffer didn't understand how important the tasks were and offering to work with her to find a solution? A second moral test will follow this one. Entering another break room, the agent will find a few other trainees griping about the same junior staffer. Will he join in on bad-mouthing a team member just to fit into the group? Or will he show loyalty to her and refrain, mindful that the staffer just made an innocent mistake?

    Such tests might seem trivial, but as Martin tells me, how agents-in-training handle them matters. Agents confront ethical dilemmas in the field all the time. They might have to befriend a violent drug dealer in hopes of sending many others in their network to prison, or they might have to bend the truth to convince a hardened criminal to cooperate with them. Good agents know where the moral and legal lines are, and they don't cross them, even under duress. An agent-in-training who can be manipulated during a relatively low-stress situation to sacrifice their ethical standards and berate or bad-mouth a team member might be liable to misbehave in other, more serious situations.

It's reassuring to see law enforcement doing its best to uphold standards of decency and morality. Even more interesting, I think, is the agency's recognition of how deeply social situations influence human behavior. In everyday life, we downplay context, preferring to regard a person's actions as directly reflecting their underlying character. This bias is so pronounced that scientists have a name for it: "fundamental attribution error."[1] And yet, if we seek to strip out toxic behavior from our lives, we can't just focus on personality, avoiding those who score high on psychopathic traits. We must attend to the external conditions that can turn people—including ourselves—into situational psychopaths.

Girls' Weekend Gone Bad

Many situations can lead otherwise good people to behave badly. We all know, for instance, that the crowd we hang out with can lead us astray. When bad behavior in our group becomes a norm, we can feel drawn to adopt it ourselves, even if we know better. Students cheat more when cheating has become normalized.[2] In countries where tax evasion, corruption, and other forms of rule-breaking are rampant, people become more inclined to break rules in mundane settings, such as when playing a dice game.[3]

Even when bad behavior isn't a norm, other aspects of our environments can induce antisociality. Research in psychology flags three types of situations that are especially prone to producing out-of-character bad behavior. The first are settings in which others around us become frustrated in some way. Psychologists think of frustration not as a feeling per se but as an objective condition: the state of being blocked from achieving your goal.[4] We all struggle with goals large and small that are important to us. The emotional strain of such struggle can make us behave in ways we later regret.

In 2009, I took a road trip with my mom and sister, driving from my home in Kelowna, British Columbia, to Vancouver. I can't remember what music we were blasting on the radio, but I do know we were excited to enjoy a girls' weekend in the big city. We were driving in my Volkswagen "City Golf," or as my roommate Tara called it, Shitty Golf. The car did have cruise control, so I set it a few kilometers an hour over the speed limit and took my foot off the gas.

The highway was scenic, taking us over soaring mountain passes. At one point, during a long stretch of flat road, I pulled into the fast lane and passed a truck before returning to the slow lane. Shortly afterward, we reached a steep incline. My car wasn't equipped for this kind of elevation gain. Despite being on cruise control, my car slowed considerably, struggling to make it up the hill. The truck passed us and then moved into the slow lane ahead of us. When we again reached flat road, my car regained its target speed.

When I overtook the truck once again, its driver seemed pissed. Taking my variable speed as a personal slight, he pulled up beside me and gave me the finger. Then, he jerked his wheel to the right, veering into my lane and forcing me abruptly onto the shoulder. Holy shit—this guy was literally trying to drive me off the road! We all screamed. My mother grabbed on to the door handle, eyes wide. My heart was exploding out of my chest. I hit the brakes, letting this guy get well ahead of us. He was clearly a poisonous person, acting on impulse and aggression—or was he?

Aggressive driving, sometimes accompanied by road rage, is a serious problem, accounting for two-thirds of deaths due to crashes, by some estimates.[5] Drivers often experience road rage when they become frustrated, feeling that another driver is impeding their progress or has disrespected them. In a common move, they might misattribute hostile intentions to others' actions, thinking that other drivers are just being mean and trying to ruin their day. But if we look more closely, an even more complicated picture can emerge. They might have had a tough day at work. Their kids might be shouting at one another in the back seat. They might be in a rush to get somewhere. Their boss might have just sent them an email that annoyed them. They might find driving inherently unpleasant. These and other factors stress people out and reduce their frustration tolerance, leaving them less capable of regulating their negative emotions. Insert a triggering incident, and they explode.[6]

It's much harder to behave well when we feel stressed, and stress in many forms can lead to aggression. Just a single night of poor sleep leaves us more inclined to react impulsively to negative triggers.[7] Research has linked a lack of sleep to decreases in empathy, the ability to detect others' emotions, and the ability to regulate our own.[8] Put a tired person into a tense situation and you'll find they're less likely to accept blame or resolve conflict.[9] Among adolescents, fatigue is also related to a wide variety of risky—and potentially dangerous—behaviors. Studies have found, for instance, a link between lack of sleep and the likelihood that a teen will carry a weapon.[10] In children especially, poor sleep leads to unstable moods and a tendency to overreact to small setbacks.[11] A feedback loop can arise in which bad sleep and a tendency to act out affect each other, making both of them worse.[12]

Other physical stressors can lead us to behave aggressively. We're angrier and more irritable when we haven't eaten enough.[13] Hunger leaves us with lower levels of glucose in our blood, which leads to the release of the stress hormone cortisol and that unpleasant "stressed out" feeling. Hungry people are more likely than sated ones to see the world around them negatively. Misattributing their experience of hunger to the situation they're in, hungry participants in one study experienced more "hate" and perceived others as more judgmental, evaluations that may make them more prone to conflict and aggression.[14]

Heat can also turn us into situational psychopaths. An influential review of research by the psychologist Craig Anderson provides compelling evidence that hotter days, years, and countries see increased aggression, including more homicides, sexual assaults, domestic violence, and riots.[15] Still other environmental factors, such as exposure to pollution and bad smells, can make us more likely to behave aggressively, as can physical pain.[16] Stress can exert a particularly potent effect on our behavior if it's chronic and consistent in our lives, and if the cognitive processes that we use to control and calm ourselves are already weak or underdeveloped.[17]

Stress gives rise to aggression so easily because it prepares us to act. Stress increases right-left activity asymmetry in our frontal brain, which is associated with what researchers call an "approach motivation."[18] When we're under strain and provoked, we're more likely to act out than if the same insult or shove came our way when we were more relaxed. Normal inhibition processes that might lead us to say "Hey, that person who offended me isn't so bad," or "Hey, I'm losing my cool," or "Hey, bad stuff might happen to me if I lash out" fade into the background. When we're drunk or high on drugs, our ability to control ourselves is similarly compromised.[19]

At the time of my road rage incident, it seemed bizarre to me that this truck driver would lash out as he did. Who *does* that? Now I recognize that the real question in that situation might not have been "who," but "why." I wonder what else might have been going on in this man's life that could have induced him to put three strangers in mortal danger, just because they offended or irritated him in some minor way. The economy was in a recession back then, so maybe he was worried about losing his job. Maybe he'd been driving for ten hours straight, with only a truck-stop burrito to eat. Maybe his spouse, upset because he was gone for long stretches of time for work, had just left him. The possibilities are endless, and perhaps they all worked together, until a tiny car passing him over and over set him off.

Why You Should Never Mess with a Yankees Fan

Even when others around us aren't provoked or frustrated, a second class of situations might lead them to behave like situational psychopaths: us-versus-them scenarios. Riots often are fueled by a shared sense of identity coupled with antagonism toward some "other," such as the police, an ethnic group, or institutional systems.[20] Animosity between groups can trigger a process of dehumanization, and a diminished sense of empathy for the members of that group. We've seen this dynamic play out in any number of genocides during the twentieth century, from the Holocaust to Rwanda to Bosnia.

In recent years, Russian leaders and soldiers dehumanized Ukrainians as a prelude to their country's 2022 invasion of that country. "We are fighting not against people but against enemies," one extreme Russian nationalist said, "not against people but against Ukrainians."[21] Graffiti scrawled by Russian soldiers on barroom walls conveyed the sadistic pleasure they took in harming a subhuman "other." "It doesn't count as a war crime if you had fun," read one message. Another proclaimed: "With a happy smile I will burn foreign villages."[22] You might recognize this remarkable absence of empathy as a hallmark of psychopathy, but many people experience temporary reductions in empathy or even a bit of sadistic joy when their enemies suffer. We may even feel compelled to physically harm someone we deem to be an "other."

It isn't only in extreme, wartime settings that we enjoy seeing members of an out-group feel pain. Baseball fans know how serious the rivalry is between the New York Yankees and the Boston Red Sox. In one fascinating study, researchers studied fans of the two clubs, choosing those who nurtured especially intense feelings for their respective team. When queried, fans reported feeling more pleasure in seeing videos of the rival team failing to score against their favorite team than they did in seeing another club—the Baltimore Orioles—failing to score in its game against a different opponent. Taking functional magnetic resonance imaging (fMRI) scans of their brains, researchers found that this pleasure was physiological: reward centers of the brain were activated when rival teams failed. Participants also felt more pain at seeing a video of their team failing to score against the rival than they did upon seeing a more neutral sports clip. In turn, parts of their brain associated with receiving punishment lit up on the scan. When our rivals beat us, it hurts, and when we beat them, it feels good. Researchers also found evidence that such internal feelings could lead to unsavory behavior. In surveys taken after the scan, fans of both teams indicated that they were more likely to abuse rival fans—spewing insults, say, or barking out threats—than they were Orioles fans.[23]

Tough Guy with a Stuffie

Talk of wartime experiences and sporting events points us toward a third class of situations that prompt our inner psychopath to emerge: contexts in which we melt into groups and feel anonymous.[24] On the evening of June 15, 2011, twenty-nine-year-old Timothy Kwong was out at a club drinking with friends in Vancouver, British Columbia, as the city's hockey team, the Canucks, took on the Boston Bruins in the National Hockey League's Stanley Cup Final. When the Bruins won the game, clinching the league championship, emotions in Vancouver boiled over, leading to a massive riot in which scores of people were injured, including nine police officers. As a judge later remarked during court proceedings for participants, the riot was "a terrible example of civil disorder, the likes of which this country has rarely seen."[25] Kwong said he happened to step outside for a smoke as the rioting was occurring. He saw a large group of people overturning cars and lighting one of them on fire. Spotting a stuffed animal nearby, he grabbed it, used his cigarette lighter to set it aflame, and threw it toward an overturned car. Since gasoline was pouring from the car, the stuffed animal was enough to create a raging inferno that engulfed the vehicle.[26]

Kwong doesn't seem to have been a bad person out to cause harm. As the judge presiding at his court appearance recounted, Kwong turned himself in to the police the next day after learning that he'd been caught on camera—in fact, he was the first of thousands of rioters to do so. Although that action didn't necessarily speak to altruistic motives, Kwong showed considerable remorse, apologizing for his actions on social media and trying to make amends. Before his sentencing by a court, he had already performed on his own initiative at least twenty-six hours of community service, including with an organization dedicated to cleaning up the city, and he had gone to counseling.

As the judge remarked, there was "no dispute" that Kwong was a person of "good character." He had no criminal record and presented letters written by community members saying that he was a good guy and confirming how "ashamed" and "embarrassed" he felt because of his actions.[27] Here we find an otherwise ordinary, decent person who, in addition to being drunk, got carried away after stepping into an anonymous situation where ordinary norms of conduct seemed to be suspended. He behaved poorly only to deeply regret it afterward.

Temporarily Terrible

Many people will misbehave when they find themselves feeling anonymous or in a group that condones immoral behavior. There's the otherwise nice kid who, when a group of bullies are harassing a classmate, blurts out something mean, too. There's the late-night motorist who, after dinging a parked car, takes off unseen rather than leaving a note with his contact information. And there are those countless people who partake in mischief and nastiness online under the cloak of made-up usernames.[28]

You might feel tempted to condemn people who lose their moral bearings when their identities become obscure, but science suggests that such behavior is natural. We evolved to treat people whom we know better than strangers. Across the generations, individuals who managed to survive were better than others at ensuring the propagation of their own genes. Helping people who are related to us aids in the survival of our genes, or at least some portion of them. Although most of us probably don't calculate the degree of genetic similarity before helping or harming another person, clues in our behavior support this reasoning. For instance, people are more likely to trust people who look like them, and parents abuse stepchildren—who lack a genetic link to them—more than they do their biological children.[29]

Looking beyond family ties, we're nicer to those we know because it works to our advantage. We might shovel our neighbor's driveway when they're on vacation because we hope that they'll cut our grass when we go on our big summer trip. In addition to such direct reciprocity, we're nicer to those closest to us because our reputations benefit from it, particularly in the kinds of small, intimate communities in which we've lived during most of our species' history.[30] When someone sees us lending a hand to our friends and neighbors, they'll think better of us, enhancing our reputation. We gain from maintaining a good reputation, since others around us will respect and reward us for it. When we're anonymous, these benefits disappear. Our reputations won't improve, since others don't observe our good deeds or know who we are.[31] Take away our identity, and that imperative to behave well falls away.

Research in economics bears out this connection between altruistic behavior and identity. In an experiment called the dictator game, researchers divide participants into pairs, give each pair a pot of money, and assign one member of the pair to be the dictator. This dictator gets the power of the purse, deciding how to divvy up the cash. They can split it any way that they like. Big surprise—studies have found that people scoring high in psychopathic traits keep more of the money for themselves.[32] But the anonymity of participants matters, too.

One study had two groups of participants play this game, giving each group a pot of ten euros. Researchers told some participants that they would eventually learn one another's identity, and others that they would remain anonymous. Among the group that didn't remain anonymous, the most common offer made by the dictator was five euros—in other words, the fairest offer. Among the anonymous dictators, it was zero. Anonymity produced behavior that was far more selfish and less equitable.[33] When people's identities are obscured, they feel temporarily released from constraints that arise out of their self-conscious guilt and shame. They become a bit more like people with psychopathy, who lack these emotions in all situations.

Steering Clear of the Darkness

Now that we know the kinds of situations that can turn otherwise good people into situational psychopaths, let's explore what to do about them. Research points to two basic strategies. First, we can *become more situationally aware*, learning to spot dangerous situations we might have stumbled into and then extricate ourselves from them. If we're just arriving at our company holiday party, is everyone drunk on their fourth eggnog? If we're stepping into a new role at work, does the culture permit—or even reward—cheating to get ahead? If we join an online forum, are people commenting under their actual names or hiding behind obscure screen names and avatars? If we're attending a rock concert or soccer game, are group dynamics and a sense of anonymity taking hold?

Many parents of teenagers warn their kids about the risks that can arise around alcohol and drug use. But parents would do well to educate their children about the full array of potentially combustible situations, as well as the possibility that multiple situational factors might emerge at once. If our kids knew to look out for situations of apparent anonymity or erosion of personal responsibility, they might be less inclined to "go with the flow" and cheat on a test just because their classmates are doing it. If they knew to pay attention to situations where insider-outsider dynamics are at play *and* emotions are running high, they might be more inclined to avoid potentially dicey situations on a night out with friends.

Awareness of situational factors can allow all of us to be more understanding when others misbehave. Because of the fundamental attribution error, we often explain away our own bad behavior by pointing to situational factors: *I said something cruel in an online forum because I was anonymous.* However, we take others' transgressions as evidence of their personality or character: *other commenters in the online forum were cruel because they're poisonous people.*

If situational factors did play a role, we can temper our judgments and punishments. As parents, teachers, or bosses, we might want to treat these episodes as valuable teaching opportunities, alerting offenders to potentially toxic situations and how to avoid them in the future.

We can also pursue a second strategy to protect ourselves from situational psychopaths: we can *change our circumstances*. When we're in an anonymous situation, changing it is as simple as introducing ourselves. One study from the 1970s tracked behavior among kids out trick-or-treating on Halloween in Seattle. One homeowner—a person involved in the study—sometimes asked kids their names and where they lived when they shouted "trick or treat!" and sometimes didn't. Rather than hand out candy, this homeowner told kids to each pick a piece from a bowl and then went back inside. Some kids felt free to help themselves to lots of candy, effectively stealing. The ones who were least likely to take extra were those who had identified themselves to the homeowner.[34]

When anonymity reigns, avail yourself of opportunities to make yourself known to others. If you're taking a massive university class with hundreds of students, reach out to make friends. Be that homeowner who becomes a presence in the neighborhood. When dealing with customer service representatives on the phone, introduce yourself and make small talk. Even if this person doesn't reciprocate, sharing a bit of information about yourself can have real benefits.

We tend to assume that people whom we know also know us in return. This belief of ours is often true, as in relationships where we've met someone and had meaningful conversations, but even learning just a bit about a total stranger makes us feel less anonymous to them. When presented with basic information about an interaction partner, such as their age, marital status, and where they work and live, participants in one study believed that their partner would be better at detecting deception and were less likely to lie to them.[35] Likewise, a field experiment in New York City found that when apartment residents received flyers describing the favorite food and hobbies of their neighborhood police officer, reports of crime went down. Learning about others makes us feel less anonymous, more visible, and more likely to get caught if we do something wrong.

We should also pay attention to the insider-outsider tensions that competition fosters.³⁶ When we perceive that our group is fiercely competing with another for scarce resources, we can feel hostility and prejudice toward the "others." Fortunately, social psychology has identified steps we can take to reduce the out-group animosity.

During the mid-1950s, researchers had a bunch of preteen boys come to a summer camp near Oklahoma's Robbers Cave State Park, dividing them into two groups.³⁷ For the first week of the three-week session, organizers kept the two groups apart from each other and unaware of the other group's existence. Boys in each group developed a strong sense of group identity as they engaged in camp activities.

The second week, organizers had the two groups compete against each other in team sports. This new competition led members of each group to act out against the other group. Tensions quickly grew: Insults flew, with boys calling one another "communists"—fighting words during the Cold War. Members of the two groups threw food at one another and raided one another's bunks. In week three organizers gave the boys some higher goals to collaborate on. They had to work together to fix a clogged valve that left the camp without running water. They pooled their money to rent a movie that neither group could afford on their own. And they banded together to push a stalled truck in order to get it started. They needed one another to complete a shared goal and so, instead of competitors, they became part of a single team. Their mutual antagonism dissipated.³⁸

In case a group of young boys in the 1950s banding together in the woods strikes you as a little trite, consider another example. Todd Ashker is no Boy Scout. A member of the violent Aryan Brotherhood gang, he is spending his life in Northern California's Pelican Bay maximum-security prison on a murder conviction. Ashker has done more than twenty-five years in solitary confinement, housed in the facility's security housing unit (SHU), away from members of rival gangs.[39] And yet, this enforced separation wound up bringing them closer together.

The gang members couldn't see or touch one another, but they could hear one another's voices. As they began to talk, they became better acquainted, sharing stories about their families, neighborhoods, and past experiences.[40] They also talked about the profound pain they felt living in the SHU, where inmates were almost entirely cut off from the world, spending twenty-three hours a day alone in small, windowless cells. The regimen was so severe that many inmates suffered psychological trauma and even contemplated suicide.[41] Their commiseration led them to unite around a shared purpose: remedying the abuses of solitary confinement.

On July 8, 2013, Ashker started a hunger strike to protest the long-term use of solitary confinement. His protest spread by word of mouth until more than thirty thousand imprisoned people in California had joined his hunger strike.[42] A group of lawyers sued California for failing to observe the US Constitution's ban on cruel and unusual punishment and in 2015, a court decided in the inmates' favor.

When an insider-outsider dynamic exists, connecting with members of the out-group—whether it's a different race, class, religion, sexual orientation, and so on—can ease tensions. People often avoid such contact, expecting it to be uncomfortable and fearing how out-group members will receive them. But keeping to our own corner can perpetuate stereotypes and biased thinking, since we never have a chance to expose ourselves to other perspectives and lived experiences. Moreover, intergroup interactions often go much better than we expect.[43] Studies of Black and white residents in housing projects that had been desegregated found that they thought better of one another than residents in projects that hadn't been integrated.[44] Studies of college roommates revealed similar results: white students paired with an other-race roommate regarded members of other racial groups more positively and felt more comfortable in interracial interactions.[45] Just a little social interaction can go a long way toward humanizing others in our eyes, and vice versa.[46]

Encourage your kids to reach out to others who are different. When you have an opportunity to attend a cultural festival that takes you out of your comfort zone—go. And, ask questions. Research suggests that others perceive us as more responsive and likable when we're curious.[47] In the workplace, create opportunities for your team members to interact across silos and to cultivate a culture of curiosity. You can also accomplish a lot by using questions to promote understanding. One study found that leaders who ask clarifying questions, take notes on the answers they receive, and show that they comprehend others' concerns are more trusted and get more buy-in from subordinates on their decisions.[48]

Proximity matters, too: collaboration and agreement will more likely occur when people are in close contact. But be sure to set a shared goal before convening groups that perceive others as adversaries. Research by my colleagues Drs. Chris Liu and Sameer Srivastava has revealed that US senators who sat closer to each other in the Senate chamber converged in their thinking: they voted the same way on bills and even worked together to cosponsor one another's bills. However, this only held true within parties; the closer a senator sat to a member of the opposing party, the more their voting patterns diverged.[49] Proximity without a shared goal can push people further apart.

When it isn't competition or anonymity that causes bad behavior but an individual's own internal loss of control, we can help to change the situation by de-escalating emotions. We can't directly control what others do or feel. But we can control how *we* behave. If emotions are raging, we can minimize the chances that others will direct aggression our way by moderating our own behavior. Sometimes that's as simple as choosing precisely when we do and don't intervene.

Gloria worked in an office with Tonia, a lawyer who handles divorces and child custody arrangements. The office had high turnover; the work was stressful, and employees rarely lasted more than a few months. Tonia's behavior was a big part of the problem. When stressed, she fell into fits of rage, calling her colleagues names and smashing objects around the office. At these times, Gloria—who worked as an independent mediator—became the office spokesperson, interceding with Tonia on behalf of the other employees and reasserting some boundaries. She would choose her moment carefully, however, waiting until Tonia had calmed down. She also took care to validate Tonia's frustration, although not her behavior. "You can feel frustrated," she would tell Tonia, "you can feel stressed out, you can feel exhausted. You can feel like these clients and their files are wearing on you. But you cannot take it out on any of your employees or colleagues."

An intern named Jane wasn't so adept at "picking her timing" with Tonia. She tended to "go in hot" to complain about Tonia's supervision of her, escalating an already volatile situation. Tonia became so upset with Jane's complaints that she fired her. When you see someone getting angry, know that time can be your friend. Giving them a moment to cool down can reduce the likelihood that they'll lash out and increase the odds of a productive conversation.

We also know that provocation on our part or a tit-for-tat exchange of verbal insults can lead to aggression.[50] But that predictable progression means that we retain power to short-circuit escalating bad behavior; it takes a show of calmness on our part, a conscious decision *not* to react. A man I interviewed, Brenner, attended a game during the same series between the Vancouver Canucks and Boston Bruins that ended in a riot. Although this game was held in Vancouver, he took the liberty of attending as a proud, swag-wearing Bruins fan. He didn't get a warm welcome from the hometown fans. A one-way food fight broke out, with Canucks fans showering Brenner and his wife with popcorn, beer, ice, hot dogs, and pizza. Fortunately, the two knew that retaliation would only turn the Canuck fans into full-blown situational psychopaths. They kept their heads down and showed no reaction. As they were heading out of the stadium and onto the street, they elected to remove their Bruins jerseys, aware that wearing them was provoking the crowd. Another member of their party, Gabe, wasn't so savvy. He turned around and taunted the Canucks fans, which made them throw more and bigger objects. Gabe eventually got into a fight on the train back to his hotel and suffered a bloody nose.

If we occupy positions of authority, we can not only change poisonous situations but prevent them from arising in the first place. We can reset social norms by instituting rules, removing perverse incentives, and demonstrating the values that we want others to espouse. We can also design social interactions with behavior in mind. If you're a corporate manager organizing a team-building retreat, make sure that everyone is well-rested, well-fed, and not overly plied with alcohol.

When we're selecting talent for our teams and organizations, or when we're choosing playmates for our children, we can look to surround ourselves with good people. Martin's law enforcement agency was right to weed out young agents incapable of withstanding situational pressures. Although situations can strongly influence our behavior, some people can withstand that pressure better than others. In one study, researchers triggered participants' subjective experience of power by asking them to write about a time when they felt powerful. A control group of participants simply wrote what they did the day before. Researchers then had participants play a dictator game, giving them each ten lottery tickets and asking them how many they'd like to share with some other, anonymous person. To incentivize participants to want more points, they dangled a prize: at the end of the session, the more points they had racked up, the better their chances of winning a hundred dollars. Researchers also measured how important morality was to each person's self-identity. Overall, people who felt powerful offered to give away fewer tickets than did members of the control group. Power made people more selfish and less fair. However, power didn't affect everyone equally. Participants who had a strong sense of moral identity experienced the opposite effect—power made them *more* generous in sharing their tickets.[51]

In assembling teams or selecting playmates for our kids, we have much to gain by seeking out people whose sense of moral identity can withstand strong situational forces. Some people regard being honest, fair, and compassionate as an important part of who they are. As a result, they're more likely to make the moral choice over the easy one. Having just one person like this in a group speaking up at the right time can puncture the power of conformity, potentially leading others to take the moral high road as well.[52]

The story of Peter Buxtun is a good example. As a social worker and epidemiologist working for the US Public Health Service, Buxtun was tasked with conducting interviews with men who had contracted sexually transmitted diseases. Through this work, he came to learn about the Tuskegee Experiment, which was created to observe the effects of syphilis over time if left untreated. The experiment, Buxtun discovered, involved only poor Black men. They were never informed of their diagnosis or of the study's purpose, nor did researchers offer them penicillin after it became clear that the drug could effectively treat their infections.

Astonished that a public health agency could behave so callously, Buxtun prepared a report on his findings, comparing the CDC's behavior to that of the Nazis.[53] When he shared that report with his superiors, he got nowhere—they were well aware of the experiment and wanted it to continue. So, Buxtun decided to speak to the press. The resulting publicity led to the end of the experiment, a reckoning for the broader research community, and eventually, a formal apology from President Bill Clinton for the agency's "shameful" behavior.[54] In this instance, the moral courage of one man led to widespread awareness of researchers' abuses and the creation of the Belmont Report, the ethical code that millions of scientists use today to guide their research.

As research shows, organizations that allow room for dissenting voices perform better. According to one study, firms that built cultures "that support debate and diverse opinions, truth, fact, and transparency" grew faster, delivered better returns, and had more highly engaged workforces than other companies.[55] Just as one bad apple can ruin the barrel, changing social norms and corrupting group cultures, so one *good* apple committed to upholding moral principles can help to stop the rot from spreading, instilling kinder, gentler ways of interacting.

We've explored how to spot poisonous people from a distance before they ensnare us, and also how to recognize and extricate ourselves from dangerous social settings before a situational psychopath can torment us. Science also has answers for us if we're already in a relationship with a dark personality. The next two chapters provide advice for how to survive a brush with someone possessing psychopathic traits. We begin by considering the big question that everyone in a relationship with a bad apple entertains at some point: should I stay or should I go?

6

Should I Stay or Should I Go?

Since people with dark personalities love to wield power, we might not expect them to pop up in more nurturing environments such as nursery schools, museums, or religious institutions. But as Nicholas found, they're there, too.

Nicholas's two small kids loved attending the art museum in their city, and Nicholas himself was impressed by the impact the museum was having on their community. Being a generous, civic-minded person, he decided a few years ago to join the museum's board on a volunteer basis. For the first several months, everything went well, until Nicholas started working on a small committee with another board member, Clark.

The committee oversaw the museum's personnel and employment policies, including the evaluation and compensation of key employees. At meetings, Clark dominated the conversation. He just had to be right and couldn't stand being contradicted. Worse, he was deceitful, saying one thing during a meeting to seem agreeable to his colleagues and then, when they weren't around, saying or doing the exact opposite.

Should I Stay or Should I Go?

Nicholas didn't like Clark's behavior, but it didn't seem hugely disruptive or harmful at first. Then Nicholas made the mistake of disagreeing with Clark. The previous year, the museum's director had griped about how the board was evaluating his performance, claiming that he hadn't received the compensation and bonuses he deserved. Since it was now performance evaluation time again, Nicholas argued that the committee needed to overhaul the process, making evaluations more rigorous and quantitative and less subjective. Clark disagreed, arguing that they didn't need to change performance evaluations; all that mattered was that the director was happy with his assessment. They could simply be more generous with him and everything would be fine. Nicholas countered that in fact, based on what he'd seen in his professional work, the organization *did* need a rigorous process. It wasn't just about the director. The museum received funding from outside sources, and it needed to show accountability for its decision-making.

During one of the committee's meetings, Clark assented to Nicholas's position. It seemed that the issue was settled. But then Clark went behind his back, gaining informal support from others in the organization for keeping the performance evaluation process as it was. Convinced that this was an important issue for the organization, Nicholas wrote an email to other board members in which he politely reminded everyone about what Clark had agreed to during the meeting. He quoted Clark's exact words and suggested that Clark was undermining what had been a consensus view. Aware of how sensitive Clark was about being right, Nicholas chose his words carefully and vetted the email with others before sending it to make sure it was kind, reasonable, and inoffensive.

Clark was incensed. He asked Nicholas to come to his office before the committee's next meeting for a conversation. It turned out to be an ambush. When Nicholas arrived, he found that Clark had invited two other members of the committee. For a good hour,

Nicholas said, Clark and one of these other members—Steve—demeaned him, not merely complaining about the email but questioning Nicholas's professional judgment and qualifications for serving on the board. The tone was aggressive and hostile—Clark and Steve hurled insults, many of them delivered in a manipulative, passive-aggressive way. As Nicholas remembers, "ninety percent of the time, Clark was saying, 'Not to be rude,' and would then say a rude thing. He'd say 'I don't mean this personally,' but what he'd say would be very personal."

Nicholas realized that there was little use in standing his ground during this attack. Clark and Steve hadn't come to talk, but rather to disparage and intimidate. Although neither of them became violent, both were bigger and stronger than Nicholas, and he picked up a menacing undertone. So, he remained silent and absorbed their insults. The other committee member present kept quiet, too, seemingly afraid to speak up on Nicholas's behalf lest they be targeted too. " 'Vicious' is the best word to describe the situation," Nicholas says. "It was very, very heated"—one of the most disturbing encounters he'd ever experienced.

What happened next was even more bizarre. The committee had a scheduled meeting right after this conversation, and Nicholas felt obliged to attend. When they arrived, Clark and Steve acted as if nothing had happened. Clark even said something nice to Nicholas, no doubt for the benefit of others who hadn't been invited to the earlier, private conversation. At another meeting the next day, it was more of the same: a total denial of their previous ambush of Nicholas. Everybody was suddenly friends again. "It just felt super inconsistent, totally unpredictable. Like, is it Jekyll? Is it Hyde? Who is showing up?"

Nicholas was so upset that he had trouble sleeping and concentrating. During the ensuing weeks, he found interacting with Clark and Steve to be extremely stressful, but he wasn't sure what to do about it. He thought about quitting the board. He really liked the organization, wanted to see it succeed, and felt he had a lot to contribute. He wondered whether over time he'd be able to salvage a working relationship with Clark and Steve; they didn't have to be friends, but perhaps they could at least function well as a committee. But Nicholas also had to think about his own happiness and sanity. If he couldn't manage to feel good in Clark's and Steve's presence, and if he didn't think he could trust Clark in particular, maybe it wasn't worth it to continue.

Many of us face quandaries like this one. It's easy to become trapped in a relationship with a poisonous person. Even when we're aware of their toxicity, breaking it off with them can feel so difficult or in some cases dangerous that we talk ourselves into staying, downplaying the risks that sticking with the status quo might bring. Science helps by clarifying a series of Hard Truths about the trials of leaving these relationships. If we can understand aspects of our own psychology that discourage us from leaving, we might find the strength we need to say goodbye to our poisonous person. If we do decide to stay, we can feel better knowing that our decision was made with eyes wide open.

Hard Truth 1: Feeling Conflicted Is Normal

We might feel reluctant to pull the cord on a relationship because we feel torn about ending it. In practical terms, breaking up with a dark personality will likely be hard, even if leaving is clearly in our best interests. We might feel we need to stick around because there are kids involved, a breakup would be financially devastating, we like parts of our partner's personality, or we fear being alone.[1] Saying goodbye to a bad-apple boss might leave us unable to pay our bills or make landing a new job harder. A board pondering whether to fire a CEO with a dark personality might fear the disruptions that this would cause the organization, including blowback from investors if the CEO had been delivering strong financial performance. In politics, voting a malevolent leader out of office might feel perilous if we like that leader's policies—even if we dislike their personality—or fear that their opponent's policies would prove disastrous or morally reprehensible.

If you feel a strong drive to stay, you also can chalk it up to human psychology. People often regard loyalty toward others as a core moral value, one that can trump other ideals such as honesty.[2] Other common biases incline us to stay in relationships once we've formed them, even if we don't find them satisfying. We might feel an impulse to stick with our current behaviors, even if they don't help us—what scientists call "commitment bias."[3] We also feel an inner drive to form and deepen romantic relationships. In the dating pool, we cast a wide net and then do a bad job of disqualifying possible partners who don't meet our professed standards. Even when we're getting warning signs that a person isn't for us, we may feel inclined to keep things moving with that person—we'll sooner change our own romantic goals rather than disqualify a person who doesn't meet them. We often rush into big relationship decisions, like moving in with the other person or introducing them to our friends. As we do, we become more invested in the relationship, lowering the odds that we'll leave, even when that relationship becomes toxic.[4]

We're so bent on building romantic relationships in part because we're influenced by cultural demands that tell us we must have a special someone by our side to feel happy and fulfilled.[5] But we can also pin the blame on human evolution. Our ancestors couldn't afford to be choosy. They had more to gain from finding *any* mate rather than the perfect one. Because individuals who sought romantic perfection might have been more likely to wind up childless, they didn't pass on their genes as readily as those who adopted a "perfection is the enemy of progress" mindset. As a result, we're primed to make decisions that emphasize forming and nurturing *some* committed relationship rather than holding out for the ideal one.[6]

Given how attuned we are to maintaining relationships, it's no surprise that the prospect of leaving would unsettle us a little. We're not wired to break up with important people in our lives. That's a good thing most of the time, but it can keep us stuck in toxic relationships. So, don't misinterpret your trepidation about breaking up with a dark personality as a sign that it's the wrong move. Ending the relationship might be difficult, but it doesn't mean that it's wrong.

Hard Truth 2: Dark Personalities Persist

Poisonous people aren't likely to change very much. Personality traits are, by definition, enduring. Although some evolution of our character happens naturally, it takes decades. Data suggests that people become a bit more agreeable over time, and research with incarcerated men finds that even those with clinical levels of psychopathy are less likely to reoffend as they get older.[7] Even so, waiting it out is likely to be a painful strategy. One study asked more than a thousand people who knew individuals with psychopathic traits for a long time whether their behavior had improved past age fifty. Almost all respondents—93 percent—said that, as researchers put it, "the behavior was just as bad or worse after age 50" than it had been previously.[8]

It would be nice if we had an effective treatment for adults with psychopathic traits—a pill they could take or a therapy they could undergo. But no treatments have fundamentally transformed people with psychopathy. We might hope anger management interventions or training in social skills would turn bad apples into good, but one study of offenders with psychopathic traits revealed that it made them *more* likely to reoffend. One interpretation of these findings is that "psychopaths learn less about themselves [in treatment] than they do new ways of manipulating and deceiving others, and that they are able to convince therapists and staff that they have made good progress when in fact they have not."[9] Together, these early studies have led some psychologists to regard people with psychopathic traits as largely untreatable. Although the picture has brightened a bit in recent years (more on this in a moment), researchers still view people with psychopathy as extremely difficult to treat.[10]

Evidence suggests that treatment *can* help children who display proto-psychopathic traits, enabling them to become more empathic.[11] That's good news for parents, but even there, we shouldn't expect that treatment will magically flip a switch. Most of us who have tried to adopt new habits know that doing so is really tough, especially if one is not motivated and committed to it. If you expect that the dark personality in your life will one day become loving, warm, honest, conscientious, and humble, you're setting yourself up for disappointment.

Hard Truth 3: Leaving Only Gets Harder

Some people believe that they can't abandon their poisonous partner, boss, or political leader because they have too much invested in the relationship. Before you jump to that conclusion, I'd advise caution. We feel less inclined psychologically to break with projects in which we've invested resources. This "sunk cost fallacy" leads us to stick with a project or relationship that's not working out because we've put in time, energy, or money and can't bear to see that go to waste.[12]

To help neutralize this fallacy, we can reframe these "wasted" resources, seeing them as a kind of tuition we paid to learn how to avoid poisonous people going forward. We can also shift our focus from past costs that are already on the balance sheet to the future costs that will likely pile up. This can be particularly effective when we consider the harms that *others* will experience if we elect to "stick it out." In one study, researchers asked participants to imagine they were babysitting their niece and nephew and decided to take them to the movies.[13] It was an expensive endeavor; the tickets alone were fifty dollars. Five minutes in, one of the kids found the movie terrifying. How likely would the participants be to continue watching the movie?

As researchers found, people were less likely to fall victim to the sunk cost fallacy if they believed the movie led to real harm—if the kids were afraid of the film, in this case—than if the kids were simply bored by it. Similarly, while we might be willing to bear the personal costs of a toxic relationship, we might be much less willing to violate our duty of care to others. Considering carefully how a boss or romantic partner who is a dark personality is impacting our children or others we care about might help us cut ties before the sunk costs pile up too high.

Focusing on the potential for future harms to others might have led the acclaimed Canadian author Alice Munro to make a different decision when her adult daughter, Andrea Skinner, revealed that she'd experienced sexual abuse years earlier at the hands of Munro's second husband, Gerald Fremlin.[14] It's unclear whether Munro knew of the abuse when it was happening, but she certainly did after Andrea wrote her a letter detailing it and its devastating effects. Instead of supporting her daughter, Munro took the allegations as a personal assault, focusing on her own feelings of humiliation and betrayal.

Claiming that she had been "told too late," she briefly left Fremlin only to return to his side within a few weeks.[15] This kind of "what's done is done" thinking can keep us from walking away from a relationship that likely will bring further harm. Andrea was deeply hurt by her mother's decision to continue her relationship with Fremlin. He did in fact continue to harm Andrea by threatening her with retribution if she ever went public. He blamed her for the abuse and told Munro that he would kill Andrea if she went to the police.

We also should consider all that *we* might lose if we don't walk away. In addition to the harms we might experience, we're missing out on the benefits we might have enjoyed had we cut that person loose. We might have found a boss who doesn't constantly abuse us. Or a life partner who doesn't lie and cheat at every turn. Or a political leader who doesn't spread vitriol and chaos. Or, in the case of Nicholas, an opportunity to serve the community that doesn't leave us stressed and depleted.

To make sure you're fully accounting for the opportunity costs of staying, work through the pros and cons in more depth. Think about the types of benefits that could come to you if you leave and that you'd forgo if you stayed. How might you benefit financially, emotionally, socially, physically, or spiritually once you're free of the dark personality in your life? It's easier to list the tangible advantages of staying, since that's the status quo and therefore well known to us. In thinking through the benefits of leaving, our challenge is to imagine the many as yet unbounded realities that *could be.*

Play out the thought experiment of your life without this person, really letting your imagination run free. What wild and crazy decisions might you feel tempted to make that you can't make now? What new experiences might open up to you? What might you be able to accomplish if you weren't bogged down by the constant stress of dealing with a person who treats you poorly? How might you feel about yourself? What kinds of relationships could you have? What kinds of new goals or ambitions might you pursue? The answers to such questions point to the opportunity at hand, one that you might pass up if you think only about losing what you've already invested.

To understand the possibilities that might await us, consider the story of Melissa. When she started to date her ex-husband, Vince, her friends told her not to. He was a know-it-all, they said, someone who dominated conversations and made others around him feel inferior. There were other warning signs to suggest that Vince wasn't such a great catch. He had a checkered work history and had been accused by a former colleague of sexual harassment. He held grudges: he regularly emailed a former boss who fired him just to say "fuck you." He had a reckless streak, drinking and gambling too much at times. He told Melissa straight up that he didn't experience empathy for others—their suffering didn't affect him. And in fact, the only time she ever saw him express something akin to sadness was when he called her to complain that he had just lost $100,000 in the stock market on a risky trade.

Melissa ignored these warning signs during their first few months of dating because, as she told me, she enjoyed being with Vince. She also decided to overlook a serious incident in which he callously embarrassed her in front of a friend, sparking a fight between them. She reasoned that this sort of thing happens in relationships, and she took comfort in knowing that the two shared similar life goals. On their second date, she had told Vince that she wanted children. She had also divulged that they might need a surrogate to carry the baby, since she'd had chemotherapy as a child and suspected that fertility would be an issue. Vince had expressed enthusiasm for starting a family on these terms—a big deal for Melissa, and something she would continue to bear in mind during rocky moments.

Unfortunately, there were more of these moments than she liked, especially once they were married. Vince was never physically abusive, but he was constantly critical of Melissa, making her feel "stupid" even about topics she had expertise in. When they fought, Vince portrayed himself as the victim, berating Melissa for being selfish and unkind. Melissa felt she had to tread lightly around him lest she trigger more harsh commentary about her shortcomings. "I think a lot of the time his personality structure caused him to act like an asshole," Melissa reflects. "I think it was just him trying to get what he needed, right? Like we all are. It's just in really toxic ways a lot of the time."

Despite these problems and her mounting unhappiness, she stayed with Vince, as they were making progress toward their shared goal of starting a family. Or so she thought. When the surrogate they found was ready to move forward, Vince announced that he no longer wanted to have children. This was the breaking point: Melissa finally decided to leave him.

When she broached the subject with Vince, it didn't go over well. "From that day, it felt like this mask that he'd been wearing that I'd occasionally, like, caught glimpses of underneath came off . . . he had no motivation to keep it on anymore if I was going to break up with him. So it came off and it stayed off. And then the worst fucking year of my life followed suit."

Vince lashed out even more harshly at her. He sent barrages of text messages and emails, calling her every name imaginable and blaming everything on her. All of this caused Melissa great suffering, but her decision to leave also led to a pleasant surprise. During their marriage, they had kept their finances largely separate, and after Vince's stock market losses, Melissa had assumed that he was broke. In fact, as she discovered, he had somehow managed to squirrel away a huge sum of money. In their divorce settlement, Melissa received a good portion of it—a windfall she hadn't anticipated.

She used this money to open a small art supply shop. Today, the business is thriving, and she has a whole new life filled with friends and colleagues who lift her up, not bring her down as Vince once did. She doesn't feel on edge anymore and has started a relationship with a man who makes her feel safe and valued. Reflecting on why she stayed with Vince for so long, she notes that ambivalent feelings "often keep people in it because they're like, 'Oh, it's not all bad, right?' But it also keeps you from thinking about how good life could be if you weren't in this relationship." Ultimately, Vince taught her a great deal about what she *didn't* want in a partner.

Hard Truth 4: Your Commitment Doesn't Guarantee Their Improvement

Despite their terrible suffering, victims of poisonous people sometimes pin the blame for their abusive relationship on themselves. *Their* behavior triggered the abuse. *They're* the ones causing discord. *Their* understanding of events is skewed. As a result of such thinking, victims might stick with the relationship, reasoning that if only they can change their own attitudes or behavior, the relationship will improve, and a benevolence buried deep inside someone with dark traits will finally emerge.

If the poisonous person in your life is anything like the ones I've studied, they want you to think that your suffering is your fault, not theirs. In fact, they want you to think that you're harming *them*. Dark personalities are more likely than the rest of us to present themselves as victims, even though in reality they're the destructive ones. They do this cynically, as a strategy to extract resources from others around them that they wouldn't otherwise receive, including money or influence.[16] In the context of a relationship, a dark personality might claim victimhood as a way to garner your sympathy or your continued commitment to the relationship.

Although the damage a poisonous person causes might be plain to see, these malicious personalities are skilled at twisting our sense of reality. We've seen how prone people with psychopathic traits are to lying and deceiving in general, but they also gaslight, making their victims question their sanity. If the dark personality is the one lying, they try to convince you that you're lying. If they're wrong, they claim that you're wrong. If they're guilty, they claim you're paranoid. If they make poor decisions, they assert that your judgment is poor. If you contradict them, they criticize you.[17]

As evidence of their innocence and good nature, the dark personality might point to times when you were thrilled to be with them. You might remember those times, too. But are those memories as pure as they seem? Was their good behavior really a genuine expression of their true personality, or were they faking it?

People with elevated psychopathic traits are skilled at making a good first impression when it's in their interest. In romantic relationships, they often engage in "love bombing," a classic bait-and-switch ruse. Aware of the affection, kindness, and support that most of us seek from relationships, they provide it at first—not because they actually feel those positive emotions or seek to commune with another person, but because they want to lure us in. Once we've become emotionally dependent on them, they reveal their true nature. "Hiding selfish intentions and convincing others of one's genuineness and trustworthiness . . . may be a 'skill' in psychopathy," one group of researchers has observed.[18] This capacity for manipulation allows people with psychopathy to establish committed relationships while simultaneously perpetrating abuse toward their partners, uninhibited by remorse or guilt.[19]

In workplaces, people with psychopathic traits can come across positively at first on account of their charisma and strong communication, only to reveal over time that they struggle to maintain positive relationships with others.[20] Narcissists, too, are skilled at making a great first impression that wears thin as we find them to be self-aggrandizing and untrustworthy.[21] As we've also seen, dark personalities not only talk a good game in order to wheedle their way into our boardrooms and bedrooms; they specifically target those of us whom they perceive to be emotionally vulnerable, even paying attention to physical cues such as our gait.[22]

We'd be mistaken if we recalled our early experiences with a poisonous person and regarded that as evidence of their "true" personality, while discounting all the contradictory evidence we've gathered in the intervening months or years. Their apparent goodness early on was a facade. Occasional acts of concern or kindness on their part might be similarly opportunistic or exploitative, intended to ensure their dominance over you. In a phenomenon known as "trauma bonding," people who experience intermittent or cyclical abuse (violence followed by acts of contrition or devotion) often develop strong feelings of attachment to abusive partners.[23] Be cautious about taking sole responsibility for problems in your relationship, or thinking that more effort on your part will make things better.

Hard Truth 5: You Probably Aren't the Only One Suffering

If you share children with a poisonous person, you might feel inclined to stay because you fear the impact that leaving might have on your kids' development. It's true that children of divorced parents generally don't do as well across a number of measures as those in intact families.[24] At the same time, it's important to consider *why* divorce can be harmful. Children can suffer because one or both of the parents is absent, and because divorce can affect a family's financial stability. But as research suggests, the chief reason children of divorce suffer is parental conflict.

Children growing up in homes where their parents are constantly shouting at each other, muttering insults, lashing out physically, not talking to each other, and so on are likely to experience negative effects on their emotional health, their academic performance, and their behavior.[25] As we've seen, people with psychopathic traits abuse their romantic partners in a slew of ways. If you're a parent concerned about your child's welfare, you might find it extremely difficult to create a calm, peaceful environment in the home if you stay with your malevolent partner. Leaving might well be the better option.

Poisonous people also can cause direct harm to children in the home. People with psychopathic traits are more likely to abuse or neglect their kids. They might bully kids, lie to them, fail to see to their needs, use drugs or alcohol around them, gaslight them, and shame them. They also might play favorites, targeting one child for abuse while lavishing affection on another. Kids might experience a mix of positive, loving experiences and painful, abusive ones—a contradiction that can be confusing and traumatic in its own right.[26]

To understand what living with a psychopathic parent might feel like, consider the story of Charlie. His parents divorced when he was a baby, and he spent his early childhood living with his father and stepmother. Although his stepmother was kind and loving, his father exhibited seriously dark traits. He was verbally abusive, yelling and screaming when displeased—behaviors that worsened thanks to his drug and alcohol use. He was also a habitual liar who refused to take responsibility for his actions. No wonder, then, that Charlie's father soon divorced for a second time. He neglected Charlie, failing to protect him from his abusive brother and on some occasions absenting himself from the family for long stretches. As Charlie later discovered, his father spent a couple of weekends in jail on charges related to his alcohol use. "I didn't exactly have a happy life," Charlie says. "If it wasn't my dad screaming at me, it was my brother pushing me around, that sort of thing."

When Charlie was eleven, he was home sick from school one day, a fact that his father didn't realize. From the next room, Charlie heard his father trying to inject his new girlfriend with narcotics against her will. As he recalls, "I heard her saying, 'No, no, I don't want that. No, I don't want that.' I just lay in my bed and was horrified by that. I did eventually fall back to sleep, and when I woke up, they were gone."

Charlie knew he had to do something. What he'd witnessed was "fucked up," and he didn't want it to be "part of my normal," nor did he want his father's girlfriend or others around his father to suffer. Going into the next room, Charlie found two syringes and hid one of them. He called his aunt for help, and she arrived to confront his father. "He just denied everything," Charlie says, "even after I pulled out the syringe." When Charlie's aunt left, his father continued to call him a liar and warned him never to go through his things again. Charlie no longer wanted to be around his father. He just couldn't stand it. Three days later, his aunt returned to take him away. Charlie moved to a different state to live with his mother, where he'd stay for the rest of his childhood.

The episode caused a permanent rupture between Charlie and his father. "For a kid to do something, it's so scary, and to be ridiculed for it and called a liar for bringing about the truth. That was an area that became heightened sensitivity between me and my dad for the rest of our lives." Looking back on it, Charlie believes that the time he spent living with his father and that incident in particular had a profound impact on his life. "I feel like it probably stole a lot of my childhood away," he says. "I think I became an adult real, real fast right then." Breaking up a household certainly impacts children negatively, but as Charlie's story suggests, so can staying.

Concern about harming others might also prevent companies from severing ties with poisonous leaders. Executives and board members might fear that firing such leaders will disrupt their teams or organizations, especially if these leaders happen to be strong performers. But remember the severe impact that bosses with psychopathic traits can have if they remain in place. We've seen that bosses who are dark personalities treat their employees poorly, leading them to head for the exits. Those who leave include many good people, employees who care about ethics and see doing good as part of their identity.[27] Bullying at work causes employees to feel stressed out, to perform poorly, and to behave destructively.[28] And the bad behavior spreads, with others taking their cues from the dark personality in charge.

Hard Truth 6: Treatment Will Be a Long and Bumpy Road

Perhaps the poisonous person in your life has agreed to go to therapy to help salvage your relationship, and you're starting to see glimmers of improvement in their behavior. It's not likely, but it could happen. One class of interventions—cognitive behavioral therapies—can improve the behavior of criminal offenders, even those scoring highly in psychopathic traits.[29] Such therapies focus on changing problematic patterns of thought. For example, someone who becomes enraged when they are offered challenging feedback at work might learn to reframe such feedback as not a challenge at all, but another person's sincere attempt to be helpful. By practicing that skill of reframing, dark personalities might contain their impulse to blow up at their colleague or sabotage them to get revenge.[30]

Among criminal psychopaths, staying in therapy longer appears to yield better results. In other words, improvement requires a strong "dose" of treatment. According to one study, men who had elevated PCL-R scores and had completed seven or more treatment sessions were nearly four times less likely to behave violently ten weeks after treatment than those who had attended six or fewer sessions.[31] The catch is that it's not easy keeping people with psychopathic traits in treatment—they ditch it more quickly than others.[32] In general, people with psychopathic traits lack motivation to change this part of their personality. Their thoughts and behaviors don't cause *them* distress, so why change?³³

Although people with psychopathic traits might not feel driven to attend therapy on their own, we can motivate them to improve. As we'll see in the next chapter, dark personalities respond better if you offer them rewards for good behavior than if you threaten to punish bad behavior. They're fundamentally selfish, focused on advancing their own interests, so if you can make it worth their while to do something, they're more likely to comply. For example, describing a criminal lifestyle as "low status" and touting the virtue of self-sufficiency can align with a dark personality's desire for status, lowering the odds that they'll tangle with the law or make parasitic lifestyle choices.³⁴ Framing therapy in a way that's consistent with their goals may motivate them, too. In a workplace setting, for instance, that might mean telling a poisonous person that therapy might put them on a faster track to a promotion and a raise.

Even if a dark personality sticks it out in therapy, the progress they'll make will probably be limited. Therapy can improve behavior, but it won't eliminate the risk entirely, and it won't fundamentally change their character. If you're hoping that your spouse will fundamentally alter the dark parts of their personality, you're out of luck. They'll still be lacking in empathy, be inclined to manipulate, and feel few emotions. But they may become better at keeping their toxic character traits from translating into harmful action.³⁵ Perhaps they won't cheat or lie to you as much as they once did, but progress will look more like reduced destruction than total transformation.

A psychologist friend of mine treats husbands who cheat serially on their wives. As she told me, "I don't know if these men will ever be the men that these women are hoping for. They're not going to become, all of a sudden, caring individuals that are warm and compassionate. They might stop some of that behavior, but will it become a rewarding relationship for them or their spouse? I don't know about that."

There's an exception to this grim picture: children. Kids with callous-unemotional (CU) traits *can* see big improvements with treatment, especially when interventions happen early. Ideally, treatment would begin when parents first notice difficulties with empathy in their children and before more serious behavioral issues arise. We can reliably measure CU traits in children ages two to five, reflected in behavior such as hurting others in order to win a game.[36] The most promising treatment approaches train parents how to model and reward good behavior while extinguishing the bad. With certain kinds of treatment, parents of preschool-age children can even see reductions in problematic personality traits, not just behavioral improvements.[37] Kids with CU traits can learn to become kinder and more empathetic.

We shouldn't get too excited, though. While these kids might improve, they will still have far to go. Dr. Daniel Waschbusch, a clinical psychologist at Pennsylvania State University who studies and works with kids with CU traits, notes that kids who see big improvement often "still end up pretty bad," simply because their skills related to empathy and emotion were so poor to begin with. Parents also must be prepared for a tough road ahead. Skill-building takes time, and it happens in fits and starts. "On a day-to-day basis," Waschbusch says, progress is "variable. Some days it feels like it's fantastic. Some days it feels like it's having no effect. Some days it feels like it's making things worse. You're not doing it for any given Tuesday, Wednesday, or Thursday. You're doing it for two or three years down the road."[38]

If you decide to maintain your relationship with a dark personality, think realistically about what the future might hold. The good news is that there's hope for behavioral improvement among adults, and a reduction in CU traits among kids with the right treatment. But it will be a long and challenging process.

Hard Truth 7: Leaving Can Be Risky

Leaving a toxic relationship can be extremely dangerous, particularly in romantic relationships. Decades of research shows that the likelihood of serious injury or death soars when a victim in a romantic relationship tries to leave their abusive partner.[39] One study of men who had committed a domestic homicide found that 70 percent killed their partner in the context of a relationship separation. Before extreme violence erupts, there are usually warning signs. This study also found that homicides were more likely to occur in relationships marked by constant jealousy and attempts to control the victims' daily activities.[40]

As frightening as the act of leaving might be, we can take steps to exit relationships more safely. Experts in domestic violence recommend, first of all, that we put a plan in place. Having a concrete plan increases the odds that we'll follow through with our intentions to break off the relationship. It also might allow us to make our move at the safest possible time. As part of our plan, we can collect important documents we might need to obtain housing or new jobs, put aside money to help us get on our feet, and arrange for people or organizations to stand by ready to help us. If applicable, we can also gather any evidence we might need in future legal proceedings, such as police reports or pictures documenting the abuse we suffered.[41]

When it comes to actually saying goodbye, you'll want to consider how a malevolent personality might take this news. Research suggests that narcissistic romantic partners often deal with rejection or perceived threats to their authority by lashing out verbally or physically.[42] Hurling insults at a narcissistic person can cause them to behave aggressively, while physically provoking a person with psychopathic traits—for instance, shoving them on your way out the door—will likely invite retaliation.[43] To ensure your safety, you might wish to make a stealth exit and then convey afterward in a phone call or email that your relationship is over.

We should make a clean break if possible. Dark personalities might feel inclined to stay in touch with an old flame after a breakup, not out of love but because they hope to gain access to resources the relationship provided them, such as sex or money.[44] If you maintain contact, you might find yourself trapped in a toxic relationship by a partner who is unrestrained by remorse.[45] You also might increase the odds of a catastrophic outcome: research shows that when highly psychopathic men murder domestic partners, they don't necessarily do it right away as an act of passion; rather, they act in a cold, calculating, premeditated way.[46]

Making a clean break prevents you from wasting time, energy, and resources on a relationship that is already over and that brings you little fulfillment or satisfaction. If dark personalities stay in your life after a breakup, they might try to manipulate themselves back into a controlling position. Soon, you can find yourself stuck once again in the toxic relationship you tried to end.

Once we've left, we can stay safe by changing our routines and phone numbers, installing alarm systems, and reaching out to local police or social services for support. Similar precautions might help when leaving a boss with dark traits. In workplace situations, our concern might not be violence but bullying or a poisonous boss's efforts to damage our professional reputation. Here, too, we can form a plan of action that might limit our exposure to harm, including coordinating with human resources, making other colleagues aware of the situation, and arranging for a transfer to a different location.

Sometimes even those who try to help victims of dark personalities must take precautions. Meghan, a divorce mediator, told me of an instance when she and colleagues at her law firm were handling a negotiation with a couple going through a separation. Allison, the wife, appeared to be utterly broken thanks to years of abuse inflicted by her husband, Tom, who exhibited many psychopathic traits. Tom had quickly sucked Allison into a relationship, wining and dining her and professing his love. Once they were married, he became controlling, making Allison cut herself off from her friends, family, and career. The situation grew much darker as Tom started to molest underage girls, including Allison's daughter from her previous relationship, and rape Allison herself. Tom even took away her birth control, forcing her to have a child with him.

Meghan says that Tom was a "monster," someone who was "as bad as they come." When Allison told Meghan about Tom, "she'd shake. Her voice would tremble. She'd sweat. She was fully traumatized by him." She "just wanted to die because he was so scary." As their relationship drew to an end, Tom would try to terrorize Allison into submission. He would leave bullets around Allison's house as well as notes with musings such as "I will kill you, but will I kill you? Kill I will." Meghan and her colleagues felt threatened, too. A restraining order intended to protect Allison prevented him from coming within two hundred feet of Meghan's law firm, since there was a chance Allison might be present. "He used to basically just measure out two hundred feet," Meghan says, "and he'd stare at us."

Having worked with many divorcing couples, including some with abusive husbands, Meghan knew that Tom wasn't a run-of-the-mill jerk—he was a real threat. She and her colleagues, who were all women, had to protect themselves.

The firm came up with a comprehensive plan to stay safe. At first, nobody was allowed to work alone in the office with the doors unlocked. Rather than unlock the door to accept deliveries of documents, they had the delivery people slide envelopes under the door or come back later when other colleagues were around. Then the firm required that nobody could work in the office alone at all. They also installed panic buttons colleagues could press to notify police if

Tom tried to hurt any of them. They started walking to the parking lot in pairs. They kept pepper spray with them at work. Thanks to these and other precautions, Meghan and her colleagues stayed safe. "I think he thought, 'I'm going to get this office full of women.' And he just picked the wrong office." Making a clean break from a dark personality probably won't be easy. But we're not powerless. Planning and caution can make a big difference.

Making It to the Other Side

Understanding and internalizing the seven Hard Truths I've outlined here can save you from making an unwise choice, but it doesn't necessarily render your decision-making easier. Leaving a poisonous person can be wrenching, even when the stakes are relatively low. Take Nicholas, the man at the beginning of the chapter who crossed a dark personality while volunteering at an art museum. He didn't face the prospect of losing his job or suffering physical abuse, but he was still upset and unsure of what to do. He pondered for a while whether to resign his post. The turning point came when he spoke to a confidant inside the organization who had seen the email Nicholas had sent. This person helped Nicholas realize that if he stayed, he would be consistently stressed and miserable, and that Clark might even take legal action against him. Staying just wasn't worth the cost, this confidant said, regardless of how much Nicholas loved the organization. Nicholas had to agree.

Although sad to leave, Nicholas felt relieved that he no longer had to deal with Clark. Nicholas has maintained relationships with some on the board and visits the art museum with his kids from time to time. He feels scarred by his experience with Clark. He still wants to give back to the community, but he plans to be more diligent in researching organizations and the people he'd be working with before making a commitment.

Even if we've been scarred, we often can find ways to open ourselves again to new relationships. If we decide to stay, there's hope, too. As we better understand these dark personalities, we can learn to see through their deception and manipulation. We can learn techniques for managing poisonous people, minimizing the pain they cause us, and reclaiming some comfort and control.

7

Seven Rules for Managing Poisonous People

Chelsea, a multitasking, high-achieving woman now in her fifties, had the misfortune of serving as an executive assistant for Frank, a wealthy CEO. He was charming and affable but also callous, manipulative, and exploitative. Although Chelsea had no illusions about Frank, she needed the money and didn't want to do anything that would jeopardize her regular paycheck. Instead of quitting, she decided to stay and try to manage her boss. Her strategy was what we might call the "more" approach. The best way to improve her relationship with Frank, she thought, was to give him more effort, more dedication, more patience. If she complied with his outrageous requests and even tried to exceed his expectations, he'd value her and come to treat her better.

In fact, Frank's behavior only worsened as he realized that he could dominate her and suffer no consequences for it. Again and again, he abused his authority, asking her to stay late, work on weekends, or handle extra requests that were beyond her job description, such as cleaning his office or running personal errands. Lingering in the background was a subtle threat that if she didn't comply, he would replace her. Often he would charm her into doing him a favor but then offer nothing in the way of extra compensation or recognition—not even a thank-you.

A turning point came when Frank made his most outrageous request yet. A dangerous storm was blowing in, bringing massive waves that could flood his art-filled, oceanfront mansion. Rather than hire professionals to build a protective wall of sandbags, Frank asked Chelsea to show up after work in the storm to do it. Oh, and she also had to enlist others at the office to help with the task.

As usual, Chelsea complied, convincing four or five colleagues to join her on the beach in front of Frank's house. "It's pouring rain," she remembers, "and we spent hours filling sandbags. We were absolutely drenched to the bone, exhausted, cold." You might think Frank would have joined them during this all-hands-on-deck moment, but as Chelsea remembers, "he was sitting in his house sipping on a glass of wine" while they toiled away. When they finally finished late in the evening, Frank barely acknowledged their efforts. "And then the next day his attitude was like, 'Well, what have you done for me lately?'" As usual, neither Chelsea nor her colleagues received extra pay for their troubles. Frank didn't even buy them dinner.

After this incident, Chelsea was done. She had taken her "more" approach as far as she could and decided she just wouldn't work for Frank any longer. If we're dealing with someone who has a conscience and is capable of empathy and gratitude, then the idealism embodied in Chelsea's "more" approach might be warranted. With a poisonous person, it's an invitation to abuse. To maintain long-term relationships with them, we must don some psychological armor. By understanding their tendencies and tactics, we can try to manage their destructive impulses and behaviors. The following seven rules can help ensure that the dark personalities in our lives will treat *us* as we would wish to be treated, or at least in a manner tolerably close to that standard.

Rule 1: Establish Clear Boundaries

Let's begin by considering how we might best structure relationships with dark personalities at the outset, or how we might *re*structure them once their malevolent tendencies come to light. Our first move should be to *specify in no uncertain terms what's allowed in the relationship, and what's not.* Setting boundaries and communicating them is important to any healthy relationship.[1] But when we're dealing with a poisonous person, it's vital to make these rules clear and explicit, and also to clarify the consequences that will occur if the rules are broken.

Most of us don't need explicit rules the way people with psychopathic traits do. We behave a bit like sheep in social situations—in a good way. It's not that we don't have minds of our own, but we cue into unwritten rules that govern behavior and follow the lead of others around us, which generally makes for harmonious social relationships. People with psychopathy do no such thing. A defining feature of their personality is breaking rules. Unwritten ones are the easiest to break, since there's room for doubt about what the rule actually is and fuzziness about the consequences of breaking it.

In her memoir, M. E. Thomas, a self-described "sociopath," describes how she maintained a "lifelong policy of following only explicit rules, and then only because they're easiest to prove against me." She disregarded "other unspoken rules with little consequence."[2] This is classic behavior among people who score high in dark traits. If a rule isn't clearly delineated, they think, "why bother with it?"—especially if breaking the rule serves their interests.

Research in workplaces suggests that clear rules can rein in people with psychopathic traits. In one study, researchers gave bosses in an organization a pot of money and let them hand it out as they pleased. With some bosses, researchers clearly articulated norms of ethical conduct and let the bosses know that the rules would be enforced. These bosses had to read the following text, which defined both guidelines for how to distribute the money as well as potential consequences for not sticking to the rules: "In our way of doing things, we always want people to treat each other with respect and dignity. We would like you to do the same and distribute fairly. We will monitor how you distribute the money, and if in our opinion you did not distribute fairly and appropriately, we might intervene and lower your bonus payment." With other bosses, researchers were much looser in laying out the rules, and they didn't promise accountability for living up to them. Participants read that they were expected "to distribute the money how you see fit. Your distribution will remain anonymous, and your decision is final. What you decide to keep for yourself will be your bonus payment."[3]

Researchers also evaluated these bosses for psychopathic traits. As they found, when rules and oversight are lax, bosses with more of these traits took more of the bonus payment for themselves. But when there was clarity about rules and accountability, dark personality traits were neutralized: highly psychopathic bosses split the bonus in the same ways everyone else did. Additional studies found that clarity about the rules in particular, rather than the presence of mechanisms for holding bosses accountable, induced poisonous bosses to refrain from abusing their team members. Clearly stated boundaries imply their enforcement, and even people with psychopathic traits can see compliance as serving their self-interest. In this sense, the presence of rules in a social setting can have, researchers claim, a "wholesome influence."

If you oversee others in the workplace, put unstated cultural norms in writing, framing them as a "respectful workplace" policy and drawing everyone's attention to them. Such formality might seem excessive; most people don't need a handbook on how to treat others decently. But such a policy might restrain a poisonous person's worst impulses. Better yet, you'll be able to refer back to this policy if violations occur. In the absence of a formal policy, you might find it hard to reprimand or fire a person with psychopathic traits, since they might not technically be breaking any rules.

You can also do more to make norms and expectations explicit in the moment. Before an important meeting, remind attendees that you expect them to arrive "ready to listen as well as to share." Stating this out loud puts you in a better position to jump in when a poisonous person dominates the conversation, interrupts others, or takes the discussion off course. Narcissistic personalities often dominate conversations as a way to convince others that they're leadership material. By proactively managing conversations, you can reduce the likelihood that dark personalities with narcissistic tendencies ascend the corporate hierarchy before more qualified coworkers.[4]

If you're embarking on a romantic relationship with a dark personality, jot down some basic rules—for instance, "We always treat each other with respect," or "No cheating on me with your old flame," or "We will always be honest with each other when it comes to money." Make clear what the consequences for breaking the rules are. Create red lines—behavior that would lead you to break off the relationship immediately—and put these in writing. Revisit your red lines from time to time. Is your partner respecting your values and concerns? Or are your red lines fading? To keep yourself honest, ask a friend to keep an eye on you and tell you when you're letting things slide.[5]

The writer Anne Lamott once wrote, "Expectations are resentments waiting to happen."[6] My friend and communications scholar Dr. Elena Svetieva added to the phrase, "especially when not communicated."[7] These are some wise women. With dark personalities, you have an extra burden to define and communicate what is acceptable in a relationship. If you don't, you won't just feel resentful, you may also suffer serious harm.

Rule 2: Don't Hand Them Power over Others

Another move you should make early in a relationship with a poisonous person—or when undertaking a reset—is to consider whether to grant them power over other people. If you're a teacher, you already know you don't put the class bully in charge when stepping away from the classroom. In the workplace, making smart choices about power might mean preventing your charming but devious employee from leading a team.

The evidence is clear: people with psychopathic traits create toxic workplace environments, reduce the productivity of subordinates, and degrade their mental health. We've all heard that power corrupts, and absolute power corrupts absolutely. But power is far more liable to corrupt dark personalities. Remember that research I described in chapter 5 showing that people with a strong sense of moral identity behaved more generously when placed in positions of power? That same study found that people overall became more selfish, and that those with a weak sense of moral identity became especially so.[8]

Power activates our latent tendencies, making us more of who we already are. The psychologist Dr. Ana Guinote has written that "power intensifies the active self"; it "helps people strive for salient goals" that reflect the ideas they hold dear and their personality traits.[9] When we hold power, we're more directed and focused in our pursuit of goals and interests, since we have the ability to effect change in the world. If you're a kind, generous person, possessing power will incline you to try to do more good. By the same token, we shouldn't be surprised if a dark personality uses their authority to pursue what they care about most—money, domination, popularity, pleasure, stimulation—while neglecting priorities that interest them less, like others' well-being or ethical behavior.[10]

If a dark personality is excelling at work, they deserve a reward just like anyone else. But rewarding them with a position of power over others is setting them up to fail. Most employees today believe that leaders with high EQ (emotional intelligence) will perform better.[11] People with psychopathic traits aren't inclined to feel what others feel and respond compassionately. In her memoir, M. E. Thomas quotes a reader of her blog who apparently has psychopathic traits and who wrote in to describe their struggles managing others in the workplace. "I've often been promoted to levels where my personal style becomes a liability," this reader said. Managing others or overseeing relationships "require[s] a great deal of sensitivity to the interests of others over a longer term. This is the level where I seem to make mistakes. Then I have to go somewhere else and start all over again."[12] When I interviewed Thomas, she shared a similar experience, noting that because she lacks empathy for others, she has to fake it. When the facade inevitably erodes, others ostracize her for faking it. To her, it feels like a catch-22.

Thomas and her reader possess a self-awareness that others with dark traits lack. If you put a poisonous person in charge of others, they're unlikely to say they're ill-suited for the job. Rather, they'll seize the opportunity to dominate others. Save yourself and others the trouble. Reward these folks in different ways—with a new title, an office with a view, a bonus, or genuine praise.

Rule 3: Look for Win-Wins

Now that we've explored how to set up and clarify relationships with dark personalities, let's consider what we might do to motivate good behavior. In 2012, I packed my bags and moved to Berkeley, California, to start a postdoctoral fellowship. My best friend, Tara, flew down with me and spent two days assembling IKEA furniture in my new apartment. When she left, I felt so alone that I coped by throwing myself into my work. My advisor had set up a pretty sweet gig for me: tutoring students in her introductory class on organizational behavior. At one point in the semester, the students learned about negotiation—a topic I'd never before studied—and I got a chance to hash out the material with them. It occurred to me that many social interactions involve negotiation in some way, and that our personalities likely affect how we approach these moments. That insight led to an interesting research question: How do psychopathic personality traits impact a person's ability to negotiate? Do these traits help them get what they want or hinder them?

My obvious next move: run a study. My research team and I convened a group of our students, gathered data on their personalities, and had them perform a negotiation exercise. We found that psychopathic traits often helped people make more money in a negotiation, but not always. That's because psychopathic folks are particularly susceptible to what business types call the "myth of the fixed pie."[13] They see the world as an antagonistic place where people either win or lose and where winning comes at the loser's expense. For this reason, they tend to take more than their fair share when their interests are diametrically opposed to their negotiation partner. By contrast, in situations where their interests and their partner's partially overlap, they leave value on the table. People with psychopathic traits aren't good at trade-offs. In their mind, compromise and collaboration are for losers—and they are winners. In our study, they couldn't "give a little" here to "get a lot" there. This rigidity sometimes hurt them.[14]

Our team did turn up one type of negotiation situation where people high in psychopathic traits did do just as well as everyone else: when they wanted the same thing as their partner. We often think of negotiations as oppositional, especially when we're confronting a poisonous person or a competitive situation, but that may not be true. If we talk it through, we might discover that we actually agree on a relevant point, and that no compromise is necessary: a simple win-win solution is at hand. In this case, psychopathic negotiators are good at getting what they want, and happily, their partners also achieve their goals.

To the extent that your interests align with the high psychopathy individual, you may be able to avoid becoming their victim. Find ways to work with dark personalities by looking for potential win-win opportunities. That in turn means staying alert to what they care about—money, power, pleasure, status, excitement—and thinking how those might align with your goals.[15]

In any negotiation, grasping your partner's personality traits can yield important insight into what their interests truly are. One psychologist I interviewed used his insight on psychopathic personalities to dramatic effect. During hostage negotiations, police would ask him for advice on how to maximize their chances of a peaceful resolution, or at least buy time for the SWAT team to arrive. When the hostage taker had psychopathic personality traits, he told police not to ask them to imagine how the hostages were feeling or appeal to them to do the right thing. Empathy and morality, as we know, aren't strong suits of psychopathic personalities. Rather, he advised the police to lean in to the hostage taker's selfishness: framing the release of hostages as a means of improving their own lot, say, by reducing their likely prison sentence. Recognizing egocentricity in its various forms is an insight we can deploy in everyday settings, too. It's worth considering: what's in it for them?

Let's say you're a boss supervising a poisonous person who strikes others as charming, affable, and charismatic. If you know this employee gets a narcissistic rush out of being in the limelight, and your organization could benefit from having this person represent it in the media, you might put them in a front-facing, public relations role rather than keep them cooped up in the back office. The employee will get the attention from others that they crave, while your organization will achieve a reputational benefit. Win-win.

Of course, you don't want to go too far and bend your goals to meet theirs. You also should be mindful of *how* a dark personality is achieving your shared goals. Make certain that your employee really will help the organization, not hurt it, by serving as its spokesperson. If they're making a good first impression by lying about your company's accolades, that should cross a red line you set for employee behavior. But if they're simply adept at being charming and bringing in new customers, this could be the mutually beneficial scenario you've been searching for.

During the 1970s and '80s, the legendary filmmaker Werner Herzog made five films with the actor Klaus Kinski. By many accounts, Kinski was an extremely difficult person to work with: volatile and violent. Kinski also had a monumental ego. Just prior to working with Herzog, he starred in a one-man show, performing a thirty-page monologue that he wrote called *Jesus Christus Erlöser* (Jesus Christ Savior). When the audience heckled him, he replied, "Can't you see that when someone lectures thirty typewritten pages of text in this way, that you must shut your mouths? If you can't see that, please let someone bang it into your brain with a hammer!"[16]

Kinski likely wasn't joking. An extra on the set of *Aguirre, the Wrath of God* (his first film with Herzog, in which he stars as a Spanish soldier leading the search for gold in the Amazon) still bears a scar on his head that Kinski gave him during a fit of rage. Likewise, Kinski was once confined to a psychiatric hospital for a brief period after stalking his theatrical sponsor and attempting to strangle her. The doctors came to a decisive diagnosis: "Conclusion: Psychopathy."[17]

During the filming of *Aguirre* in Peru, Kinski threatened to leave, a move that would have derailed the project. He had broken dozens of contracts in the past, so his threat was serious. Herzog had to figure out how to convince Kinski to stick it out. In a documentary that Herzog made about their relationship, he said he calmly approached the actor and said, "You can't do this. The movie is more important than our personal emotions, and even more important than our persons. This can't be permitted. This simply will not be."[18] Herzog followed up this measured appeal by threatening to shoot Kinski if he left.

That conversation seemed to do the trick. Afterward, Kinski was "very docile" for the remainder of the filming. While Herzog seemed to credit his threats as the motivating factor for Kinski's change of heart, I see it differently. We know that dominance contests with dark personalities only serve to inflame a situation, so it's not likely that Herzog's threats were decisive. But Herzog's invocation of the movie's importance likely was. In just a few words, he implicitly reminded Kinski of all the actor would gain from the movie's successful release, including fame, attention, and status in the industry. Of course, Herzog, too, wanted these things. By subtly reminding Kinski of what was in it for him, Herzog framed the situation as a win-win, and he got Kinski back on board.

Rule 4: Use the Carrot, Not the Stick

A similar logic of aligning interests applies when we're figuring out how to deal with behavior lapses on the part of dark personalities, or, for that matter, dogs. Let me tell you about Archie, my seven-year-old golden retriever. Leave it to the universe, in all its irony, to send me a dog with many of the hallmark psychopathic traits. Compared with my other golden retriever, Fischer, Archie is a taker. In his mind, humans exist to entertain and feed him, and that's about it. Well, we also exist to admire his beauty. If it's possible for a dog to be narcissistic, this dog is. When you pet his chest, he points his nose to the sky in pride and quiet contentment: he was born to be adored, and all is right with the world when he's receiving attention. Archie is also fearless and needs to dominate his brother, as well as the rest of us. He acts like the despotic ruler of our household, barreling over others to make sure he's the first through the front door and rearranging the pillows on the couch so that he can sleep in luxury. To my knowledge, there is no formal test for canine psychopathy, but perhaps there should be.

Like human psychopaths, Archie is impervious to punishment. While most of us will change our behavior to avoid penalties, people with psychopathy respond differently: they struggle to learn from them. This tendency might have a biological basis. Buried in each of our brains is a little almond-shaped structure called the amygdala. It's associated with emotional memory and the fear response, and people with psychopathic traits appear to have smaller and less active amygdalae than the rest of us.[19] That's important, because the amygdala has been found to play a role in "passive avoidance," the process of avoiding something that we know from experience will cause us pain. As a means of shaping behavior, punishment works by prompting passive avoidance: we remember having been punished in the past, so we refrain from the behavior that got us in trouble. People with psychopathic traits don't have the wiring required to perform passive avoidance. Like Archie, they're more inclined to shrug off a punishment and perform the offending behavior again.[20]

This is not to say that punishment is entirely useless for these folks. Some research suggests that people with psychopathic traits can learn better from being punished if we make a point of calling their attention to the penalty.[21] Evidence also suggests that people respond better to punishments when they're smaller in magnitude but predictably delivered.[22] In other words, if you're going to remove a portion of your bad-apple employee's bonus for messing up, draw their attention to the penalty and levy it in small bites each time they violate the rules, without exception. They're more inclined to get the message and improve their behavior.

Another way to get dark personalities to follow rules is to take a softer approach, placing less emphasis on punishment and instead offering rewards for *good* behavior. By dangling a carrot, you're in effect turning the situation into a win-win. You get the behavior you want, and they receive some benefit they care about. Children with callous-unemotional traits respond especially well when their good behavior is rewarded.[23]

To get the most out of positive reinforcement, identify the types of rewards that the dark personalities in your life will value. Dr. Pevitr Bansal, a former counselor at a summer treatment camp for kids with CU traits, told me that the camp had an arcade-style store in place where kids could buy prizes on Fridays with points they had earned for good behavior during the week. There were some pretty legit rewards on offer. "We had a giant Hot Wheels set that was a really big prize," Bansal recalled. "So, when someone walked out with that thing in week six or seven, everyone's like, 'Oh, my God, you got it!' . . . but there was something in there for everyone. So even a child who had a really rough week, if they only accumulated fifty points, there was something there for them."[24]

To make sure you're hitting the mark, ask the dark personality in your life to help you come up with the rewards. Bear in mind, rewards don't always have to be tangible benefits like money or special perks. You can also reward good behavior with praise or more attention.[25] If you catch a dark personality behaving well, let them know it—again and again.

In addition to favoring the carrot over the stick, watch how you react when a poisonous person breaks the rules, or, more broadly, when any kind of conflict arises. You might get upset and fly off the handle. My advice: stick with a softer approach and ask questions instead of showing frustration or toughness. If you frame a concern of yours as a query, you get your point across in a way that is less likely to be perceived as a direct affront. Let's say you're collaborating with your colleague Jerry, and you catch him bad-mouthing your work product with your mutual boss, Michelle. You could say, "Hey, asshole, you should come to me before you complain to Michelle about my work." Or you could say, "Jerry, what do you think about coming to me first when you see an error in my work? That way, I'll have a chance to correct any mistakes."

In a series of studies with bosses and employees, researchers found that questions were more likely to generate a positive response from the leader than declarations, especially if the leader had a dominant or aggressive style.[26] We find something similar in prisons. Dr. Mark Olver, a professor at the University of Saskatchewan who specializes in treating incarcerated men with psychopathy, told me how important it is for him to take a restrained approach with his patients when they act out. Because these men are likely to commit future crimes upon release, they require lots of therapy now. Kicking them out of a treatment program for being disruptive or insubordinate isn't really an option—that's the whole reason they're there to begin with. Instead of writing these men off as hopeless because of their bad behavior, psychologists should show more understanding, recognizing that this is precisely why they *need* the treatment. Therapists must keep their cool instead of getting frustrated by the antics of a person with psychopathy. "You need to be the biggest professional in the room there," Olver says, "and you need to role-model those prosocial behaviors you want them to pick up. It's a major credibility buster if you wind up acting unprofessionally to a group of people that you want to behave differently."[27]

We also can rise above the fray and role-model desirable behavior in conflict situations. I'm not suggesting we tiptoe around poisonous people and let them have their way, just that we carefully consider how to deliver our own messages. In addition to asking questions, we can deploy humor, getting our point across while also easing potentially combustible emotions. We also can focus on listening intently and engaging empathetically. "Just trying to understand their perspective" can help, Olver advises. "They're not just trying to [get under your skin] and make things difficult. A lot of times people have a valid point; they just might not be trying to make it in the most appropriate way."

Where dark personalities go, conflict and drama will likely follow. But the more we can bring ourselves to be calm with them in conflict situations, while sticking to our own positions and asking for what we need, the more we stand to benefit. Greeting conflict with understanding and restraint can be a strategic choice that serves our own interests. As a bonus, we'll also ensure that our conduct stays true to our own ideals and values.

Rule 5: Emphasize Your Common Identity

To inspire a poisonous person to behave in desirable, prosocial ways, we can adopt another soft tactic: mobilizing the power of in-group solidarity. In chapter 5, we discussed the perils of us-versus-them thinking and the animosity toward outsiders that it can cause. But we can turn the insider-outsider dynamic to our advantage. As researchers have found, creating a shared identity—a strong sense of "we"—promotes prosocial behavior *within* groups, even for those with psychopathic personality traits.

In one study, researchers asked participants either to accept or pass on a series of paired betting opportunities. One of those opportunities concerned their own personal finances and came with pretty good odds: participants learned they had a 60 percent chance of winning ten points, and only a 40 percent chance of losing one point. The other opportunity concerned a stranger's finances and came with poor odds: participants learned they had only a 20 percent chance of winning one point and an 80 percent chance of losing seven points. The researchers wondered how people with psychopathic traits would behave when a stranger's welfare was at stake, in addition to their own. Would their decision be swayed by both their odds of a big return *and* the stranger's prospects, or would they ignore the stranger's odds altogether, choosing to focus only on their personal gains?[28]

As you might suppose, high-psychopathy participants' decisions were swayed more by their personal outcomes than by a stranger's welfare. But there was an interesting exception. When researchers told participants that they had been assigned to a team and that the stranger affected by their gambling choices was also a team member, that neutralized the dark personality's selfishness. All of a sudden, they started to pay more attention to the stranger's odds of winning, too, when making a decision to accept or pass on the pair of bets. People with subclinical levels of psychopathy may not normally be *motivated* to show concern for others, but they can take others' well-being into account when they identify with the others in some way.

Finding some shared aspect of identity also may mitigate aggressive responses from people with narcissistic tendencies. People who possess an inflated sense of their own greatness often react when others appear to chastise or criticize them, sometimes retaliating aggressively.[29] But when the person cutting them down to size shares their identity in meaningful ways, this behavior changes. In one set of studies, organizers told participants with narcissistic traits that a person evaluating them had the same birthday or rare fingerprint type that they did. When these evaluators delivered harsh feedback, participants responded less aggressively. The sense of sharing an insider status with evaluators made all the difference.[30]

As such research suggests, it might be worthwhile to consider points of similarity between yourself and the poisonous people in your life. If you're supervising a dark personality at work, did you go to the same college? Do you root for the same football team? Did you grow up in the same geographic area? Did you listen to the same music growing up? Referencing these shared identities periodically can prevent them from thinking of you as the enemy. When you know you're about to deliver critical feedback, start the conversation by discussing points of commonality. If you remind them that you're both on the same team, you're more likely to avoid a knee-jerk, aggressive response.

Rule 6: Become a Detective

As much kindness and compassion as we might show toward dark personalities, there's one thing we can't do: trust them. We know they have a penchant for lying and deception, so the old rule of "trust but verify" doesn't hold. With them, it must be all "verify" all the time.

Earlier in this book, I described cues that can alert you to deception. Mastering these cues will help if you're in a relationship with a poisonous person, but that's just the beginning. Research surveying how people detect lies in the real world reveals that it's often a protracted process, lasting days, weeks, or even longer. Behavioral cues can be important early on in that they arouse suspicion, but then truth-seekers must follow up, performing informal detective work to validate or disprove their suspicions. To establish what actually happened, they must look for proof, whether that's physical evidence such as a text message, information they received from a third party, facts that don't line up, a confession they elicit, or some combination.[31]

In the workplace, your employee might claim to be a highly effective leader, a clear communicator, or the team's strongest performer. This could be true—or it could be narcissistic delusions and outright lies. Instituting a 360-degree review where team members weigh in confidentially on each other's performance can provide third-party verification of their self-assessment. A study using this type of assessment in a corporate setting found that employees with more psychopathic personality traits were rated as more strategic and innovative thinkers by their subordinates, peers, and bosses, but also as poorer team players with a caustic management style.[32] Colleagues have an important perspective that you as a boss should consider.

At home, your child might claim to have attended school and to have done their homework the past week. Call the school to see whether your child really was in class. Ask to see the completed homework. If they claim to have been treating their siblings and friends well, do their siblings concur? If they went to a friend's house after school, did the friend's parent see them behaving respectfully?

If you parent a teenager, you could require that they share their location with you on their phone so you can track their whereabouts. You might have them friend you on social media and share their passwords with you, with the understanding that you'll be checking their online activity on a regular basis. Instead of giving them their allowance in cash, you can have them use a designated credit or debit card that you fund so you can track their spending.

This is to say, you can build into your relationship regular mechanisms of verification. If you're managing a dark personality at work, you can require them to give you and others on the team regular updates on important issues, and to provide rationales for big decisions they make. Making these updates public creates less opportunity for the bad apple to manipulate you by telling different stories to different people. You also might ask an employee to keep a log of their daily activities so you can review it periodically, and you might schedule more check-in conversations with them and others.

You can take notes so that you have a record of what you discussed and agreed upon. You can also require that employees conduct any significant communication via email, so that you can keep a record of it.

Documentation and recordkeeping often bring a dark personality's transgressions to light. In chapter 5, we met Tonia, a bad-apple lawyer who terrorized her receptionist, clerks, and the mediator in her office. What ultimately did her in was a mechanism of transparency: accounting. It turns out that she was up-charging clients for services from her office. When she was holding a large amount of a client's money in escrow, she'd bill like crazy, leading the client to believe that there were additional legal steps she needed to take on their behalf. She'd also bill for her paralegal's work, charging the client her own, much higher rate. She was stealing clients' money, and there were records to prove it. Her bookkeeper discovered these irregularities and reported her to the relevant authorities, eventually getting her disbarred. Tonia had committed a litany of transgressions, but in the end she went down for financial misconduct, thanks to a paper trail.

It might seem time-consuming to constantly verify someone's claims, but instituting transparency not just for a problem employee but as a workplace norm can have tangible benefits that make the effort worthwhile. Open communication is critical for effective coordination. It builds trust and can keep team members from duplicating efforts unnecessarily. Transparency also reduces self-dealing in the workplace; in one study, employees making corporate purchasing decisions were less likely to select the more expensive supplier (who offered a personal kickback) than the cheaper supplier when their decisions were transparent to their coworkers.[33]

As a manager, parent, or teacher, *you* should be transparent about your thoughts, goals, and decision-making, too. The more openly and honestly you communicate, the more trusted and effective you'll be with all your team members.[34] Don't try to beat a dark personality at their own game by practicing subterfuge yourself. Instead, build transparency into the ground rules you establish up front for the entire team. If you set expectations in this way, a poisonous person will be less likely to push back when you insist on making their behavior visible.

Rule 7: Avoid Face-to-Face Negotiations

Just as you shouldn't trust a dark personality, you also must be careful how you handle negotiations with one. Despite your best efforts, you might not be able to align your interests with those of a poisonous person, creating a win-win situation. In that case, you'll have to work out a solution together through negotiation, a possibility that renders you vulnerable to their manipulative dark arts. You can help to protect yourself and get the best possible outcome by making a simple adjustment: holding your negotiations in writing rather than in person.

Earlier in this book, I shared research showing that men with psychopathic traits who had committed serious crimes were more than *twice* as likely as other inmates to have been paroled, even though their personality profiles made them likelier to reoffend. The very people who posed the greatest risk to the community wound up getting out early. The reason for this, I think, is that criminals with psychopathic traits are better able to plead their case in person before a parole board. They're more charming and can "put on a good show" better than the average felon.[35]

Nonviolent dark personalities also might have an advantage when interacting with us face-to-face. One study found that students high in dark traits outperformed others when negotiating the sale price of concert tickets—but only when the discussions happened in person. When the negotiation occurred via written messages, the opposite held true. Students with fewer dark traits came out ahead.[36] I spoke to the senior author of that work, Dr. Michael Woodworth of the University of British Columbia, and he advised negotiating with psychopathic personalities by text rather than in person. Doing so deprives them of their persuasive advantage, and it allows you to document the conversation.[37]

One rationale for conducting face-to-face negotiations with a poisonous person might be that it allows us to better tell whether they're lying, since we'd be able to scan for nonverbal cues of duplicity. In fact, in-person interaction may make us *less* accurate when it comes to spotting deception.[38] We overinterpret nonverbal behaviors such as a shifty gaze or fidgeting that, as you'll recall, don't tell us much about whether someone is lying. The most accurate indicators of deception are verbal ones, so we would do best to drop the visuals and either focus on the words someone speaks or read what they have to say.

Such advice can help us in business, in our personal lives, and even on the world stage. In 1961, the Central Intelligence Agency (CIA) presented President John F. Kennedy with a dossier that unpacked the personality of Soviet leader Nikita Khrushchev. Khrushchev had some dark traits. The report described him as impetuous, ruthless, and prone to taking risks. He was at least somewhat narcissistic. "On more than one occasion," the report noted, "he has revealed an exaggerated sensitivity to imagined personal slights or reflections on his country's prestige, while, on the other side, he takes delight in private conversations in dropping the names of world statesmen with whom he has corresponded or who have sent him gifts."[39] Khrushchev was also a wily manipulator. On one occasion, he made a big deal of calling off a highly anticipated appearance on American TV, only to let the show go on at the last minute. This put the reporters who were interviewing him off balance, and put him in control.

As the report suggested, Khrushchev also had the capacity to charm and smooth-talk others to his advantage. He did well in unscripted, face-to-face interactions with others. The journalist Joseph Alsop apparently came away impressed, saying of Khrushchev: "I thought him one of the most intellectually powerful, tough, pragmatic, and energetic-minded men I have ever run into." The CIA's analysis noted that he was something of a chameleon, capable of playing different roles depending on the situation. "His personality," the report observed, "has more impact than his words."

If the CIA's analysis was correct, negotiating via written messages likely would have neutralized some of the advantages Khrushchev's personality gave him. A diplomat negotiating with Khrushchev also would have had more of a chance to step back, take their time, think critically about what they were saying, and craft thoughtful retorts of their own. And they'd have had a record of what was said and not said, preventing Khrushchev from taking on new guises in different situations, shifting positions, and potentially gaslighting them.

If you're a boss overseeing a "bad apple" employee, make sure your annual reviews have a strong written component to them. If you're starting a project with a colleague with dark traits and trying to figure out a working arrangement, do it via email or text. Likewise, text and email are a more productive medium for sorting out separation details with an ex who harbors dark traits. These forms of communication give you time and space to manage your emotions before responding, and they help to keep you safe by putting physical distance between you and the poisonous person.

The Power of Realistic Expectations

As these seven rules suggest, navigating relationships with poisonous people comes down to taking a more unsentimental, pragmatic approach than we would with others. The truth is that they'll never be the kind, caring, loving person we'd like to see. They'll never impress us with their genuine displays of affection or their consistent honesty. They'll never inspire us with their acts of humility and self-sacrifice. We can make the most of our relationships with dark personalities by reconciling ourselves to these realities. If we go into these relationships with our eyes wide open, reminding ourselves along the way of whom we're dealing with and calibrating how we deal with them, we won't be disappointed, and we'll keep ourselves and others safer.

In chapter 6, we met Charlie, the man who broke with his abusive father as a child after a horrifying episode in which his dad forcibly injected his girlfriend with narcotics. As a young adult, Charlie wound up moving back to where his father—Brian—was living, getting back in touch with him, and for a time even going to work for him. By this time, Brian had become sober, so Charlie believed there might have been hope for a healthier relationship. He soon realized that his father was just as dishonest, callous, and manipulative as he'd always been. He refused to admit to past misdeeds, including the narcotics episode with his girlfriend. He continued to cheat Charlie out of money he owed him and abuse him emotionally.

At first, Charlie suffered from Brian's behavior. But as he grew older and started a family of his own, he developed a new, healthier approach that included some of the strategies described in this chapter. He established clear ground rules, requiring that any business arrangements between him and his father be put in writing. When Brian seemed to be lying, Charlie saw through the deception, and he refused when his father asked him to take actions Charlie thought were inappropriate. On one occasion, Brian reconnected with his old girlfriend and wanted Charlie to go out to dinner with them, acting as if nothing bad had happened back when he was eleven years old. Charlie didn't hesitate to say no. Although he felt empathy for his father's girlfriend, he couldn't bear to relive the trauma of that episode, especially since Brian still wouldn't admit that it had happened.

Perhaps the single most important step Charlie took in managing his relationship with his father was simply recognizing who the man was and adjusting his own expectations. Charlie came to expect that Brian would mistreat him, so he stopped seeking love and support from him. He would keep Brian in his life, but he would remain independent, relying on himself and on other, healthier relationships. Charlie also made a conscious decision to behave differently as a parent with his own children.

A poignant instance of this new stance came when Charlie underwent surgery for a brain tumor. A severe storm came through as Charlie lay at home recovering, knocking out power and heat for a week. His father promised repeatedly to bring over a portable generator so that Charlie could get the furnace going, but he never showed up. Charlie's mother was taking care of him, and she made a fire in the fireplace to keep warm. Brian's clear lack of concern bothered Charlie, but not unduly. This was who his father was. Charlie simply couldn't count on him for support. He would look elsewhere for it rather than getting overly stressed or upset.

Looking back on it, Charlie thinks about his old tendency to expect Brian to behave in a loving, compassionate way as "my insanity." He found that he was happier after he'd come to accept his father for who he was, and that their relationship improved. Charlie stopped trying to change Brian or tell him what to do, as he had in the past. In return, his father seemed to develop a new respect for him and to open up to him more. On his deathbed, he even managed to acknowledge in a broad sense that he'd caused Charlie harm. "The best thing he ever said to me," Charlie recalls, "just prior to his passing was, 'I wasn't always fair to you.'" That might have been the understatement of a lifetime, but it was something, and Charlie appreciated it.

With the right approach, we can learn to live with dark personalities in ways that minimize their capacity to cause harm. In so doing, we reduce in some small measure the overall pain and suffering that exists in the world, benefiting others as well as ourselves. But we can do even more to look out for others and make the world a kinder, happier place. For starters, we can cast a critical eye on our own behavior. Although we might count ourselves among the good apples of the world, we might not be spreading nearly as much compassion, empathy, and respect as we think.

8

I'm the Problem, It's Me

Imagine that for the past year, you've worked at a small but busy real estate brokerage. You've had an opportunity to collaborate closely with two fellow brokers whose personalities are very different.

Angelica, who sits in the cubicle to your right, is a joy to be around. She smiles or makes a funny remark when passing you in the hallway, and in the break room she asks friendly questions about your life, showing genuine interest. She speaks kindly about her clients, even when they aren't within earshot, and takes pains to lower her voice when they call to avoid distracting you. She also goes out of her way to be helpful. When she makes a coffee run, she asks whether you'd like one, too. At times when you're struggling to sell one of your properties, she commiserates with you and offers useful advice. She even organized a toy drive for a local charity last Christmas.

Dierdre, who sits in the cubicle to your left, has a much less agreeable personality. Her idea of a friendly conversation is to talk about herself—the new ring her boyfriend bought her, the latest big sale she closed, the "Realtor of the Year" accolade she received, the tennis championship she won in college. Occasionally, she asks about your life, but it's obvious she's not interested. What she cares about is her own success. In the short time you've worked with her, you've seen her steal clients from colleagues and attack team members she thinks are trying to challenge her. She reacts harshly to the smallest perceived slight but can switch just as quickly to smiles and laughter if a prospective client walks in the door.

Now let's say that you arrive at work one day to learn that Angelica and Dierdre were in a car accident on the way to a shared listing, and that they both sustained serious injuries. There's a chance Angelica will never walk again, while Dierdre has excruciating pain in her neck and has permanently lost sight in one eye. Both of them will require lengthy rehabilitation before they return to work, and their lives will be much different than they were before. Both will need kindness and support.

Would you empathize with both of them equally, going out of your way to show compassion to them both? Or would you direct more of your kindness toward Angelica, whom you like and who has treated you well? Be honest!

The science suggests that most of us would empathize more with Angelica's pain than with Dierdre's. Although we can instinctively connect with others' suffering, moral concerns influence how much empathy we feel. When we regard people as bad actors, we become more coldhearted and less sensitive to their pain. When someone like Dierdre is hurting, part of us might think, "It's wrong to empathize with someone who is so awful," or even, "They got what they deserved!"[1] Sometimes we even *enjoy* seeing bad luck befall another person. We experience schadenfreude—the German word for feeling pleasure at another's misfortune—when we dislike them and feel as though they deserve it.[2]

In other words, we might be good people, but our benevolence isn't infinite or equally distributed. Without thinking about it, we might show less kindness and compassion when confronted with the Dierdres of this world. But that response says as much about us as it does them. When we cast judgment on dark personalities, we ourselves become a bit more callous and cynical.[3]

My point isn't that you're a bad person. But I do hope to inspire some self-reflection. The danger in reading—and frankly, in writing—a book about people with psychopathic traits is that we'll fixate unduly on others' darkness, forgetting about our own defects. Dark personalities can serve as a convenient foil. As the psychopathy researcher Dr. Abigail Marsh at Georgetown University points out, many of us find dark traits interesting precisely because their existence reaffirms our own sense of ourselves as good by comparison. "Hearing about psychopathy makes people feel superior," she says. "It's like, 'Ah, well, I may not be perfect, but I'm better than *that*.'"[4]

The science of dark personalities challenges any sense of moral superiority we might have. As we've seen, people with psychopathy aren't fundamentally different from us—they simply have higher levels of common human traits. But that also means *we're* not fundamentally different from *them*. We harm others as well with our uncaring, callous ways. We don't do it nearly as often or as severely, but we still do it. If we're serious about containing dark traits and improving life in our homes and workplaces, we can't just spot and contain the poisonous people around us. We must also tamp down the malevolence within. We must acknowledge, in the immortal words of Taylor Swift, that sometimes, "I'm the problem, it's me."

Nurturing Our Better Angels

I've tried to do some of this work myself over the years. At one point I had the misfortune of working an unpaid summer internship under a malicious boss named Gene. Despite his slick, attractive veneer, he was abusive to the more junior staff. He made unreasonable demands and demeaning comments, and was constantly trolling for dates with staffers half his age. Gene's leadership style had me in tears more than once. But it's not accurate for me to portray myself as the blameless victim who valiantly stood up against the toxic work environment he created. I sometimes found myself perpetuating it.

Gene was adept at teaching basic skills we'd need to win in the corporate world: how to work efficiently, analyze sales data, craft winning strategies, give impressive presentations, make persuasive pitches to clients. Unfortunately, though, his workplace didn't make me a better person. In some ways, it changed me for the worse, turning me into someone who valued competition over collaboration and who at times behaved callously.

The office was a pressure cooker. We had to churn out as much work as quickly as possible and compete aggressively for sales and accolades. As we've seen, dominant, ubercompetitive leaders increase zero-sum thinking among their subordinates, and that was true here for me.[5] Somewhere along the line, I started to see some of my colleagues as competitors, not team members. If someone else excelled on an assignment, my gut reaction was to criticize their work rather than appreciate its value. Once, when someone asked me what I thought about a colleague's latest project, I called it "unoriginal and uninspired." Who did I think I was? And what a terrible thing to say!

On one occasion, a close friend and office-mate told me that the other interns were all afraid of me. I laughed it off, attributing it to my expression when I concentrate, which strongly resembles a "resting bitch face." But maybe it was more than that. Maybe over time that environment had turned me into a person who wasn't always kind, who created an air of competition instead of collaboration, who put people on edge.

I'm not a dark personality. But those of us who score relatively low on these traits owe it to others around us to avoid putting ourselves in settings where we can become situational psychopaths, or to try to change these situations entirely. Are you toiling away in a toxic work environment? Think about leaving—not just because of the harm you might sustain, but because of the unpleasant person you might become. If you find yourself in rotten circumstances, take the steps I've outlined to make it better. Become more social. Connect with others outside your in-group. Look for win-win situations. Lower the emotional temperature. Check your own emotions. All of these measures will protect you from others who might become situational psychopaths, but they'll also help prevent *you* from behaving badly and becoming part of the problem.

We must think, too, about the parts of our personalities that cause us at times to harm others. We might not be bursting at the seams with dark traits, but if we were to complete a measure of our own personality, we'd probably find that at least some of them are more elevated than we'd like. The more aware we can become of these problem areas, the more we can correct for them, and the quicker we can be to take responsibility and apologize when our efforts fail.

Take a look back at the Dark Behavior Scanner from chapter 4 and apply it to your own behavior. Do you have a vindictive streak? Do you find yourself telling self-serving lies relatively often? When there's something you really want, do you resort to manipulative behavior? Do you dominate conversations or relationships more than you should? Are you a tad too competitive?

To help you identify dark traits you might have at low levels, let's play a round of "never have I ever." Put a check mark next to any act you've committed at least once.

Poisonous People

Bucket 1: How You Relate to Others

Never have I ever . . .

- told a lie to get what I want.
- manipulated my family, friends, or coworkers to my own advantage.
- pretended to like someone to get what I wanted.
- thought other people were "suckers" for believing my lies.
- felt cynical, believing that everyone is willing to screw you over to get what they want.
- wanted to be the center of attention.
- felt like I'm special, and others are inferior to me.

Bucket 2: How You Experience Emotions

Never have I ever . . .

- enjoyed watching someone else fail or experience pain.
- picked on someone just for the fun of it.
- been described as cold or callous.
- felt nothing when I saw someone else in pain.
- thought I was tougher than everyone else.
- enjoyed watching violent sporting events or movies.
- ignored a friend when they stopped being useful to me.
- thought that people respond far too emotionally at funerals, weddings, or graduations.

Bucket 3: How You Weigh Risks

Never have I ever . . .

- sought out dangerous situations.
- responded aggressively to someone without thinking.
- considered myself a "thrill-seeker."
- had sex with a stranger.
- enjoyed gambling for a significant sum of money.
- been easily bored.
- driven recklessly, just to feel alive.
- been described as reckless or irresponsible.

Bucket 4: How You Handle Social Rules and Conventions

Never have I ever . . .

- shoplifted from a store.
- taken illegal drugs.
- gotten in a fistfight.
- been arrested or charged with a crime.
- gotten kicked out of a restaurant or other establishment for breaking their rules.
- broken into a car or building.
- tricked someone into giving me money.
- been suspended or expelled from school.

Having engaged in a behavior once doesn't amount to a personality trait, but if you are seeing a lot of check marks on the page, that might suggest a concerning pattern. All of us have areas in which we can improve, and an understanding of our less flattering tendencies can serve as a basis for self-improvement. As we spot areas to work on, we can challenge ourselves to behave more generously, helpfully, and collaboratively than we might if left to our own devices. In fact, there are simple, proven strategies for becoming better, more agreeable people.

Research by Dr. Nathan Hudson and his colleagues asked people to take on "agreeableness" challenges over fifteen weeks. These were tasks such as writing down parts of your life for which you feel grateful, attending a volunteer event, or trying to take someone else's perspective during an argument. Those who followed through on these challenges found that their personalities became more agreeable over time.[6] These same challenges also reduced dark traits, making people less psychopathic, Machiavellian, and narcissistic.[7] These results were self-reported, so it's possible that participants overestimated the benefits of the agreeableness challenges. Still, the findings paint a hopeful picture, suggesting that people who commit to becoming more agreeable can make gradual progress toward that goal.

The Case for Goodness

Evidence suggests that striving to be more empathic and kinder than you currently are can make a significant difference in the wider world. First off, refraining from mistreating others helps *us* live healthier, more fulfilled lives. Consider the phenomenon of lying. As upstanding as we may be, we still lie with some regularity—on average, once or twice per day.[8] These are, tellingly, "white" lies, for the most part.[9] We say "no" when our spouse asks whether they've gained weight. We nod agreeably when a friend voices an opinion we consider a bit batshit. We smile and say "I loved your book" when we meet an author, even though we didn't read it.

Research that my colleagues and I performed suggests that these lies have an insidious effect on us. When we lie, we become suspicious that others might be lying, too. And so, we believe and trust them less. What do they *really* think about us? Is their kindness toward us just a veneer? We might not realize it, but telling a little white lie sets off a cascade of thoughts that can ultimately affect our mental health. We have a harder time building relationships, and as a result we feel lonelier and more alienated. Telling fewer lies yields the opposite result.[10]

We would also benefit from performing more acts of kindness than we currently do. Although we might expect that lavishing money on ourselves will make us happy, in fact we become even happier when treating *others* generously.[11] We might wish to be left alone during our bus ride home from work, but our state of mind improves more if we chat someone else up.[12] Research also shows that expressing gratitude has a surprisingly big impact—people *like* being thanked.[13] Showing appreciation strengthens our relationships, contributing in turn to our own well-being.

We should also probably apologize more often than we do. It can be hard to admit we're wrong, but as Dr. Alison Wood Brooks, a professor at Harvard Business School, told *The Washington Post*, "There's really no apology researcher who will ever tell you that apologizing is bad. There's just no evidence that zero apology is ever better than at least one."[14] Research suggests that apologizing and taking responsibility usually isn't as hard as we anticipate.[15] Further, it can make a positive difference in our lives, prompting those we've hurt to see us in a better light, feel less animosity toward us, and be more willing to forgive us and move on. When we apologize, we feel relieved and our relationships improve.[16]

If you represent an organization, saying sorry and really meaning it can yield financial benefits. We've all heard those trite public apologies that corporate leaders offer after companies commit misdeeds. Working together at London Business School, the organizational psychologist Dr. Gabrielle Adams and I gathered videos of these apologies issued between 2007 and 2011, analyzing the extent to which the facial expressions of the person saying sorry matched the sentiment of their message.[17] Was the person grinning while they were begging for forgiveness, or was sadness written on their face? To gauge the business impact of these mea culpas, we gathered data about how companies' stock prices fared after company representatives expressed their regret. We controlled for variables such as how severe the transgression was, how much media attention the apology received, and how much time had passed between the misdeed and the apology.

It turns out that when a CEO is smiling while apologizing profusely for, say, fouling the environment via a massive oil spill, people doubt whether the leader really means it. That's probably not so surprising. What was striking, though, was the tendency of investors to penalize companies for issuing these seemingly insincere apologies. According to our analysis, companies' stock performance fared worse in instances where the company representative smiled while giving the apology. And this effect could last for months. Apologizing helps mend relationships, including economic ones, so long as we perceive them as sincere.

One of the best reasons to apologize, express gratitude, or help someone else isn't that our own lives will improve but that the broader society will. Just like bad behavior and negativity are contagious, darkening our social world, so the goodness we project ripples outward to lighten it. Take gratitude. When people receive expressions of thanks, they don't just feel good—they feel *valued*, which in turn leads them to show more kindness themselves.

Imagine that you help someone out, and they respond with a follow-up request for additional help. Experiments suggest that you'd lend them a hand a second time if they had said a simple thanks for your initial efforts.[18] Likewise, people tip more in restaurants when their server writes "thank you" on the check.[19] We all want to feel valued by others, and acknowledging what a good deed means to you tells a helper that in fact you do value them. Their interest in helping out further will probably intensify.[20]

When you show empathy or behave kindly, you serve as a role model. Others get the message, feeling and behaving in prosocial ways, too. Their response isn't simply a rote mimicking of your behavior. Studies have found that when people observe others reaching out to help, they're more inclined to behave generously in ways that might be entirely different.[21] Goodness cascades, sometimes multiple times.

A bystander might observe you donating ten dollars to canvassers for the Salvation Army. Then, when they see their elderly neighbor struggling to carry bags of groceries, they might run over to lend a hand. That elderly person, in turn, might come away from an encounter and think to call an ailing friend to offer support. In this way, your single act of goodness might do double or triple duty.

If we're parents, offering as much kindness, compassion, and honesty as we can becomes especially important, as it has a profound influence on our kids' development. They're watching us all the time. They're sizing us up, noticing our smallest actions and mannerisms. For this reason, our warmth and responsiveness to them helps shape how they will behave toward others as they grow up. The more goodness we project, the better. Children who behave altruistically are more likely to have parents who do the same and who treat them with warmth and affection.[22] As Dr. J. Stuart Ablon, a psychologist at Harvard Medical School, explains, "Empathy is a skill, and the only way you build any skill is first by modeling it for somebody so they have some idea of what it looks like, what it feels like for them, before you're asking them to do it as well."[23]

Current approaches to treating children with behavioral issues, including the Collaborative Problem Solving model that Ablon helped develop, aim to teach parents how to show their kids more warmth and understanding. When a child with CU traits breaks the rules, acts defiantly, yells, or steals, parents might crack down harshly in an attempt to regain control over the child and situation.[24] Even if our kids lack CU traits, we might still lash out at them in frustration when they behave aggressively or defiantly. Such a response, while understandable, is far from ideal. In an approach called Parent-Child Interaction Therapy, therapists coach parents as they play with their children, teaching them how to create a warm and responsive relationship while maintaining safe, consistent limits.[25] Parents of a preschooler learn to pay attention when their child shows kindness to a person or toy, to repeat kind words their child uttered, and to praise their child's good deeds. At the same time, parents learn to reduce disruptive behavior by either ignoring it or using time-outs.

This protocol works as preventative medicine in typical households as well as in families with CU kids.[26] Interventions in which parents attempt to model empathic and prosocial behavior, practice it, and reward kids for doing well produce positive changes over time.[27] Research also suggests that kids with or without behavior problems might benefit when teachers and others learn these approaches.[28] If authority figures in our children's lives can learn to project more warmth, kindness, and compassion, they can help our kids learn the skills associated with empathy. This isn't always easy for frazzled parents or teachers to do, but the effort they put in can make a big difference.

Be Good... Even When They're Not

At risk of sounding overly idealistic, let me go further and contend that we should try to muster more empathy and compassion for dark personalities of *all* ages. Consider the colleague who is undermining you, that neighbor who seems to delight in flouting all the community bylaws, that politician whose aggressive behavior makes you switch off the news. I want to inspire you to show more understanding and concern for these folks—not necessarily for their sake, and certainly not because you approve of their behavior, but for the good of our broader society.

I know I've spent an entire chapter of this book (chapter 2) detailing how much harm dark personalities cause. I'm not backtracking on that. I'm just suggesting that to the extent we have these dark personalities in our lives and safely can extend our empathy, we should, even if we don't think them capable of returning the favor.

These individuals didn't *ask* to be cold and callous, incapable of feeling the emotions that others consider central to the experience of being human. They were born that way, or they became that way as a result of abuse suffered early in life.[29] Because empathy is such a core human trait, we dehumanize those who don't display it, regarding them as "animals" or "monsters."[30] Dr. Mark Olver has spent decades studying and working with dark personalities. "Ultimately," he says, "psychopathic people are people, too. We often think of them as reptilian and something 'other,' but they are people, too."[31]

Bear in mind, showing more empathy and compassion to dark personalities is also in our self-interest. Punishing dark personalities isn't particularly effective at modifying their behavior. Attempts to cancel or publicly shame them aren't likely to change them fundamentally, either. As a society, we've gotten used to reflexively canceling someone when they behave in ways we find noxious. Commentators have objected to this practice on ethical, practical, or political grounds, but there's a scientific basis for opposing it, too. As much as we might find it satisfying, canceling others doesn't help us address their problematic behavior. Dark personalities feel little remorse, and because their social connections are weak, they feel less motivated than the rest of us to apologize and reestablish relationships. They're inclined to move on and perpetuate the same behavior, only with someone new. Canceling them might actually cause them to act out even more. As research suggests, being ostracized makes people *more* rude, selfish, callous, and manipulative.[32]

If we want people with dark traits to change their behavior, we must take a different approach, which is precisely what forensic psychologists do with psychopathic individuals in prison. They recognize that we can train these people—albeit with some difficulty—to behave in more prosocial ways. And as with CU kids, the way to do that is in part by showing them warmth and empathy. It's a strange irony, but as Olver points out, people with psychopathic traits might actually need *more* warmth and empathy than the rest of us do. "That's the funny thing," he says. "They're really crappy at giving it, and they stomp all over people. But they actually benefit from it and actually do need validation."[33] Rather than recoiling from dark personalities, we can make progress with them if we extend our empathy, while still taking steps to protect ourselves.

Most of us have built-in emotional capabilities that nudge us toward doing the right things. We feel empathy, which encourages us to help others who we perceive to be in pain. We feel guilt, which keeps us from behaving badly. We feel fear, which stops us from behaving impulsively. We feel love, which causes us to delight in others' happiness and encourages us to cooperate for mutual benefit. But people with dark traits lack these predispositions and as a result exert a noxious influence on others. It's not that they *can't* act in moral ways. They're just less inclined to do so. We can encourage them to behave more prosocially by modeling that behavior and rewarding them for adopting it. Rejecting and punishing people with high levels of dark traits might feel morally righteous, but it doesn't solve the problem. Real change requires that we engage with poisonous people as much as we can instead of pushing them away.

Some dark personalities can articulate this need. "David," a person with psychopathy, has shared his story on a website dedicated to the condition. As he recalls, he had the good fortune of being "identified very early on [as a psychopath] due to conduct and hit real hard with kindness." Instead of expelling him, as other schools might have, his school "taught me stuff no one bothered to . . . mostly how to human: how to read faces . . . why and how to change my voice in social situations." The person who was helping him "taught me about her love of prosocial behavior. She was the only one who had paid me attention in a way that felt good, so I was going to damn well hear everything she wanted to tell me. And that was to learn to categorize choices along an axis I could actually comprehend."[34]

Over time, David did improve his behavior—not because he was punished, but because a kind soul in his orbit fought her instinct to push him away and instead patiently welcomed him in. Just as abuse can embed dark traits and create a cycle of abuse, we have the power to create an upward spiral of goodness, especially with the kids we encounter.

Choose Better Leaders

Although we can brighten our immediate social environments with our own good behavior, we shouldn't stop there. Regardless of our station in life, most of us help to determine who holds positions of authority and influence. We elect political leaders. We make hiring decisions in the workplace or provide input on who should lead our teams, departments, or organizations. We serve on the boards of directors of companies or nonprofits in our communities, tasked with hiring suitable people to serve as CEO or in other executive roles. We can ensure that values such as kindness, compassion, and truthfulness prevail inside our organizations and societies, and that manipulative, deceitful, and abusive acts are sidelined.

Most of us take many factors into account when vetting potential leaders. In politics, we might consider their experience, personal background, policy preferences, and, of course, their party membership. In business, we might consider what's on their résumés as well as their ideas about business, leadership, strategy, and so on. What we often neglect to consider adequately is their *personalities*, and specifically whether they have any of the damaging character traits described in this book. As a result, we aren't on the alert for poisonous people, nor are we necessarily seeking out kind, empathetic ones as deliberately as we should be.

Chip, a corporate recruiter, told me that the companies he's worked with generally don't consider personality directly. Rather, they claim to seek candidates who, in addition to having the right skills, seem to "fit the culture." The analysis is hazy and unscientific, and that's because, as Chip notes, "a lot of companies don't spend enough time and resources on establishing their company culture. You can come up with some words and put it up on a wall and hope everyone reads it and operates that way, but that's just not how human beings operate."

With only a foggy sense of the culture, Chip says, those doing the hiring often wind up being unduly influenced by other factors, including their own biases, their flawed first impressions, or whether they already know the candidates. They lack a clear understanding of candidates' personalities, and they're not particularly alert to dark traits. No surprise when a manipulative, charismatic, poisonous person manages to wheedle their way in.

Selecting kindhearted executives and board members is especially important, since it sets the tone for the whole organization. Middle managers in companies often feel caught between frontline employees, who want to be treated compassionately and to do purposeful work, and senior leaders, who feel pressure from shareholders for the organization to perform financially.[35] By hiring leaders at the executive and board levels whose identity and sense of personal purpose relate strongly to serving others and treating them well,

I'm the Problem, It's Me

and who understand the connection between empathetic, compassionate leadership and financial performance, companies can lessen the burden on middle managers. They'll understand that the company is prioritizing a kinder, gentler brand of leadership, and they'll feel more liberated to treat their own team members well in addition to aiming for high performance.

In politics, too, many of us might give the personality of candidates a passing glance, placing far greater weight on whether we like the candidate's policies or track record.[36] We've seen this in recent years among supporters of President Donald Trump who purport to recognize his character flaws but vote for him anyway because they like his conservative positions on hot-button issues such as abortion and immigration, or share his resentment toward establishment elites. For voters of this mindset, even Trump's legal problems and felony convictions aren't enough to make them place more weight on his personality. As one young voter told ABC News, "He might be a bad person, but he is a good president."[37]

We should remember that when we opt for strong leaders with dark traits, we're signing up for the downward spiral we discussed in chapter 3. Poisonous people create division and chaos, breaking long-standing norms, defecting from partners whom they perceive as offering them little value, and sowing distrust in institutions and among community members. They act impulsively and create gridlock by showing themselves unwilling to aim for win-win solutions. Chaos in turn scares us, leading us to believe we need a "strong" leader to fix it—and we gravitate toward these dark types who claim that only they can fix it. But we don't get a fix. We get more of the same. The next thing we know, we have a whole government full of people more interested in seeking win-lose solutions than negotiating and building consensus. We have leaders who would rather bring the entire economy to its knees than arrive at a compromise with their political opponents.

None of us can fix big, complex problems on our own. We need generous, empathic, trustworthy leaders to broker deals in which everyone feels understood, gets some of what they desire, and wants to continue working together. To get these leaders and contain dark personalities, we of course must allow leaders to show compassion and seek compromise with the other side. If we oust every leader who doesn't get us exactly what we want when we want it, we create fertile ground for poisonous people to make big promises, entrench competitive thinking, and sow division. But we must also change how we select leaders, placing far more weight on personality and less on policies, experience, party affiliation, or other factors. The data I've presented in this book is clear: personality matters when it comes to governance. Politicians and corporate executives with dark personality traits are objectively worse at their jobs, and we must weigh the chaos, destruction, and cultural rot they cause against any successes they claim. We do best to vote in benevolent, ethically minded, consensus-driven leaders, even if we happen to disagree with them on the issues.

In addition to selecting individual leaders who would seem to score low in dark traits, we can push to change our broader political system in ways that inhibit poisonous people from taking power. Here's a thought experiment: instead of allowing voters to choose from among a slate of candidates, let's simply pick them randomly from among a pool of citizens. Any voting-age citizen would be eligible for selection, regardless of their background, education level, and so on. Under such a system, *you* might wake up one day to learn that you've been selected as the next congressperson or senator from your state.

As unlikely as this scenario sounds, it has a distinguished history, harkening back to the cradle of democracy, ancient Greece. The Athenians believed strongly that we shouldn't just let elites govern but open up our institutions to the common man. Yes, it was just

Athenian men back then. Women and slaves couldn't participate. So clearly there was room for improvement, but I think they were onto something. Two institutions figured prominently: an assembly that in theory at least anyone was welcome to attend, and a council that decided on specific issues the assembly would take up and offered recommendations for how the assemblymen should vote. To get onto the influential, five-hundred-member council, you didn't campaign for others to vote for you. A lottery was held, and you were selected at random from a pool of all citizens thirty and over. You served a one-year term and then made way for the next person. The Athenians also picked government administrators and jurors by random selection.[38]

If you wanted to open up governance to the common folk, lotteries were the way to go. As the Athenians understood, and as we see today, elections are vulnerable to manipulation by moneyed elites. Wealthy people can bankroll candidates, unduly influencing policy decisions. And with their connections to other wealthy people, they have an edge in becoming candidates themselves and putting together winning coalitions. Lotteries took money out of the selection process. Every citizen stood an equal chance of being selected, no matter how wealthy they were. To ensure that potential public servants were both willing and eligible to serve, citizens had to opt into the pool of applicants. Once chosen, they had to prove to an assembly that they met basic citizenship qualifications (both of their parents had to be Athenian) and that they had followed through on their civic responsibilities, such as paying taxes and serving in the military.[39]

While the Athenians might have been willing to gamble with their government, most people today probably wouldn't be excited to return to this system if it meant giving up their right to vote. But the psychologist and Wharton School of Business professor Dr. Adam Grant makes a persuasive case that we should. As he's noted, selecting government officials at random would give us much more of a fighting chance in keeping dark personalities out of politics. People with dark traits are more interested in running for office because they love the rush of power. With their charismatic ways, they're more likely to win—but also, as we've seen, less likely to make progress once in power. Although picking leaders at random might make it harder for us to select those with unusual talents, no system is perfect and in Grant's estimation, lotteries at least allow us to avoid the worst outcomes. "As lucky as America was to have Lincoln at the helm," he wrote in the *New York Times*, "it's more important to limit our exposure to bad character than to roll the dice on the hopes of finding the best."[40]

Studies suggest that leaders who are randomly selected make better decisions, perhaps because their egos are smaller on average and aren't inflated by having won an election.[41] Selecting leaders at random also helps to rein in the abuse of power. If you think you're smarter and better than everyone else because you won a competitive race, you won't be as inclined to accept limitations on your behavior as randomly selected leaders are, and you'll more easily cross ethical lines.[42] Maybe you'll take personal vacations on the public dime, or use your position to give family members plum appointments. Random selection helps minimize actions like these that aren't in the public interest. Lotteries also attract people—especially women—who have less of an appetite for competition.[43] Since women, on average, harbor fewer psychopathic traits than men, bringing in more women will only increase the odds that we'll have fewer leaders with dark personalities.[44]

Other, less radical changes to our electoral process might offer similar advantages. Typical elections, where the candidate with the most votes wins, are highly competitive and zero-sum. Your victory comes at someone else's expense, and vice versa. As a result, these contests give the edge to candidates who are more cutthroat and conniving than others. Particularly in close races, candidates get dirty in the midst of campaigning, calling their opponents names or spreading negativity about them.[45] The result is that voters *don't* learn what they really need to know: can these candidates empathize and collaborate with others?

By contrast, ranked-choice voting provides space for candidates to spotlight their collaborative nature. It works like this: You don't vote only for your favorite candidate. Instead, you look at the slate of candidates and rank them from first to last place according to your preference. If one candidate receives a majority of first-place votes, great—we have a winner. But if they don't, the lowest-ranked candidate is eliminated and the election goes into a runoff. If you voted for the least popular candidate, your vote now goes to the candidate you ranked second. The election proceeds in this way, with the ongoing elimination of least popular candidates, until one candidate can claim a majority. If you're a candidate, you have less incentive to eviscerate other candidates, since you need their voters to rate you highly, even if they didn't rank you number one. You can even collaborate with other opponents, campaigning together so that your voters can rank each of you highly. In other words, elections cease to be zero-sum contests that favor poisonous people.

Ranked-choice voting has been used in the United States since the early twentieth century and has spread in recent years.[46] As of 2022, dozens of US localities have embraced it, often finding that the format increased turnout.[47] A recent research project of mine tested whether ranked choice can help us elect more collaborative and less divisive candidates. One early finding is that people have different expectations about winning candidates and their personalities depending on the way an election is set up. We told participants about the difference between traditional, single-choice elections and those built around ranked choice. That way, they'd understand how a voter would complete a ballot in both systems, and how each system allows for the identification of a winner. Then we prompted participants to consider the character traits that winning candidates might have. We asked them to fill out a questionnaire about the candidates called the B-Scan, which, like the PCL-R, measures psychopathic personality features.[48]

Participants presumed that winning candidates in a conventional, single-choice election would display higher levels of psychopathic traits, relative to a ranked-choice election. In other words, voters in a ranked-choice election seemed to think that *fewer* psychopathic traits gave politicians an edge. Our current research is testing whether people actually shift their voting preferences in ranked-choice elections to vote more good people into government and keep out the poisonous ones. Like random selection, ranked-choice elections may offer a structural solution for choosing better leaders.

Rethinking Success

As important as it is to attend to our own behavior and to choose leaders more carefully, we have a deeper kind of soul-searching to do if we are truly to contain the darkness in our midst. To convey what that is, let me tell you about an unusual encounter I had some years ago at a posh New York City ballroom.

A prominent investment firm was holding its annual conference for its biggest customers, large institutions that collectively oversaw billions of dollars in assets. I'm not a part of this world, but I happened to attend on account of some consulting work I was doing. Hundreds of financial executives representing these institutions packed the room, eager to hear the firm's senior leadership team discuss the performance of its investments. As the event got underway, the firm's wealthy CEO took the stage. He was a slender, middle-aged man with piercing blue eyes and perfectly coiffed black hair. Exquisitely dressed in a dark blue power suit and bright blue tie, he looked exactly like the titan of industry he was. Some people might have felt intimidated before such a crowd, but not him—he seemed confident, even arrogant. His booming voice echoed off the opulent room's marble pillars as he boasted about the firm's recent performance and took digs at his firm's competitors.

After a short soliloquy, the main program began. The CEO introduced his chief legal counsel, a distinguished industry veteran in his early sixties, inviting him to stand up and give a short presentation. As this man prepared to speak, the CEO made a snide remark in front of all these people about what a doddering, forgetful old guy he was. I had never witnessed someone embarrass and demean another person so openly before, with no hint of conscience or remorse. The older man laughed it off and began his presentation, but he seemed a bit diminished—his cheeks reddened and his voice wavered.

Unfortunately, the CEO wasn't finished. Every twenty or thirty seconds, he interrupted the man as he spoke, correcting perceived inaccuracies and taking credit for the legal team's wins. I couldn't help but cringe: everything this senior manager and his team had accomplished, it seemed, was because the CEO had a hand in it. This was the legal counsel's moment to shine, but the CEO wouldn't let him have it. He seemed to have an insatiable—and insufferable—urge to be the star of the show.

I wondered whether the CEO had it in for this guy. But as other senior managers came up to speak, the CEO doled out similar humiliation. He made a disparaging comment about one executive's tie. He commented on how another was too fat. He presented these as jokes, but they were clearly malicious attempts to diminish his subordinates in public. He also interrupted each of them repeatedly, correcting them before the audience.

There was a moment when, as one of the managers was making

an important point, the CEO's cell phone rang. "Hold on, hold on," he said from his place at the podium. Incredibly, everyone waited as he took a call from his wife. Without divulging that he was standing on a stage before a large audience, he held a brief conversation with her. Hanging up, he revealed that she had been at an expensive boutique and forgot her credit card, so he would need to have his assistant get that to her. This, too, occasioned a mildly derogatory remark: he was, it seemed, the only competent person in the world. It wasn't enough for him to look smart, important, and rich onstage. He needed to cut down everyone around him, regardless of how it made them feel. That way, he could make it clear: he was the alpha dog.

Audience members, too, took a hit—and remember, they were the firm's paying customers. Midway through the proceedings, as one of the CEO's team members was speaking, a door in the back opened and latecomers entered. These guests seemed content to linger quietly in the back so as not to disturb anyone. But the CEO wouldn't have it. Again, he stopped the proceedings, this time remarking on the latecomers' tardiness and inviting them to take some empty seats right in the front. It was punishment masquerading as kindness: to reach their seats, these poor souls had to take an extended walk of shame through the crowd, with all eyes focused on them. Once again, the CEO had established his dominance, without any concern for how others around him felt. He even seemed to experience a rush of sadistic pleasure at other people's shame or embarrassment; a smug half-smile was one of the only expressions I saw on his face that evening.

I thought that this behavior would alienate audience members, but on the contrary, they seemed to love it. They hung on his every word. When he interrupted someone or made a joke at their expense, they didn't cringe—they laughed. Again and again. And when the CEO's wife called and he made derogatory remarks about her, howls of laughter filled the room. As he handed over his credit card and phone to his assistant, asking her to come to his hapless wife's rescue, people clapped.

We've talked about how leaders can corrupt behavioral norms when they behave poorly, and perhaps that happened here. But I think there was more to their fawning. It seemed to me that this audience found validation of their closely held beliefs about power, authority, and success in this CEO's antics. Somehow, his insults and hurtful behavior didn't clash with his position of authority. They enhanced and validated it. His hubris seemed to be a sign that their money was in good hands and that they could profit off his cunning. This man might have been a jerk, but the audience delighted in knowing that he was *their* jerk. Never mind our research, which suggests that leaders with psychopathic traits make less money for investors than those without these traits.[49]

As a society, we remain in thrall to poisonous people, especially when they occupy positions of authority. The successful people we love to hate are the brilliant disruptors who swagger into meetings and rack up VC funding for their big new idea. They're the CEOs who spew vulgarities on social media and receive a landslide of "likes." They're the brash, aggressive politicians whom we find endlessly entertaining. The TV shows and movies we watch affirm the apparent links between dark personality traits and success. Just think of memorable characters such as Mr. Burns from *The Simpsons*, Logan Roy from *Succession*, Miranda Priestly from *The Devil Wears Prada*, and Gordon Gekko from *Wall Street*. Such examples affirm the common and wrongheaded belief that while this behavior is despicable, it also begets success.

We all have the power to improve our organizations and societies, and it starts with changing our underlying beliefs about success. Rather than smiling upon people who excel, regardless of who they might have hurt in the process, we should celebrate individuals who behave well *and* achieve great results. We should broaden our definition of what "winning" is to include not just the ends but the means.

Every community has people who not only achieve material success but make a profound and positive difference in others' lives. A review of eighty-nine academic papers found that agreeable leaders—with personalities opposed to the antagonistic core of darkness—took a more empathic, ethical, and collaborative approach to their work.[50] One such leader was the late Herb Kelleher, cofounder of Southwest Airlines; Kevin and Jackie Freiberg eulogized him in *Forbes* as having showed that it is "possible to love people (employees and customers alike), have fun, and make money simultaneously."[51] In an interview about his leadership style, Kelleher specifically denounced tactics that dark personalities often adopt when they attain leadership positions, including "false promises, backstabbing, or lying."[52]

A similarly virtuous corporate leader is Accenture's CEO, Julie Sweet, who since her appointment in 2019 has emphasized caring for her company's employees by paying attractive wages and giving them opportunities to learn and advance. Sweet also has worked to make Accenture more inclusive, pledging that the company would achieve gender equality among its workforce. She has led Accenture to make electricity use across all its locations 100 percent renewable.[53] She has spoken out against antisemitism and other forms of hate, earning the Anti-Defamation League's 2024 Courage Against Hate Award.[54] In accepting the award, she applauded Accenture's workforce, noting its "values of respect, equity, inclusion of all people and zero tolerance of hate and bigotry of any kind." She exhorted her audience to "build the foundation of trust, understanding and shared humanity that will be the opposite of hate."

Sweet's kinder, more ethical approach—a marked contrast from that of other leaders we've met—hasn't come at the expense of financial performance. Between September 2019 and March 2024, the company's revenues have grown from around $43 billion to $65 billion, while profits have risen from about $13 billion to $21 billion.[55]

Instead of presuming that the most successful people have dark personality traits, let's affirm our idealistic belief—which also happens to be scientifically supported—that the best and most effective leaders feel a profound sense of responsibility to others.[56] Let's venerate and support kindness and collaboration rather than callousness and competition. Instead of hitching our wagons to selfish leaders in hopes that we can draft off their personal success, let's find leaders who seek to engineer collective gains rather than personal dominance—who want *everyone* to win. And let's spread our prosocial values far and wide. In case any Hollywood writers happen to be reading this, please make a lot more shows like *Ted Lasso* and a lot fewer like *Succession*. Until then, the rest of us should vote with our remotes, our "likes," and our "follows," applauding compassionate people when we spot them and downvoting the callous ones.

If we want to escape the poison, we must take responsibility and realize that we, too, are part of the problem. We should look hard at our own behavior and try to improve it, and we should rethink our basic notions of success. Individuals, organizations, and even entire societies can generate wealth, influence, and power by tearing others down or by building them up. The true cost of success achieved by dark personalities only becomes clear when we count all its victims.

Epilogue

The Ultimate Arms Race

This book began by posing a simple question: is humanity fundamentally good or evil? As the science of social and personality psychology suggests, the question doesn't help us much because the notion of good versus evil is an oversimplification. It can't account for personality traits, which lie on a continuum rather than conforming to a dichotomy. It can't account for research suggesting that even people with clinical psychopathy can curb their criminal behavior with the help of intensive therapy. And it can't account for everyday situations that lead generous, kind, compassionate people to commit atrocious acts.

At the same time, some people really do behave worse than others. For roughly 20 percent of the population, antisocial behavior isn't just an occasional lapse but a defining part of their personalities. Whether on account of genetics or their life experiences, members of this group feel driven to dominate, manipulate, and deceive.

For most of human history, members of the prosocial majority might have sighed and shrugged their shoulders at the malevolent few, presuming that there was nothing they could do about their misbehavior. Today, a different response is possible. Decades of scientific research have given us the ability to quantify dark aspects of human personality to understand their effects, and, to an increasing extent, contain and mitigate the damage. Although we haven't yet invented a treatment that will dramatically and immediately change dark personalities, we now have powerful tools to keep them at bay, both in our own lives and at the societal level. And the science is getting better with each passing year.

At the same time, poisonous people also have more tools and opportunities than before to wreak havoc. They might even seem to have gained the upper hand. Democracy is in retreat around the globe, with dark politicians ushering in a new era of authoritarian rule.[1] In business, too, domineering leaders erode norms of cooperation among their employees.[2] Social media platforms allow poisonous people to expand their reach, targeting masses of people and causing a range of serious harms, at very little risk or expense to themselves. Around the world, people are increasingly individualistic, seeing themselves as less connected to other people and more self-focused.[3] Distrust has grown, while interest in cooperation has waned.[4] With conflict and economic uncertainty mounting, populations increasingly come to value the tough guy over the good guy.[5]

Taking a longer view, we find that the picture isn't quite so grim. Poisonous people might be winning, but only for now. Mobilizing some of the strategies in this book to spot and avoid people with psychopathic traits, the rest of us might soon be able to swing the pendulum back the other way. Some might consider this the ultimate goal: to sideline dark personalities from our families, workplaces, and governments.

In fact, such marginalization won't be enough. Once thwarted, dark personalities will likely catch on to these strategies, developing workarounds that give them the upper hand once again. Psychological science will then have to develop newer, better tools. Spinning this out over decades, it seems that neither darkness nor light will reign supreme, either now or in the foreseeable future. Rather, humanity is in an ongoing arms race, with no end in sight.

Such a dynamic is a basic biological process. Among many kinds of living organisms, some members of a population try to survive by engaging in cooperative, prosocial behavior, while others do so by cheating or free-riding.[6] Over time, as genetic and social evolution take place, both cooperators and cheaters evolve new capabilities. Individuals who excel at cooperating and at avoiding the cheaters flourish. That in turn puts pressure on the cheaters—the shrewdest of them find a way past the cooperators' defenses, allowing *them* to survive and pass on *their* genes and strategies. The presence of better cheaters in turn prompts the cooperators to up their game. And on and on we go.

Humanity has so far managed to sustain such an arms race between light and dark, but it might not be able to do so for much longer. Two dangers concern me. First, the destructive technologies coming online are so powerful that poisonous people might use them to cause cataclysmic harm. We know the damage that a single active shooter can do when unleashed in an elementary school. What happens when dark personalities mobilize technologies such as AI, robotics, drones, and genetic engineering? What happens when a country led by a dark personality tries to assert dominance by detonating a nuclear weapon? Short-term thinking, impulsive behavior, and a lack of concern for others strike me as exactly what we *don't* need to lead us through perilous times.

A second danger is more mundane but perhaps more insidious. As our norms decay, and before the forces of good have time to mount a compelling comeback, civilization is acutely vulnerable, less capable of preventing or reacting to existential threats that might emerge. We recently saw how much difficulty humanity had in responding to COVID-19. What happens if another, deadlier virus spreads around the world? Given all the distrust and instability that poisonous people have sown since COVID, will we be able to take the kind of concerted, collective action required to save our societies? Similarly, will a humanity hobbled by eroded trust and cooperation norms respond effectively if we see widespread crop failures and food shortages thanks to climate change, or if AI goes rogue and threatens to end civilization as we know it?

Given the chances of catastrophe, humanity must find a way to move beyond an unending arms race between light and darkness. It's up to the benevolent majority not just to survive the arms race in the short term but to *end* it. I think there might be a way, one that also has its roots in the biological world.

The 1990s were a difficult decade for a bird that is common in many US communities, the North American house finch.[7] A bacteria called *Mycoplasma gallisepticum* that had previously infected poultry began infecting finches. These poor birds started to come down with conjunctivitis, a swelling of the eyes and a discharge that impeded the birds' vision, preventing them from foraging for food and making them more vulnerable to predators. Happily, the finch populations managed to survive conjunctivitis. But the birds didn't simply mount an immune response that resisted the bug. They also developed a greater tolerance of the bacteria, meaning they became less sick when infected. The *combination* of resistance and tolerance allowed the birds to mount a successful defense.

If the birds had only developed resistance, an arms race would have raged on. Since the birds would have become resistant, most of the bacteria would have died out. But a few bacteria would have mutated and evaded the birds' resistance. Those bacteria would have multiplied, prompting a similar evolution on the parts of the birds. On and on this process would have gone.

Adding tolerance to the mix as a defensive strategy, the situation changes. In birds that better tolerate a bacteria, the bug lives on in their bodies, but the birds don't experience as much swelling around their eyes. These finches are sick, but not gravely so. Individual birds that can tolerate the bacteria survive and coexist with it, not simply resist it. This disrupts the arms race, with both birds and bacteria able to live in a kind of stasis without evolving ever more extreme detection and evasion strategies.

A similar situation might arise when it comes to human populations and dark personality traits. If the benevolent majority were to adopt the strategies in this book to spot and avoid poisonous people, that would be akin to a host developing a biological resistance to a pathogen. Over time, the individual dark personalities that survive and thrive would be those that figured out how to work around our strategies. An arms race would take hold.

But this book also has presented strategies for living with and managing dark personalities. That's akin to tolerance among the finches. If we were to apply those management strategies, we would be better able to coexist, while capping harm at tolerable levels. Malevolent types would perceive that they were achieving their objectives, while the benevolent masses would be able to carry on as well, largely unscathed. By applying known techniques to avoid but also manage dark personalities, and by incorporating new, science-based strategies as we discover them, we might be able to achieve a more harmonious coexistence. Over time, the arms race would become more muted, and we'd reach a kind of stasis. Since we'd be minimizing those periods in which the dark personalities temporarily gain more sway, humanity also would become less vulnerable to the catastrophic disruptions I described earlier.

I wish that science had a quick and easy solution for curtailing humanity's darkest impulses, but it doesn't. Malevolent behavior and the suffering it causes will continue to mar our collective experience. Still, by mustering our knowledge of the latest findings, we can steer our destiny in a more positive direction. As we understand dark personalities better and build resistance and tolerance to them, we can make their toxicity less potent, enhancing both individual happiness and collective success. The antidote to poisonous people isn't some magical drug or transformative therapy. It's the benevolent majority. It's *you*.

Acknowledgments

Writing this book has been a long and challenging journey, but never a lonely one. I'm deeply grateful for all those who kept me excited, engaged, and hopeful about this project.

I couldn't be more appreciative than I am to have worked with Seth Schulman, who poses the most fascinating questions and writes the clearest prose. This book would be far less without him. To our editor, Eamon Dolan, for seeing the promise in this topic, and for pushing us to make it more engaging and practically useful to the reader: thank you. I'm also deeply grateful to Ben Kalin, our diligent fact-checker, for double- and triple-checking every word on these pages. To everyone at Simon & Schuster and SEI who helped launch this book into the world, I deeply appreciate your expertise, attention, and enthusiasm. To my agents at UTA, Albert Lee and Pilar Queen, thank you for this opportunity of a lifetime.

This book brings together research undertaken by myself and countless others. I'm indebted to the community of psychological scientists who've devoted their careers to understanding personality and how it shapes our lives, and to all the research assistants and participants who've contributed to the study of dark personalities over the decades.

In particular, I am grateful for all of the current and former students of the Truth and Trust Lab. Thank you for the immeasurable time, energy, and thought that you have put into the studies I have

Acknowledgments

shared in this book and the many other studies we've done together. You make studying even the darkest topics fun.

I *love* data, but it quickly became clear to me that this book couldn't stand on numbers alone. I'm honored to have interviewed dozens of people for this book, many of whom suffered deeply in the shadow of a dark personality. Not every interviewee will find their experience detailed in these pages, but I can confidently say that every conversation helped shape this book. I am deeply indebted to every person who shared their story with me. Thank you for your trust and courage.

My interest in dark personalities began decades ago, when Ms. Louise Lorefice wheeled a TV/VHS into my high school sociology class and played a *Nature of Things* episode on psychopathy. That spark eventually led me to graduate school at the University of British Columbia, Okanagan, and a life filled with the most amazing colleagues and friends. Thank you to Tara Carpenter, Pamela Black, and Alysha Baker; every author needs a Lady Boss Gang in their corner, and I'm so lucky to have you in mine. I'd be remiss if I didn't also thank Paul Davies for encouraging me to seek out a post-doc in a business school and supporting my circuitous academic journey ever since. My years at UC Berkeley's Haas School of Business were formative in many ways, largely due to Dana Carney and Dacher Keltner, who gave me opportunities that shaped this book and my life.

I must also thank my family. I've benefited profoundly from having siblings and parents who are humble, honest, thoughtful, and kind, which is probably why I find people without these traits so fascinating. To my dad, who inspires me with his soft heart, and my mom, who displays an enviable sense of humor, drive, and focus, thank you for being with me every step of the way.

I also owe a debt of gratitude to Fischer and Archie, who've been on all the thought-clarifying walks and runs and have sat under my desk for hundreds of hours as I read, wrote, and edited. Everyone should know the love of a golden retriever—or two.

Lastly, to my husband, Wayne: I wouldn't have been confident or strong enough to take on this book without your unwavering love, support, and belief in me. Thank you for being relentlessly interested in my work and for reminding me, always, that the best adventures are the ones we take together.

Notes

Introduction

1. My account of Clive Michael Boutilier in this and the following paragraphs draws on the court's decisions in *Boutilier v. Immigration and Naturalization Service*, 387 U.S. 118 (1967), as well as Marc Stein, "Boutilier v. Immigration and Naturalization Service (1967)," *Out History*, May 22, 2017, https://outhistory.org/exhibits/show/boutilier/intro#:~:text=Notwithstanding%20the%20strong%20arguments%20made,the%201889%20Chinese%20Exclusion%20Cases; Marc Stein, "Crossing the Border to Memory: In Search of Clive Michael Boutilier," *Journal of the Canadian Lesbian and Gay Studies Association* 6 (2004): 91–115.
2. Boutilier v. INS, 387 U.S. 118 (1967).
3. Stein, "Boutilier v. Immigration."
4. Norman Dorsen, "Introduction: Douglas and Civil Liberties," in *He Shall Not Pass This Way Again: The Legacy of Justice William O. Douglas*, ed. Stephen L. Wasby (Pittsburgh: University of Pittsburgh Press, 2010), 65–67.
5. Ronald Dworkin, "Dissent on Douglas," *New York Review of Books*, February 19, 1981, https://www.nybooks.com/articles/1981/02/19/dissent-on-douglas/?lp_txn_id=1575828.
6. Boutilier v. INS, 387 U.S. 118, 125 (1967).
7. David J. Garrow, "The Tragedy of William O. Douglas," *The Nation*, March 27, 2003, https://www.thenation.com/article/archive/tragedy-william-o-douglas/; Bruce Allen Murphy, *Wild Bill: The Legend and Life of William O. Douglas* (New York: Random House, 2003), 199.
8. Melvin I. Urofsky, "Conflict Among the Brethren: Felix Frankfurter, William O. Douglas and the Clash of Personalities and Philosophies on the United States Supreme Court," *Duke Law Journal*, 1988, 71.
9. Murphy, *Wild Bill*, 408.
10. Bruce Allen Murphy, "Fifty-Two Weeks of Boot Camp," in *In Chambers:*

Notes

Stories of Supreme Court Law Clerks and Their Justices, eds. Todd C. Peppers and Artemus Ward (Charlottesville: University of Virginia Press, 2012).
11. Murphy, *Wild Bill*, 424.
12. I draw my rendition of this story, including the quotes in the subsequent paragraphs, from the account provided in Murphy, "Fifty-Two Weeks of Boot Camp."
13. Murphy, *Wild Bill*, 422.
14. Murphy, *Wild Bill*, 424.
15. Wade C. Myers, Erik Gooch, and J. Reid Meloy, "The Role of Psychopathy and Sexuality in a Female Serial Killer," *Journal of Forensic Sciences* 50, no. 3 (2005): 652–57; Tod A. Roy, Joni L. Mihura, Alan F. Friedman, David S. Nichols, and J. Reid Meloy, "The Last Psychological Evaluation of Charles Manson: Implications for Personality, Psychopathology, and Ideology," *Journal of Threat Assessment and Management* 10, no. 3 (2022): 127–50.
16. Jane M. Murphy, "Psychiatric Labeling in Cross-Cultural Perspective: Similar Kinds of Disturbed Behavior Appear to Be Labeled Abnormal in Diverse Cultures," *Science* 191, no. 4231 (1976): 1019–28; Kent A. Kiehl and Morris B. Hoffman, "The Criminal Psychopath: History, Neuroscience, Treatment, and Economics," *Jurimetrics* 51 (2011): 355–97.
17. Rebecca Evans, Minna Lyons, Gayle Brewer, and Emily Bethell, "A Domestic Cat (*Felis silvestris catus*) Model of Triarchic Psychopathy Factors: Development and Initial Validation of the CAT-Tri+ Questionnaire," *Journal of Research in Personality* 95 (2021): 104161; Robert Latzman, Laura E. Drislane, Lisa K. Hecht, Sarah J. Brislin, Christopher J. Patrick, Scott O. Lilienfeld, Hani J. Freeman, Steven J. Schapiro, and William D. Hopkins, "A Chimpanzee (*Pan troglodytes*) Model of Triarchic Psychopathy Constructs: Development and Initial Validation," *Clinical Psychological Science* 4, no. 1 (2016): 50–66.
18. Stephen Porter, Leanne ten Brinke, and Kevin Wilson, "Crime Profiles and Conditional Release Performance of Psychopathic and Non-psychopathic Sexual Offenders," *Legal and Criminological Psychology* 14, no. 1 (2009): 109–18.
19. Paul Babiak, Craig S. Neumann, and Robert D. Hare, "Corporate Psychopathy: Talking the Walk," *Behavioral Sciences & the Law* 28, no. 2 (2010): 174–93.
20. Leanne ten Brinke and Dacher Keltner, "Theories of Power: Perceived Strategies for Gaining and Maintaining Power," *Journal of Personality and Social Psychology* 122, no. 1 (2022): 53–72.
21. Cynthia Mathieu and Paul Babiak, "Corporate Psychopathy and Abusive Supervision: Their Influence on Employees' Job Satisfaction and Turnover Intentions," *Personality and Individual Differences* 91 (2016): 102–6.

22. Mary Bardes Mawritz, David M. Mayer, Jenny M. Hoobler, Sandy J. Wayne, and Sophia V. Marinova, "A Trickle-Down Model of Abusive Supervision," *Personnel Psychology* 65, no. 2 (2012): 325–57, https://doi.org/10.1111/j.1744-6570.2012.01246.x.
23. Babiak et al., "Corporate Psychopathy: Talking the Walk"; Peter K. Jonason, Minna Lyons, Holly M. Baughman, and Philip A. Vernon, "What a Tangled Web We Weave: The Dark Triad Traits and Deception," *Personality and Individual Differences* 70 (2014): 117–19.
24. Robert D. Hare, *Without Conscience: The Disturbing World of the Psychopaths Among Us* (New York: Pocket Books, 1993), 87.
25. Adelle Forth, Sage Sezlik, Seung Lee, Mary Ritchie, John Logan, and Holly Ellingwood, "Toxic Relationships: The Experiences and Effects of Psychopathy in Romantic Relationships," *International Journal of Offender Therapy and Comparative Criminology* 66, no. 15 (2022): 1627–58.
26. Mathieu and Babiak, "Corporate Psychopathy and Abusive Supervision."
27. Paul J. Frick, James V. Ray, Laura C. Thornton, and Rachel E. Kahn, "Can Callous-Unemotional Traits Enhance the Understanding, Diagnosis, and Treatment of Serious Conduct Problems in Children and Adolescents? A Comprehensive Review," *Psychological Bulletin* 140, no. 1 (2014): 1–57.
28. Julia Dmitrieva, Lauren Gibson, Laurence Steinberg, Alex Piquero, and Jeffrey Fagan, "Predictors and Consequences of Gang Membership: Comparing Gang Members, Gang Leaders, and Non–Gang-Affiliated Adjudicated Youth," *Journal of Research on Adolescence* 24, no. 2 (2014): 220–34; Mitch van Geel, Faith Toprak, Anouk Goemans, Wendy Zwaanswijk, and Paul Vedder, "Are Youth Psychopathic Traits Related to Bullying? Meta-Analyses on Callous-Unemotional Traits, Narcissism, and Impulsivity," *Child Psychiatry & Human Development* 48 (2017): 768–77.
29. Craig S. Neumann, Scott Barry Kaufman, Leanne ten Brinke, David Bryce Yaden, Elizabeth Hyde, and Eli Tsykayama, "Light and Dark Trait Subtypes of Human Personality—A Multi-Study Person-Centered Approach," *Personality and Individual Differences* 164 (2020): 110121; Delroy L. Paulhus, Craig S. Neumann, and Robert D. Hare, "Self-Report Psychopathy Scale, 4th Edition Technical Manual" (Multi-Health Systems, 2016).
30. Neumann et al., "Light and Dark Trait Subtypes of Human Personality."
31. Thomas Hobbes, *Leviathan* (1651; Oxford: Basil Blackwell, 1960).
32. Eric Schwitzgebel, "Human Nature and Moral Education in Mencius, Xunzi, Hobbes, and Rousseau," *History of Philosophy Quarterly* 24, no. 2 (2007): 147–68.
33. Schwitzgebel, "Human Nature and Moral Education."
34. Detlef Fetchenhauer and David Dunning, "Do People Trust Too Much or Too Little?," *Journal of Economic Psychology* 30, no. 3 (2009): 263–76.

Notes

35. Michael Tomasello and Amrisha Vaish, "Origins of Human Cooperation and Morality," *Annual Review of Psychology* 64 (2013): 231–55.
36. Joseph Henrich and Michael Muthukrishna, "The Origins and Psychology of Human Cooperation," *Annual Review of Psychology* 72 (2021): 207–40.
37. Carolyn Zahn-Waxler, Marian Radke-Yarrow, Elizabeth Wagner, and Michael Chapman, "Development of Concern for Others," *Developmental Psychology* 28, no. 1 (1992): 126–36.
38. J. Kiley Hamlin, Karen Wynn, and Paul Bloom, "Social Evaluation by Preverbal Infants," *Nature* 450, no. 7169 (2007): 557–59.
39. Grant T. Harris and Marnie E. Rice, "Treatment of Psychopathy: A Review of Empirical Findings," in *Handbook of Psychopathy*, ed. Christopher J. Patrick (New York: Guilford Press, 2006), 555–72.
40. We also contemplate what "leadership lessons" we might glean from their antagonistic approach to power: Adam Grant, "Elon Musk's Leadership Style: What It Teaches Us About Business and Education," *New York Times*, April 13, 2025, https://www.nytimes.com/2025/04/13/opinion/elon-musk-leadership-business-education.html.
41. Hemant Kakkar and Niro Sivanathan, "When the Appeal of a Dominant Leader Is Greater Than a Prestige Leader," *Proceedings of the National Academy of Sciences* 114, no. 26 (2017): 6734–9.

I: Defining Dark Personalities

1. It's possible that what I was actually observing were manifestations of psychopathic personality traits. Rapists are more likely to meet the criteria for clinical levels of psychopathy (in other words, scoring at least a thirty on the Psychopathy Checklist-Revised [PCL-R] test) than intrafamilial or extrafamilial molesters. Stephen Porter, David Fairweather, Jeff Drugge, Hugues Hervé, Angela Birt, and Douglas P. Boer, "Profiles of Psychopathy in Incarcerated Sexual Offenders," *Criminal Justice and Behavior* 27, no. 2 (2000): 216–33.
2. Kevin Dutton, "Would You Vote for a Psychopath?," *Scientific American*, September 2016, https://www.scientificamerican.com/article/would-you-vote-for-a-psychopath/.
3. Michael Woodworth and Stephen Porter, "In Cold Blood: Characteristics of Criminal Homicides as a Function of Psychopathy," *Journal of Abnormal Psychology* 111, no. 3 (2002): 436–45.
4. Hervey M. Cleckley, *The Mask of Sanity* (St. Louis: Mosby, 1941).
5. For more on this test, see Robert D. Hare, "Psychopathy: A Clinical Construct Whose Time Has Come," *Criminal Justice and Behavior* 23, no. 1 (March 1996): 25–54.

6. The American Psychiatric Association's *Diagnostic and Statistical Manual of Mental Disorders* (DSM-5) defines a personality disorder as "an enduring pattern of inner experience and behavior that deviates markedly from the norms and expectations of the individual's culture, is pervasive and inflexible, has an onset in adolescence or early adulthood, is stable over time, and leads to distress or impairment." American Psychiatric Association, *Diagnostic and Statistical Manual of Mental Disorders*, 5th ed., Text Revision (Washington, DC: American Psychiatric Publishing, 2022).
7. Martin Sellbom and Laura E. Drislane, "The Classification of Psychopathy," *Aggression and Violent Behavior* 59 (2021): 101473.
8. Robert D. Hare and Craig S. Neumann, "Psychopathy as a Clinical and Empirical Construct," *Annual Review of Clinical Psychology* 4 (2008): 217–46.
9. John F. Edens, David K. Marcus, Scott O. Lilienfeld, and Norman G. Poythress Jr., "Psychopathic, Not Psychopath: Taxometric Evidence for the Dimensional Structure of Psychopathy," *Journal of Abnormal Psychology* 115, no. 1 (2006): 131–44; Takakuni Suzuki, Douglas B. Samuel, Shandell Pahlen, and Robert F. Krueger, "DSM-5 Alternative Personality Disorder Model Traits as Maladaptive Extreme Variants of the Five-Factor Model: An Item-Response Theory Analysis," *Journal of Abnormal Psychology* 124, no. 2 (2015): 343–54.
10. Robert D. Hare and Craig S. Neumann, "Structural Models of Psychopathy," *Current Psychiatry Reports* 7, no. 1 (2005): 57–64. Other models propose two or three buckets (or factors) of traits. For example, the triarchic model characterizes psychopathy as boldness, meanness, and disinhibition. While the organization of traits and names of the "buckets" might vary, scholars tend to agree about the constituent parts of the psychopathic personality. Self-report measures that adhere to the three-factor and four-factor models of psychopathy are highly correlated; people who score high on one measure generally score high on the other, too. Christopher J. Patrick, Don C. Fowles, and Robert F. Krueger, "Triarchic Conceptualization of Psychopathy: Developmental Origins of Disinhibition, Boldness, and Meanness," *Development and Psychopathology* 21, no. 3 (2009): 913–38; Laura E. Drislane, Christopher J. Patrick, and Güler Arsal, "Clarifying the Content Coverage of Differing Psychopathy Inventories Through Reference to the Triarchic Psychopathy Measure," *Psychological Assessment* 26, no. 2 (2014): 350–62.
11. Eric W. Hickey, B. K. Walters, Laura E. Drislane, Isabella M. Palumbo, and Christopher J. Patrick, "Deviance at Its Darkest: Serial Murder and Psychopathy," in *Handbook of Psychopathy*, ed. Christopher J. Patrick (New York: Guilford Press, 2006): 570–84; Christopher J. Patrick, ed., *Handbook of Psychopathy*, 2nd ed. (New York: Guilford Press, 2018); Tod A. Roy, Joni L.

Notes

Mihura, Alan F. Friedman, David S. Nichols, and J. Reid Meloy, "The Last Psychological Evaluation of Charles Manson: Implications for Personality, Psychopathology, and Ideology," *Journal of Threat Assessment and Management* 10, no. 3 (2023): 127.

12. Peter K. Jonason, Minna Lyons, Holly M. Baughman, and Philip A. Vernon, "What a Tangled Web We Weave: The Dark Triad Traits and Deception," *Personality and Individual Differences* 70 (2014): 117–19.
13. James Ryerson, "Dirty Rotten Hero," *New York Times*, April 13, 2003, https://www.nytimes.com/2003/04/13/books/dirty-rotten-hero.html; Stephen B. L. Penrose, *Whitman—An Unfinished Story* (Menasha, WI: Collegiate Press, 1935).
14. John H. Johns and Herbert C. Quay, "The Effect of Social Reward on Verbal Conditioning in Psychopathic and Neurotic Military Offenders," *Journal of Consulting Psychology* 26, no. 3 (1962): 217–20.
15. Lucas Powe, interview with the author, September 6, 2024.
16. Ashley M. Hosker-Field, Danielle S. Molnar, and Angela S. Book, "Psychopathy and Risk Taking: Examining the Role of Risk Perception," *Personality and Individual Differences* 91 (2016): 123–32.
17. Bruce A. Murphy, "Fifty-Two Weeks of Boot Camp," in *In Chambers: Stories of Supreme Court Law Clerks and Their Justices*, eds. Todd C. Peppers and Artemus Ward (Charlottesville: University of Virginia Press, 2012).
18. David J. Garrow, "The Tragedy of William O. Douglas," *The Nation*, March 27, 2003.
19. M. Margaret McKeown, *Citizen Justice: The Environmental Legacy of William O. Douglas—Public Advocate and Conservation Champion* (Lincoln, NE: Potomac Books, 2022), 2.
20. David J. Cooke, Christine Michie, and Stephen D. Hart, "Facets of Clinical Psychopathy," *Handbook of Psychopathy* (2006): 91–106; Jennifer L. Skeem, Devon L. L. Polaschek, Christopher J. Patrick, and Scott O. Lilienfeld, "Psychopathic Personality: Bridging the Gap Between Scientific Evidence and Public Policy," *Psychological Science in the Public Interest* 12, no. 3 (2011): 95–162.
21. Murphy, "Fifty-Two Weeks of Boot Camp."
22. "Nation: Impeach Douglas?," *Time*, April 27, 1970, https://time.com/archive/6842962/nation-impeach-douglas/.
23. I hesitated to describe Trump's behavior here. The Goldwater Rule prohibits psychiatrists from diagnosing individuals whom they have never personally examined. While this rule doesn't directly apply to psychologists, the *Ethical Principles of Psychologists and Code of Conduct* set out by the American Psychological Association (APA) advises that practitioners in my field proceed

with caution. Psychologists should "provide opinions on the psychological characteristics of individuals only after they have conducted an examination of the individuals adequate to support their statements or conclusions. When, despite reasonable efforts, such an effort is not practical, psychologists document the efforts they made and the result of those efforts, clarify the probable impact of their limited information on the reliability and validity of their opinions, and appropriately limit the nature and extent of their conclusions and recommendations. . . . When psychologists conduct a record review . . . [they should] explain this and the sources of information on which they have based their conclusions and recommendations." The prominent psychopathy researcher Dr. Scott Lilienfeld noted that the Goldwater Rule was put in place before the Internet and the availability of a large catalog of public figures' behavior. He further suggested that in the case of powerful public figures psychologists may actually have a "duty to warn" the public of potentially harmful psychological traits and that psychologists may offer informed opinions, with appropriate caveats. Scott O. Lilienfeld, Joshua D. Miller, and Donald R. Lynam, "The Goldwater Rule: Perspectives From, and Implications for, Psychological Science," *Perspectives on Psychological Science* 13, no. 1 (2018): 3–27; American Psychological Association, *Ethical Principles of Psychologists and Code of Conduct*, 2003, retrieved from http://www.apa.org/ethics/code/.

24. Glenn Kessler, Salvador Rizzo, and Meg Kelly, "Trump's False or Misleading Claims Total 30,573 Over 4 Years," *Washington Post*, January 24, 2021, https://www.washingtonpost.com/politics/2021/01/24/trumps-false-or-misleading-claims-total-30573-over-four-years/.

25. "Donald Trump Under Fire for Mocking Disabled Reporter," *BBC News*, November 26, 2015, https://www.bbc.com/news/world-us-canada-34930042.

26. Luke Harding, Julian Borger, and Dan Sabbagh, "Kremlin Papers Appear to Show Putin's Plot to Put Trump in White House," *The Guardian*, July 15, 2021, https://www.theguardian.com/world/2021/jul/15/kremlin-papers-appear-to-show-putins-plot-to-put-trump-in-white-house.

27. James Hamblin, "The President Who Looked at the Sun," *The Atlantic*, August 21, 2017, https://www.theatlantic.com/health/archive/2017/08/next-steps-for-the-presidents-eyes/537528/.

28. David Montgomery, "The Abnormal Presidency," *Washington Post Magazine*, November 10, 2020, https://www.washingtonpost.com/graphics/2020/lifestyle/magazine/trump-presidential-norm-breaking-list/; Libby Nelson, "'Grab 'Em by the Pussy': How Trump Talked About Women in Private Is Horrifying," *Vox*, October 7, 2016, https://www.vox.com/2016/10/7/13205842/trump-secret-recording-women; Ayesha Rascoe, "A Year After

Charlottesville, Not Much Has Changed for Trump," NPR, August 11, 2018, https://www.npr.org/2018/08/11/637665414/a-year-after-charlottesville-not-much-has-changed-for-trump; "Gold Star Families Fault Trump on Alleged 'Loser' Remarks," Associated Press, September 10, 2020, https://apnews.com/article/veterans-archive-donald-trump-da1e4da2f0ae92fa9365afbfe819297d; Alexandra Hutzler, "Trump Says 'Can't Have a Trial' For All Migrants He Wants to Deport," *ABC News*, April 23, 2025, https://abcnews.go.com/Politics/trump-trial-migrants-deport/story?id=121080810; James FitzGerald, "Canada Vows Swift Retaliation to 'Unjustified' Trump Tariffs," *BBC News*, February 11, 2025, https://www.bbc.com/news/articles/ckgxeg9g85no.

29. Politico Staff, "Tracking the Trump Criminal Cases," *Politico*, June 13, 2023, https://www.politico.com/interactives/2023/trump-criminal-investigations-cases-tracker-list/.
30. It's also worth noting that political experts and Dutch citizens—regardless of their political ideology—also perceive Donald Trump as having high levels of psychopathic traits. On average, these groups rated him as a six . . . out of seven. Alessandro Nai and Jürgen Maier, "Can Anyone Be Objective About Donald Trump? Assessing the Personality of Political Figures," *Journal of Elections, Public Opinion and Parties* 31, no. 3 (2021): 283–308.
31. Robert R. McCrae and Oliver P. John, "An Introduction to the Five-Factor Model and Its Applications," *Journal of Personality* 60, no. 2 (1992): 175–215.
32. Donald R. Lynam and Joshua D. Miller, "The Basic Trait of Antagonism: An Unfortunately Underappreciated Construct," *Journal of Research in Personality* 81 (2019): 118–26.
33. Robert D. Hare, *Manual for the Revised Psychopathy Checklist*, 2nd ed. (Multi-Health Systems, 2003), 8; Jeremy Coid, Min Yang, Simone Ullrich, Amanda Roberts, and Robert D. Hare, "Prevalence and Correlates of Psychopathic Traits in the Household Population of Great Britain," *International Journal of Law and Psychiatry* 32, no. 2 (2009): 65–73.
34. Delroy L. Paulhus, Craig S. Neumann, and Robert D. Hare, *Self-Report Psychopathy Scale 4th Edition* (Multi-Health Systems, 2016).
35. Paulhus et al., *Self-Report Psychopathy Scale*, 22.
36. Craig. S. Neumann, Scott Barry Kaufman, Leanne ten Brinke, David B. Yaden, Elizabeth Hyde, and Eli Tsykayama, "Light and Dark Trait Subtypes of Human Personality—a Multi-Study Person-Centered Approach," *Personality and Individual Differences* 164 (2020).
37. One meta-analysis considered five samples of twins who were raised together, a sample of twins who were reared apart, and a sample of those who were adopted. The data suggested that genetic influences accounted for 52 percent

of the variability in self-reported psychopathy, while environments accounted for the remaining 48 percent. In other words, dark personalities arise out of both genetic makeup and a person's unique life experiences. Irwin D. Waldman, Seunghyeon Rhee, Devon LoParo, and Y. Park, "Genetic and Environmental Influences on Psychopathy and Antisocial Behavior," in *Handbook of Psychopathy* (2006): 205–28.

38. Ben Karpman, "On the Need of Separating Psychopathy into Two Distinct Clinical Types: The Symptomatic and the Idiopathic," *Journal of Criminal Psychopathology* 3 (1941), 112–37.
39. Rebecca Waller, Luke W. Hyde, Kelly L. Klump, and S. Alexandra Burt, "Parenting Is an Environmental Predictor of Callous-Unemotional Traits and Aggression: A Monozygotic Twin Differences Study," *Journal of the American Academy of Child & Adolescent Psychiatry* 57, no. 12 (2018): 955–63.
40. Craig S. Neumann, Scott Barry Kaufman, and Leanne ten Brinke, "Citizens in Democratic Countries Have More Benevolent Traits, Fewer Malevolent Traits, and Greater Well-Being," *Scientific Reports* 15, no. 1 (2025): 13346.
41. Ingo Zettler, Lau Lilleholt, Martina Bader, Benjamin E. Hilbig, and Morten Moshagen, "Aversive Societal Conditions Explain Differences in 'Dark' Personality Across Countries and US States," *Proceedings of the National Academy of Sciences* 122, no. 20 (2025): e2500830122.
42. Lewin believed that to understand human behavior, we need to study the whole individual, not just isolated parts. In a famous body of work called *field theory*, he posited that each person's "life space"—all the internal and external forces acting on an individual at a particular moment—involved an interplay between two factors: the person (including their personality, motivations, desires, and experiences) and the environment (including the physical and social environments, and how one interprets that context). Moreover, he believed that the person affects the environment, and vice versa. Kurt Lewin, *Principles of Topological Psychology*, trans. Fritz Heider and Grace M. Heider (New York: McGraw-Hill, 1936). More recently, researchers involved in the so-called person-situation debate have tested which predicts behavior, personality or environment. As you might expect, both do. David C. Funder, "Towards a Resolution of the Personality Triad: Persons, Situations, and Behaviors," *Journal of Research in Personality* 40 (2006): 21–34.
43. Delroy L. Paulhus and Kevin M. Williams, "The Dark Triad of Personality: Narcissism, Machiavellianism, and Psychopathy," *Journal of Research in Personality* 36 (2002): 556–63; Erin E. Buckels, Daniel N. Jones, and Delroy L. Paulhus, "Behavioral Confirmation of Everyday Sadism," *Psychological Science* 24 (2013): 2201–9.
44. Peter Muris, Harald Merckelbach, Henry Otgaar, and Ewout Meijer, "The

Malevolent Side of Human Nature: A Meta-Analysis and Critical Review of the Literature on the Dark Triad (Narcissism, Machiavellianism, and Psychopathy)," *Perspectives on Psychological Science* 12, no. 2 (2017): 183–204.

45. Angela S. Book, Beth A. Visser, Julie Blais, Ashley Hosker-Field, Tabitha Methot-Jones, Nathalie Y. Gauthier, Anthony Volk, Ronald R. Holden, and Madeleine T. D'Agata, "Unpacking More 'Evil': What Is at the Core of the Dark Tetrad?," *Personality and Individual Differences* 90 (2016): 269–72.

46. Niccolò Machiavelli, *The Prince* (1532), trans. N. H. Thomson (East Bridgewater, MA: World Publications Group, 2008).

47. Marcus Field, "Architect of Desire: Frank Lloyd Wright's Private Life Was Even More Unforgettable Than His Buildings," *Independent*, March 8, 2009, https://www.independent.co.uk/arts-entertainment/architecture/architect-of-desire-frank-lloyd-wright-s-private-life-was-even-more-unforgettable-than-his-buildings-1637537.html.

48. Charlyne Varkonyi Schaub, "Exhibiting the Master's Works Here," *Baltimore Sun*, October 23, 2018, https://www.baltimoresun.com/1996/03/31/exhibiting-the-masters-works-here-home-his-buildings-may-have-leaked-but-frank-lloyd-wright-is-still-considered-by-many-to-be-americas-greatest-architect-a-show-at-evergreen-house-pays-tribute/.

49. Erin E. Buckels, Daniel N. Jones, and Delroy L. Paulhus, "Behavioral Confirmation of Everyday Sadism," *Psychological Science* 24, no. 11 (2013): 2201–9.

50. Thomas A. Widiger and Alexandra Hines, "Personality Disorders," in *Encyclopedia of Mental Health, Third Edition*, eds. Howard S. Friedman and Charlotte H. Markey (New Brunswick, NJ: Academic Press: 2023), 761–69, https://www.sciencedirect.com/science/article/abs/pii/B9780323914970001041.

51. *Diagnostic and Statistical Manual of Mental Disorders*, 5th ed., Text Revision (Washington, DC: American Psychiatric Publishing, 2022).

52. As regards antisocial personality disorder (ASPD), for instance, research has found that about 80 percent of clinical psychopaths in forensic contexts meet criteria for this disorder, too, while only about 30 percent of individuals with ASPD would meet criteria for clinical psychopathy. Hare, *Manual for the Revised Psychopathy Checklist*; Stephen D. Hart and Robert D. Hare, "Psychopathy and Antisocial Personality Disorder," *Current Opinion in Psychiatry* 9, no. 2 (1996): 129–32; Christian Huchzermeier, Friedemann Geiger, Emelie Bruss, Nils Godt, Denis Köhler, Günter Hinrichs, and Josef B. Aldenhoff, "The Relationship Between DSM-IV Cluster B Personality Disorders and Psychopathy According to Hare's Criteria: Clarification and Resolution of Previous Contradictions," *Behavioral Sciences & the Law* 25, no. 6 (2007): 901–11.

53. As if all of this weren't confusing enough, people sometimes use the term "sociopathy" as a synonym for psychopathy or antisocial personality disorder,

or to describe people who develop these traits as a result of childhood abuse (as opposed to genetics), or because the term sounds less nefarious than psychopathy. In truth, psychologists have no widely accepted clinical measure of sociopathy. For the sake of clarity and simplicity, it's probably best to avoid the term. Scott O. Lilienfeld, Ava L. Pydych, Steven Jay Lynn, Robert D. Latzman, and Irwin D. Waldman, "50 Differences That Make a Difference: A Compendium of Frequently Confused Term Pairs in Psychology," *Frontiers in Education* 2 (2017): 37.

54. Georgia Zara, Henriette Bergstrøm, and David P. Farrington, "The Sexual Life of Men with Psychopathic Traits," *Journal of Criminological Research, Policy and Practice* 7, no. 2 (2021): 164–78.

55. Peter. K. Jonason, Bryan L. Koenig, and Jeremy Tost, "Living a Fast Life: The Dark Triad and Life History Theory," *Human Nature* 21 (2010): 428–42; Olli Vaurio, Eila Repo-Tiihonen, Hannu Kautiainen, and Jari Tiihonen, "Psychopathy and Mortality," *Journal of Forensic Sciences* 63, no. 2 (March 2018): 474–77; Peter K. Jonason, Holly M. Baughman, Gregory L. Carter, and Phillip Parker, "Dorian Gray Without His Portrait: Psychological, Social, and Physical Health Costs Associated with the Dark Triad," *Personality and Individual Differences* 78 (2015): 5–13; J. Michael Maurer, Aparna R. Gullapalli, Michaela M. Milillo, Corey H. Allen, Samantha N. Rodriguez, Bethany G. Edwards, Nathaniel E. Anderson, Carla L. Harenski, and Kent A. Kiehl, "Adolescents with Elevated Psychopathic Traits Are Associated with an Increased Risk for Premature Mortality," *Research on Child and Adolescent Psychopathology* 53, no. 1 (2025): 17–28.

56. Linda Mealey, "The Sociobiology of Sociopathy: An Integrated Evolutionary Model," in *The Maladapted Mind*, ed. Simon Baron-Cohen (East Sussex, UK: Psychology Press, 1997), 133–88.

2: The Cost of a Malevolent Few

1. What is a "successful psychopath"? Some scholars have argued that simply avoiding incarceration is one measure of success. Sharon S. Ishikawa, Adrian Raine, Todd Lencz, Susan Bihrle, and Lori Lacasse, "Autonomic Stress Reactivity and Executive Functions in Successful and Unsuccessful Criminal Psychopaths from the Community," *Journal of Abnormal Psychology* 110, no. 3 (2001): 423. Cathy Widom was one of the first to study these personalities outside of institutions. To recruit them she placed the following advertisement in Boston newspapers: "Wanted charming, aggressive, carefree people who are impulsively irresponsible but are good at handling people and at looking after number one" (675). If you see a Tinder profile with these adjectives, consider swiping left. Cathy S. Widom, "A Methodology for Studying

Noninstitutionalized Psychopaths," *Journal of Consulting and Clinical Psychology* 45, no. 4 (1977): 674–83. Others have focused on individuals in particular lines of work or those who have achieved high social status. Because we can define success in many ways, scholars don't agree on exactly what makes for a "successful psychopath." They do agree that serious antisocial behavior and criminal convictions aren't it. Jason R. Hall and Stephen D. Benning, "The 'Successful' Psychopath," in *Handbook of Psychopathy*, ed. Christopher J. Patrick (New York: Guilford Press, 2006), 459–75; Scott O. Lilienfeld, Irwin D. Waldman, Kristin Landfield, Ashley L. Watts, Steven Rubenzer, and Thomas R. Faschingbauer, "Fearless Dominance and the US Presidency: Implications of Psychopathic Personality Traits for Successful and Unsuccessful Political Leadership," *Journal of Personality and Social Psychology* 103, no. 3 (2012): 489–505; Björn N. Persson and Scott O. Lilienfeld, "Social Status as One Key Indicator of Successful Psychopathy: An Initial Empirical Investigation," *Personality and Individual Differences* 141 (2019): 209–17.

2. This account describes research published in Leanne ten Brinke, Aimee Kish, and Dacher Keltner, "Hedge Fund Managers with Psychopathic Tendencies Make for Worse Investors," *Personality and Social Psychology Bulletin* 44, no. 2 (2018): 214–23.

3. Since Dacher and I controlled for the type of investment strategy managers used, the relatively poor performance of high psychopathy managers didn't reflect specific investment practices they might have been adopting. Nor did it seem that these managers were taking on more risk than their peers relative to the profits they were yielding. Psychopathy was the only dark triad trait associated with decreased annualized (%) returns. However, narcissism was negatively related to *risk-adjusted* returns. Someone who invested with a highly versus moderately narcissistic manager wouldn't find much difference in their account balance after ten years but would have endured a lot more ups and downs (in other words, volatility) to get there. Remember how you felt when you checked your 401(k) balance in 2021 ("I'm rich!") and then again in 2022 ("I'll never be able to retire")? That's a bit what it feels like to invest with a highly narcissistic hedge fund manager. Leanne ten Brinke et al., "Hedge Fund Managers with Psychopathic Tendencies Make for Worse Investors."

4. Bennett J. Tepper, Michelle K. Duffy, Christine A. Henle, and Lisa Schurer Lambert, "Procedural Justice, Victim Precipitation, and Abusive Supervision," *Personnel Psychology* 59 (2006): 101–23.

5. Cynthia Mathieu and Paul Babiak, "Corporate Psychopathy and Abusive Supervision: Their Influence on Employees' Job Satisfaction and Turnover Intentions," *Personality and Individual Differences* 91 (2016): 102–6.

6. Donald Sull, Charles Sull, and Ben Zweig, "Toxic Culture Is Driving the Great Resignation," *MIT Sloan Management Review*, January 11, 2022, https://sloanreview.mit.edu/article/toxic-culture-is-driving-the-great-resignation/.
7. Scholars have chronicled the severe business impact that uncivil behavior in general has in the workplace. See Christine Porath, *Mastering Incivility: A Manifesto for the Workplace* (New York: Grand Central Publishing, 2016), chapter 2.
8. Sarah Francis Smith, Ashley Watts, and Scott O. Lilienfeld, "On the Trail of the Elusive Successful Psychopath," *Psychological Assessment* 15 (2014): 340–50; Sarah Francis Smith, Scott O. Lilienfeld, Karly Coffey, and James M. Dabbs, "Are Psychopaths and Heroes Twigs off the Same Branch? Evidence from College, Community, and Presidential Samples," *Journal of Research in Personality* 47, no. 5 (2013): 634–46.
9. Jochem Willemsen, Julie De Ganck, and Paul Verhaeghe, "Psychopathy, Traumatic Exposure, and Lifetime Posttraumatic Stress," *International Journal of Offender Therapy and Comparative Criminology* 56, no. 4 (2012): 505–24.
10. Diana M. Falkenbach, Sean J. McKinley, and Farren R. Roelofs Larson, "Two Sides of the Same Coin: Psychopathy Case Studies from an Urban Police Department," *Journal of Forensic Psychology Research and Practice* 17, no. 5 (2017): 338–56.
11. Christina L. Patton, Sarah Francis Smith, and Scott O. Lilienfeld, "Psychopathy and Heroism in First Responders: Traits Cut from the Same Cloth?," *Personality Disorders: Theory, Research, and Treatment* 9, no. 4 (2018): 354–68.
12. Studies conducted in business settings also found that high psychopathy employees were perceived as charismatic and persuasive communicators but were also poor team players who accomplished less than their peers. Paul Babiak, Craig S. Neumann, and Robert D. Hare, "Corporate Psychopathy: Talking the Walk," *Behavioral Sciences & the Law* 28, no. 2 (2010): 174–93.
13. Marty Steinberg and Scott Cohn, "Bernie Madoff, Mastermind of the Nation's Biggest Investment Fraud, Dies at 82," CNBC, April 14, 2021, https://www.cnbc.com/2021/04/14/bernie-madoff-dies-mastermind-of-the-nations-biggest-investment-fraud-was-82.html.
14. Clive R. Boddy, "Insights into the Bernie Madoff Financial Market Scandal Which Identify New Opportunities for Business Market Researchers," *International Journal of Market Research* 66, no. 1 (2023): 1–19. Other scholars take issue with the measure this author used to assess psychopathy, arguing that it focuses primarily on buckets 1 and 2 (interpersonal and emotional traits) to the exclusion of buckets 3 and 4 (impulsive and antisocial traits). Daniel N. Jones and Robert D. Hare, "The Mismeasure of Psychopathy: A Commentary on Boddy's PM-MRV," *Journal of Business Ethics* 138 (2016): 579–88.

Notes

15. Robert D. Hare, *Without Conscience: The Disturbing World of the Psychopaths Among Us* (New York: Pocket Books, 1993), 87.
16. Ralph C. Serin and Nancy L. Amos, "The Role of Psychopathy in the Assessment of Dangerousness," *International Journal of Law and Psychiatry* 18, no. 2 (1995): 231–38.
17. David A. Anderson, "The Aggregate Cost of Crime in the United States," *Journal of Law and Economics* 64 (November 2021). The typical murder, for instance, carries tangible and intangible costs of about $8 million. For data on the cost of specific crimes, see Kathryn E. McCollister, Michael T. French, and Hai Fang, "The Cost of Crime to Society: New Crime-Specific Estimates for Policy and Program Evaluation," *Drug and Alcohol Dependence* 108, nos. 1–2 (April 2010): 98–109.
18. Fischer Elias ten Brinke scores a zero on the PCL-R.
19. Rolfe Daus Peterson and Carl L. Palmer, "The Dark Is Rising: Contrasting the Dark Triad and Light Triad on Measures of Political Ambition and Participation," *Frontiers in Political Science* 3 (2021): 657750; Philip Chen, Scott Pruysers, and Julie Blais, "The Dark Side of Politics: Participation and the Dark Triad," *Political Studies* 69, no. 3 (2021): 577–601; William Hart, Christopher John Breeden, Joshua Tripp Lambert, and Charlotte Kinrade, "Who Wants to Be Your Next Political Representative? Relating Personality Constructs to Nascent Political Ambition," *Personality and Individual Differences* 186 (2022): 111329.
20. Alessandro Nai, "Disagreeable Narcissists, Extroverted Psychopaths, and Elections: A New Dataset to Measure the Personality of Candidates Worldwide," *European Political Science* 18 (2019): 309–34.
21. Craig S. Neumann, Scott Barry Kaufman, Leanne ten Brinke, David Bryce Yaden, Elizabeth Hyde, and Eli Tsykayama, "Light and Dark Trait Subtypes of Human Personality–A Multi-Study Person-Centered Approach," *Personality and Individual Differences* 164 (2020): 110121.
22. The following paragraphs describe the research in Leanne ten Brinke, Christopher C. Liu, Dacher Keltner, and Sameer B. Srivastava, "Virtues, Vices, and Political Influence in the U.S. Senate," *Psychological Science* 27, no. 1 (2016): 85–93.
23. Alessandro Nai, "The Electoral Success of Angels and Demons: Big Five, Dark Triad, and Performance at the Ballot Box," *Journal of Social and Political Psychology* 7, no. 2: 830–62; Alessandro Nai, "Disagreeable Narcissists, Extroverted Psychopaths, and Elections."
24. Alessandro Nai and Jürgen Maier, "Dark Necessities? Candidates' Aversive Personality Traits and Negative Campaigning in the 2018 American Midterms," *Electoral Studies* 68 (December 2020): 102233.

25. Alessandro Nai and Ferran Martínez i Coma, "The Personality of Populists: Provocateurs, Charismatic Leaders, or Drunken Dinner Guests?," *West European Politics* 42, no. 7 (2019): 1337–67.
26. Alessandro Nai and Emre Toros, "The Peculiar Personality of Strongmen: Comparing the Big Five and Dark Triad Traits of Autocrats and Nonautocrats," *Political Research Exchange* 2 (2020): 1707697.
27. Scott O. Lilienfeld, Irwin D. Waldman, Kristin Landfield, Ashley L. Watts, Steven J. Rubenzer, and Thomas R. Faschingbauer, "Fearless Dominance and the U.S. Presidency: Implications of Psychopathic Personality Traits for Successful and Unsuccessful Political Leadership," *Journal of Personality and Social Psychology* 103, no. 3 (2012): 489–505; Ashley L. Watts, Scott O. Lilienfeld, Sarah Francis Smith, Joshua D. Miller, W. Keith Campbell, Irwin D. Waldman, Steven J. Rubenzer, and Thomas J. Faschingbauer, "The Double-Edged Sword of Grandiose Narcissism: Implications for Successful and Unsuccessful Leadership Among U.S. Presidents," *Psychological Science* 24, no. 12: 2379–89.
28. Nir Grinberg, Kenneth Joseph, Lisa Friedland, Briony Swire-Thompson, and David Lazer, "Fake News on Twitter During the 2016 U.S. Presidential Election," *Science* 363, no. 6425 (2019): 374–8.
29. Claire E. Robertson, Kareena S. del Rosario, and Jay J. Van Bavel, "Inside the Funhouse Mirror Factory: How Social Media Distorts Perceptions of Norms," *Current Opinion in Psychology* 60 (December 2024): 101918.
30. Evita March, "Psychopathy, Sadism, Empathy, and the Motivation to Cause Harm: New Evidence Confirms Malevolent Nature of the Internet Troll," *Personality and Individual Differences* 141 (2019): 133–7.
31. On the connections between dark personalities and infidelity, see Daniel N. Jones and Dana A. Weiser, "Differential Infidelity Patterns Among the Dark Triad," *Personality and Individual Differences* 57 (2014): 20–24; Barış Sevi, Betul Urganci, and Ezgi Sakman, "Who Cheats? An Examination of Light and Dark Personality Traits as Predictors of Infidelity," *Personality and Individual Differences* 164 (2020): 110126; Liane J. Leedom, "The Impact of Psychopathy on the Family," in *Psychopathy: New Updates on an Old Phenomenon*, ed. F. Durbano (BoD–Books on Demand, 2017), 139–68.
32. Courtney Humeny, Adelle E. Forth, and John Logan, "Psychopathic Traits Predict Survivors' Experiences of Domestic Abuse," *Personality and Individual Differences* 171 (2021): 110497.
33. Adelle Forth, Sage Sezlik, Seung Lee, Mary Ritchie, John Logan, and Holly Ellingwood, "Toxic Relationships: The Experiences and Effects of Psychopathy in Romantic Relationships," *International Journal of Offender Therapy and Comparative Criminology* 66, no. 15 (2022): 1627–58.

Notes

34. Eva R. Kimonis and Kathleen Armstrong, "Adapting Parent–Child Interaction Therapy to Treat Severe Conduct Problems with Callous-Unemotional Traits: A Case Study," *Clinical Case Studies* 11, no. 3 (2012): 234–52.
35. Donald R. Lynam, Avshalom Caspi, Terrie E. Moffitt, Rolf Loeber, and Magda Stouthamer-Loeber, "Longitudinal Evidence That Psychopathy Scores in Early Adolescence Predict Adult Psychopathy," *Journal of Abnormal Psychology* 116, no. 1 (2007): 155–65. This study finds a correlation between psychopathic personality features in thirteen-year-olds and scores on a screening version of the PCL-R completed at age twenty-five. In other words, these traits tend to be stable from youth to adulthood. Most commonly, psychologists assess CU traits in combination with a conduct disorder diagnosis. Taken together, the impulsive and antisocial behaviors characteristic of conduct disorder, combined with CU traits, looks a lot like what we call psychopathy in adults. Paul J. Frick, James V. Ray, Laura C. Thornton, and Rachel E. Kahn, "Can Callous-Unemotional Traits Enhance the Understanding, Diagnosis, and Treatment of Serious Conduct Problems in Children and Adolescents? A Comprehensive Review," *Psychological Bulletin* 140, no. 1 (2014): 1–57.
36. "A Parent's Story: How Do You Sum Up a Lifetime of Abuse in 700 Words?" PsychopathyIs, September 26, 2020, https://psychopathyis.org/personal-stories/parent-psychopathy-story/.
37. Kostas A. Fanti and Luna C. Muñoz Centifanti, "Childhood Callous-Unemotional Traits Moderate the Relation Between Parenting Distress and Conduct Problems Over Time," *Child Psychiatry & Human Development* 45 (2014): 173–84.
38. Jennifer Kahn, "Can You Call a 9-Year-Old a Psychopath?," *New York Times Magazine*, May 11, 2012, https://www.nytimes.com/2012/05/13/magazine/can-you-call-a-9-year-old-a-psychopath.html.
39. Roxanne Khan and David J. Cooke, "Risk Factors for Severe Inter-Sibling Violence: A Preliminary Study of a Youth Forensic Sample," *Journal of Interpersonal Violence* 23, no. 11 (2008): 1513–30; Leedom, "The Impact of Psychopathy on the Family"; Jim Snyder, Lew Bank, and Bert Burraston, "The Consequences of Antisocial Behavior in Older Male Siblings for Younger Brothers and Sisters," *Journal of Family Psychology* 19, no. 4 (2005): 643–53.
40. "Police: Boy Calm as Friend Drowned," *Orlando Sentinel*, July 24, 2021, https://www.orlandosentinel.com/1986/11/12/police-boy-calm-as-friend-drowned/. It's not clear whether the toddler was a sibling.
41. Barbara Bradley Hagerty, "When Your Child Is a Psychopath," *The Atlantic*, June 2017, https://www.theatlantic.com/magazine/archive/2017/06/when-your-child-is-a-psychopath/524502/.

42. Kahn, "Can You Call." Research supports the link between CU traits and cruelty to animals. Mark R. Dadds, Clare Whiting, and David J. Hawes, "Associations Among Cruelty to Animals, Family Conflict, and Psychopathic Traits in Childhood," *Journal of Interpersonal Violence* 21, no. 3 (2006): 411–29.
43. Leedom, "The Impact of Psychopathy on the Family."
44. Laura C. Thornton, Paul J. Frick, Elizabeth P. Shulman, James V. Ray, Laurence Steinberg, and Elizabeth Cauffman, "Callous-Unemotional Traits and Adolescents' Role in Group Crime," *Law and Human Behavior* 39, no. 4 (2015): 368–77.
45. See, for instance, Kostas A. Fanti, P. J. Frick, and S. Georgiou, "Linking Callous-Unemotional Traits to Instrumental and Non-instrumental Forms of Aggression," *Journal of Psychopathology and Behavior Assessment* 31 (2009): 285–98; Rebecca S. Levine, Kelly Smith, and Nicholas J. Wagner, "The Impact of Callous-Unemotional Traits on Achievement, Behaviors, and Relationships in School: A Systematic Review," *Child Psychiatry & Human Development* 54, no. 6 (2023): 1546–66.
46. Levine et al., "The Impact of Callous-Unemotional Traits."
47. Levine et al., "The Impact of Callous-Unemotional Traits."
48. Jennifer L. Allen, Amy Morris, and Celine Y. Chhoa, "Callous-Unemotional (CU) Traits in Adolescent Boys and Response to Teacher Reward and Discipline Strategies," *Emotional and Behavioural Difficulties* 21, no. 3 (2016): 329–42.
49. Rachel E. Kahn, Paul J. Frick, Eric Youngstrom, Robert L. Findling, and Jennifer Kogos Youngstrom, "The Effects of Including a Callous-Unemotional Specifier for the Diagnosis of Conduct Disorder," *Journal of Child Psychology and Psychiatry* 53, no. 3 (2012): 271–82. It's worth noting that this research used a well-validated self-report screening measure called the Children's Symptom Inventory-4 to measure conduct disorder. Similarly, parents and teachers rated CU traits on a well-validated measure called the Antisocial Process Screening Device. While these are good approximations, official diagnosis would require assessment by a psychologist or psychiatrist. Paul J. Frick and Robert D. Hare, *Antisocial Process Screening Device (APSD)* (Toronto, ON: Multi-Health Systems, 2001); Kenneth D. Gadow and Joyce N. Sprafkin, *Manual for the Child Symptom Inventory*, 4th ed. (Stony Brook, NY: Checkmate Plus, 1994).
50. This account relies closely on a case study of Hanssen: J. Scott Sanford and Bruce A. Arrigo, "Policing and Psychopathy: The Case of Robert Philip Hanssen," *Journal of Forensic Psychology Practice* 7, no. 3 (2007): 1–31; "Devoted Father of 6 Lives Modestly," *Tampa Bay Times*, February 21, 2001, https://www.tampabay.com/archive/2001/02/21/devoted-father-of-6-lives-modestly/;

Niles Lathem, "Neighbors Wondered Where He Got The $$," *New York Post*, February 21, 2001, https://nypost.com/2001/02/21/neighbors-wondered-where-he-got-the/.
51. Sanford and Arrigo, "Policing and Psychopathy: The Case of Robert Philip Hanssen"; Sanford and Arrigo, "Devoted Father"; Lathem, "Neighbors Wondered."
52. David Ensor, "What Made the American Turncoat Tick," CNN, May 10, 2002.
53. David A. Vise, *The Bureau and the Mole: The Unmasking of Robert Philip Hanssen, the Most Dangerous Double Agent in FBI History* (New York: Grove Press, 2002), 230.
54. Sanford and Arrigo, "Policing and Psychopathy: The Case of Robert Philip Hanssen."
55. Lindsay Whitehurst, "Former FBI Agent Robert Hanssen, Who Was Convicted of Spying for Russia, Dies in Prison," Associated Press, June 5, 2023, https://apnews.com/article/fbi-spy-russia-prison-died-hanssen-f16ff609b91ba5f84946a2ccf6363df2.
56. "Robert Hanssen, Called the Most Destructive Spy in U.S. History, Dies at 79," NPR, June 7, 2023, https://www.npr.org/2023/06/07/1180665283/robert-hanssen-called-the-most-destructive-spy-in-u-s-history-dies-at-79.
57. Peter Baker, "Robert Hanssen, F.B.I. Agent Exposed as Spy for Moscow, Dies at 79," *New York Times*, June 5, 2023, https://www.nytimes.com/2023/06/05/us/robert-hanssen-spy-dead.html.
58. Josh Lederman and Jill Lawless, "US, Allies Band Together to Expel Russians Over Spy Case," Associated Press, March 26, 2018, https://apnews.com/article/700e491efa334fe8ae7d20fd576b4d1b.
59. "Damage Assessment: Convicted Spy Robert Hanssen," PBS News Hour, May 10, 2002, https://www.pbs.org/newshour/show/damage-assessment-convicted-spy-robert-hanssen.

3: How the Poison Spreads

1. Paul A. M. Van Lange, Ellen De Bruin, Wilma Otten, and Jeffrey A. Joireman, "Development of Prosocial, Individualistic, and Competitive Orientations: Theory and Preliminary Evidence," *Journal of Personality and Social Psychology* 73, no. 4 (1997): 733–46.
2. In our sample of 149 participants, only six consistently elected to dominate their partner by selecting option one in multiple trials of this task. That's good news for society—only a few bad apples! But not great for conducting statistical tests, since we had very unequal numbers of people who chose option one (n = 6), option two (n = 90), and option three (n = 43). In that

paper, we collapse across options one and three to create a larger group of "competitive" people, but the handful of people who elected to dominate their partner had a higher psychopathy score (mean = 10.50) than those who chose to win by a smaller margin (mean = 8.54) or those who elected to share points equally with their partner (mean = 7.59). Leanne ten Brinke, Pamela J. Black, Stephen Porter, and Dana R. Carney, "Psychopathic Personality Traits Predict Competitive Wins and Cooperative Losses in Negotiation," *Personality and Individual Differences* 79 (2015): 116–22.

3. Andrea L. Glenn, Leah M. Efferson, Ravi Iyer, and Jesse Graham, "Values, Goals, and Motivations Associated with Psychopathy," *Journal of Social and Clinical Psychology* 36, no. 2 (2017): 108–25.

4. Niccolò Machiavelli, *The Prince* (1532), trans. N. H. Thomson (East Bridgewater, MA: World Publications Group, 2008), 105.

5. Kristoph J. Brazil and Adelle E. Forth, "Psychopathy and the Induction of Desire: Formulating and Testing an Evolutionary Hypothesis," *Evolutionary Psychological Science* 6, no. 1 (2020): 64–81; Liane J. Leedom, Emily Geslien, and Linda Hartoonnian Almas, "Did He Ever Love Me? A Qualitative Study of Life with a Psychopathic Husband," *Family and Intimate Partner Violence Quarterly* 5, no. 2 (2012): 103–35.

6. Studies of male inmates convicted of violent crimes found that those who scored higher for psychopathy more accurately identified women and men who had previously been victimized, cueing into subtle behaviors such as posture or gait. Angela Book, Kimberly Costello, and Joseph A. Camilleri, "Psychopathy and Victim Selection: The Use of Gait as a Cue to Vulnerability," *Journal of Interpersonal Violence* 28, no. 11 (2013): 2368–83. Less violent bad apples have this superpower, too, as evidenced by research with college students. S. Wheeler, Angela Book, and Kimberly Costello, "Psychopathic Traits and Perceptions of Victim Vulnerability," *Criminal Justice and Behavior* 36, no. 6 (June 2009): 635–48.

7. Kevin Wilson, Sabrina Demetrioff, and Stephen Porter, "A Pawn by Any Other Name? Social Information Processing as a Function of Psychopathic Traits," *Journal of Research in Personality* 42, no. 6 (2008): 1651–6.

8. Judith A. Hall, Erik J. Coats, and Lavonia Smith LeBeau, "Nonverbal Behavior and the Vertical Dimension of Social Relations: A Meta-Analysis," *Psychological Bulletin* 131, no. 6 (2005): 898–924.

9. Larissa Z. Tiedens and Alison R. Fragale, "Power Moves: Complementarity in Dominant and Submissive Nonverbal Behavior," *Journal of Personality and Social Psychology* 84, no. 3 (2003): 558–68.

10. Frans de Waal, *Chimpanzee Politics: Sex and Power Among Apes* (Baltimore: Johns Hopkins University Press, 1982); Tiedens and Fragale, "Power Moves."

Notes

11. Paul Babiak, Craig S. Neumann, and Robert D. Hare, "Corporate Psychopathy: Talking the Walk," *Behavioral Sciences & the Law* 28, no. 2 (2010): 174–93.
12. Cameron Anderson and Gavin J. Kilduff, "Why Do Dominant Personalities Attain Influence in Face-to-Face Groups? The Competence-Signaling Effects of Trait Dominance," *Journal of Personality and Social Psychology* 96, no. 2 (2009): 491–503.
13. Gerben A. Van Kleef, Astrid C. Homan, Catrin Finkenauer, Seval Gündemir, and Eftychia Stamkou, "Breaking the Rules to Rise to Power: How Norm Violators Gain Power in the Eyes of Others," *Social Psychological and Personality Science* 2, no. 5 (2011): 500–507.
14. Golnaz Sadri, Todd J. Weber, and William A. Gentry, "Empathic Emotion and Leadership Performance: An Empirical Analysis Across 38 Countries," *The Leadership Quarterly* 22, no. 5 (2011): 818–30.
15. Rebecca Schaumberg and Francis J. Flynn, "Uneasy Lies the Head That Wears the Crown: The Link Between Guilt Proneness and Leadership," *Journal of Personality and Social Psychology* 103, no. 2 (2012): 327–42.
16. Karen P. Leith and Roy F. Baumeister, "Empathy, Shame, Guilt, and Narratives of Interpersonal Conflicts: Guilt-Prone People Are Better at Perspective Taking," *Journal of Personality* 66, no. 1 (February 1998): 1–37.
17. Barbora Nevicka, Femke S. Ten Velden, Annebel H. B. De Hoogh, and Annelies E. M. Van Vianen, "Reality at Odds with Perceptions: Narcissistic Leaders and Group Performance," *Psychological Science* 22, no. 10 (2011): 1259–64.
18. Emily Grijalva, Timothy D. Maynes, Katie L. Badura, and Steven W. Whiting, "Examining the 'I' in Team: A Longitudinal Investigation of the Influence of Team Narcissism Composition on Team Outcomes in the NBA," *Academy of Management Journal* 63, no. 1 (2020): 7–33.
19. Jeff Pearlman, "Barry, It's Time to Tell the Truth," ESPN, accessed July 20, 2025, https://www.espn.com/espn/page2/story?page=pearlman/060823; Larry Brown, "Barry Bonds Tries to Explain Why He Was Such a Bad Teammate," Yardbarker, August 5, 2023, https://www.yardbarker.com/mlb/articles/barry_bonds_tries_to_explain_why_he_was_such_a_bad_teammate/s1_127_39099896.
20. CC Sabathia and Ryan Ruocco, *R2C2* (podcast), "The One and Only Barry Bonds," June 30, 2023, 47 min., https://podcasts.apple.com/us/podcast/the-one-and-only-barry-bonds/id1525256191?i=1000618880796.
21. Seth Trachtman, "The Best MLB Players Who Never Won a World Series," Yardbarker, July 14, 2024, https://www.yardbarker.com/mlb/articles/the_best_players_who_never_won_a_world_series/s1_38876993#slide_5.
22. Jessica A. Kennedy, Cameron Anderson, and Don A. Moore, "When

Overconfidence Is Revealed to Others: Testing the Status-Enhancement Theory of Overconfidence," *Organizational Behavior and Human Decision Processes* 122, no. 2 (2013): 266–279.

23. Jill Lobbestael, Arnoud Arntz, Marisol Voncken, and Michael Potegal, "Responses to Dominance Challenge Are a Function of Psychopathy Level: A Multimethod Study," *Personality Disorders: Theory, Research, and Treatment* 9, no. 4 (2018): 305–14.

24. Toshisada Nishida and Kazuhiko Hosaka, "Coalition Strategies Among Adult Male Chimpanzees of the Mahale Mountains, Tanzania," in *Great Ape Societies*, eds. William C. McGrew, Linda F. Marchant, and Toshisada Nishida (Cambridge, UK: Cambridge University Press, 1996), 114–34.

25. Jon K. Maner and Charleen R. Case, "Dominance and Prestige: Dual Strategies for Navigating Social Hierarchies," *Advances in Experimental Social Psychology* 54 (2016): 129–80.

26. Christine A. Kirkman, "From Soap Opera to Science: Towards Gaining Access to the Psychopaths Who Live Amongst Us," *Psychology and Psychotherapy: Theory, Research and Practice* 78, no. 3 (2005): 379–96.

27. Hemant Kakkar and Niro Sivanathan, "When the Appeal of a Dominant Leader Is Greater than a Prestige Leader," *Proceedings of the National Academy of Sciences* 114, no. 26 (2017): 6734–9.

28. Timothy R. Levine, "Truth-Default Theory (TDT): A Theory of Human Deception and Deception Detection," *Journal of Language and Social Psychology* 33, no. 4 (2014): 378–92.

29. Charles F. Bond Jr. and Bella M. DePaulo, "Accuracy of Deception Judgments," *Personality and Social Psychology Review* 10, no. 3 (2006): 214–34.

30. Lyn Garrity, "Five Fake Memoirs That Fooled the Literary World," *Smithsonian*, December 20, 2010, https://www.smithsonianmag.com/arts-culture/five-fake-memoirs-that-fooled-the-literary-world-77092955/; Annie Lowrey, "Don't Build Schools in Afghanistan," *Slate*, May 5, 2011, https://slate.com/business/2011/05/three-cups-of-tea-scandal-the-real-lesson-is-don-t-build-schools-in-afghanistan.html.

31. Christopher A. Gunderson, Alysha Baker, Alona D. Pence, and Leanne ten Brinke, "Interpersonal Consequences of Deceptive Expressions of Sadness," *Personality and Social Psychology Bulletin* 49, no. 1 (2023): 97–109.

32. Peter K. Jonason, Minna Lyons, Holly M. Baughman, and Philip A. Vernon, "What a Tangled Web We Weave: The Dark Triad Traits and Deception," *Personality and Individual Differences* 70 (2014): 117–19.

33. Christopher A. Gunderson, Thanh Viet Anh Vo, Benjamin Harriot, Chloe Kam, and Leanne ten Brinke, "In Search of Duping Delight," *Affective Science* 3, no. 3 (2022): 519–27.

Notes

34. Jessica R. Klaver, Zina Lee, Alicia Spidel, and Stephen D. Hart, "Psychopathy and Deception Detection Using Indirect Measures," *Legal and Criminological Psychology* 14, no. 1 (2009): 171–82; Zina Lee, Jessica R. Klaver, and Stephen D. Hart, "Psychopathy and Verbal Indicators of Deception in Offenders," *Psychology, Crime & Law* 14, no. 1 (2008): 73–84.
35. Kristoph J. Brazil, Chantelle J. Dias, and Adelle E. Forth, "Successful and Selective Exploitation in Psychopathy: Convincing Others and Gaining Trust," *Personality and Individual Differences* 170 (2021): 110394; Kristoph J. Brazil and Adelle E. Forth, "Psychopathy and the Induction of Desire: Formulating and Testing an Evolutionary Hypothesis," *Evolutionary Psychological Science* 6, no. 1 (2020): 64–81.
36. Courtney Shea, "Meet the Women Trying to Catch One of Canada's Most Prolific Romance Scammers," *Chatelaine*, March 27, 2023, https://chatelaine.com/living/romance-scammer-canada-marcel-andre-vautour/.
37. Consistent with the definition of personality traits, the use of deception and superficial charm was clearly a *pattern* of behavior for Vautour. On the same day that he vanished from Jodi's life with vast amounts of her money, he was starting the charade all over again with Rosey (a pseudonym) in Vancouver, British Columbia. And these women were hardly the only ones Vautour duped. His rap sheet goes back decades and includes fraud, possession of stolen property, and auto and identity theft.
38. Albert Bandura, Dorothea Ross, and Sheila A. Ross, "Transmission of Aggression Through Imitation of Aggressive Models," *Journal of Abnormal and Social Psychology* 63, no. 3 (1961): 575–82.
39. Mary Bardes Mawritz, David M. Mayer, Jenny M. Hoobler, Sandy J. Wayne, and Sophia V. Marinova, "A Trickle-Down Model of Abusive Supervision," *Personnel Psychology* 65, no. 2 (2012): 325–57.
40. Tatiana Siegel, "'Everyone Just Knows He's an Absolute Monster': Scott Rudin's Ex-Staffers Speak Out on Abusive Behavior," *The Hollywood Reporter*, April 7, 2021, https://www.hollywoodreporter.com/movies/movie-news/everyone-just-knows-hes-an-absolute-monster-scott-rudins-ex-staffers-speak-out-on-abusive-behavior-4161883/.
41. Anne Victoria Clark, Jackson McHenry, Lila Shapiro, Gazelle Emami, Helen Shaw, Tara Abell, Nate Jones, E. Alex Jung, and Megh Wright, "Scott Rudin, as Told by His Assistants, A Portrait of a Toxic Workplace," *Vulture*, April 22, 2021, https://www.vulture.com/2021/04/scott-rudin-as-told-by-his-assistants.html.
42. Clark et al., "Scott Rudin, as Told."
43. Gerben A. van Kleef, Michele J. Gelfand, and Jolanda Jetten, "The Dynamic Nature of Social Norms: New Perspectives on Norm Development, Impact,

Violation, and Enforcement," *Journal of Experimental Social Psychology* 84 (2019): 103814.
44. Researchers have documented this in relation to academic cheating on the part of students. Peers who cheat corrupt norms, inclining more students to cheat. Donald L. McCabe, Linda Klebe Trevino, and Kenneth Butterfield, "Cheating in Academic Institutions: A Decade of Research," *Ethics & Behavior* 11, no. 3 (2001): 219–32.
45. Arwa Mahdawi, "30 Under 30-Year Sentences: Why So Many of Forbes' Young Heroes Face Jail," *The Guardian*, April 7, 2023, https://www.theguardian.com/business/2023/apr/06/forbes-30-under-30-tech-finance-prison.
46. Christine H. Hansen and Ranald D. Hansen, "Finding the Face in the Crowd: An Anger Superiority Effect," *Journal of Personality and Social Psychology* 54, no. 6 (1988): 917–24; Tiffany A. Ito, Jeff T. Larsen, N. Kyle Smith, John T. Cacioppo, "Negative Information Weighs More Heavily on the Brain: The Negativity Bias in Evaluative Categorizations," *Journal of Personality and Social Psychology* 75, no. 4 (1998): 887–900; Felicia Pratto and Oliver P. John, "Automatic Vigilance: The Attention-Grabbing Power of Negative Social Information," *Journal of Personality and Social Psychology* 61, no. 3 (1991): 380–91.
47. Andrea K. Bellovary, Nathaniel A. Young, and Amit Goldenberg, "Left- and Right-Leaning News Organizations Use Negative Emotional Content and Elicit User Engagement Similarly," *Affective Science* 2, no. 4 (2021): 391–6.
48. Cynthia Mathieu, Craig S. Neumann, Robert D. Hare, and Paul Babiak, "A Dark Side of Leadership: Corporate Psychopathy and Its Influence on Employee Well-Being and Job Satisfaction," *Personality and Individual Differences* 59 (2014): 83–88.
49. Jennifer S. Lerner and Dacher Keltner, "Fear, Anger, and Risk," *Journal of Personality and Social Psychology* 81, no. 1 (2001): 146–59; Tamar Kugler, Terry Connolly, and Lisa D. Ordóñez, "Emotion, Decision, and Risk: Betting on Gambles Versus Betting on People," *Journal of Behavioral Decision Making* 25, no. 2 (2012): 123–34.
50. Amit Goldenberg and James J. Gross, "Digital Emotional Contagion," *Trends in Cognitive Sciences* 24, no. 4 (April 2020): 316–28.
51. Mike Isaac, "Uber's C.E.O. Plays with Fire," *New York Times*, April 23, 2017, https://www.nytimes.com/2017/04/23/technology/travis-kalanick-pushes-uber-and-himself-to-the-precipice.html?_r=0. For a general portrait of Kalanick and Uber's culture, see Robert Eames, "Uber: Kalanick's Tumultuous Era," Ivey Business School Case Study W18144, 2018.
52. Mike Isaac, "Inside Uber's Aggressive, Unrestrained Workplace Culture,"

Notes

New York Times, February 22, 2017, https://www.nytimes.com/2017/02/22/technology/uber-workplace-culture.html.

53. Caroline O'Donovan and Priya Anand, "How Uber's Hard-Charging Corporate Culture Left Employees Drained," *BuzzFeed News*, July 17, 2017, https://www.buzzfeednews.com/article/carolineodonovan/how-ubers-hard-charging-corporate-culture-left-employees.

54. Hemant Kakkar and Niro Sivanathan, "The Impact of Leader Dominance on Employees' Zero-Sum Mindset and Helping Behavior," *Journal of Applied Psychology* 107, no. 10 (2022): 1706–24.

55. Irwin D. Waldman, Seunghyeon Rhee, Devon LoParo, and Y. Park, "Genetic and Environmental Influences on Psychopathy and Antisocial Behavior," in *Handbook of Psychopathy*, ed. C. J. Patrick (New York: Guilford Press, 2006), 205–28.

56. See, for example, Soroush Vosoughi, Deb Roy, and Sinan Aral, "The Spread of True and False News Online," *Science* 359, no. 6380 (2018): 1146–51; Bellovary et al., "Left- and Right-Leaning News Organizations Use Negative Emotional Content and Elicit User Engagement Similarly"; Almog Simchon, William J. Brady, and Jay J. Van Bavel, "Troll and Divide: The Language of Online Polarization," *PNAS Nexus* 1, no. 1 (2022): 1–12.

57. Jin Woo Kim, Andrew Guess, Brendan Nyhan, and Jason Reifler, "The Distorting Prism of Social Media: How Self-Selection and Exposure to Incivility Fuel Online Comment Toxicity," *Journal of Communication* 71, no. 6 (2021): 922–46; Jeremy A. Frimer, Harinder Aujla, Matthew Feinberg, Linda J. Skitka, Karl Aquino, Johannes C. Eichstaedt, and Robb Willer, "Incivility Is Rising Among American Politicians on Twitter," *Social Psychological and Personality Science* 14, no. 2 (2022): 1–11.

58. Matthew E. K. Hall and James N. Druckman, "Norm-Violating Rhetoric Undermines Support for Participatory Inclusiveness and Political Equality Among Trump Supporters," *Proceedings of the National Academy of Sciences* 120, no. 40 (2023): e2311005120.

59. Eduardo Rivera, Enrique Seira, and Saumitra Jha, "Apex Corruption Erodes Democratic Values," May 5, 2025, Stanford University Graduate School of Business Research Paper No. 4166, available at https://ssrn.com/abstract=4828343 or http://dx.doi.org/10.2139/ssrn.4828343.

4: Spotting a Dark Personality in Ten Seconds or Less

1. "Mother Charged in Death of 12-Year-Old Karissa Boudreau," *Globe and Mail*, June 14, 2008, https://www.theglobeandmail.com/news/national/mother-charged-in-death-of-12-year-old-karissa-boudreau/article18452281/.

2. "The Tragic Story of Karissa Boudreau | True Crime Documentary,"

posted September 8, 2023, by Real Crime Explained, YouTube, 25 min., 7 sec., https://www.youtube.com/watch?v=OkLCWyIpYr4. In a second press conference a few days later, Boudreau likewise appealed for Karissa to come home. "Karissa, I just want to tell you that you have lots of people who love you and want you home." "Crime Beat: Karissa Boudreau, up with the angels | S2 E5," posted November 14, 2020, by Crime Beat TV, YouTube, 10 min., 50 sec., https://youtube.com/watch?v=rMqZ7FggSso.

3. "Mother Charged in Death," *Globe and Mail*.
4. Stephen Porter and Leanne ten Brinke, "Reading Between the Lies: Identifying Concealed and Falsified Emotions in Universal Facial Expressions," *Psychological Science* 19, no. 5 (2008): 508–14.
5. Aldert Vrij and Samantha Mann, "Who Killed My Relative? Police Officers' Ability to Detect Real-Life High-Stake Lies," *Psychology, Crime & Law* 7, no. 2 (2001): 119–32.
6. David Matsumoto, Dacher Keltner, Michelle N. Shiota, M. O'Sullivan, and M. Frank, "Facial Expressions of Emotion," *Handbook of Emotions* 3 (2008): 211–34.
7. Paul Ekman, Gowen Roper, and Joseph C. Hager, "Deliberate Facial Movement," *Child Development* 51 (1980): 886–91, https://doi.org/10.2307/1129478; Pierre Gosselin, Mélanie Perron, and Martin Beaupré, "The Voluntary Control of Facial Action Units in Adults," *Emotion* 10 (2010): 266–71, https://doi.org/10.1037/a0017748.
8. William E. Rinn, "The Neuropsychology of Facial Expression: A Review of the Neurological and Psychological Mechanisms for Producing Facial Expressions," *Psychological Bulletin* 95 (1984): 52–77, https://doi.org/10.1037/0033-2909.95.1.52.
9. The previous paragraph reproduces language I used in that original email in the course of describing my analysis.
10. My curiosity about the Penny Boudreau case is described in Maria Konnikova, "How to Tell When Someone Is Lying," *New Yorker*, April 23, 2014, https://www.newyorker.com/science/maria-konnikova/how-to-tell-when-someone-is-lying.
11. Blair Rhodes, "Penny Boudreau Granted More Passes from Prison 16 Years After Killing Daughter," *CBC News*, April 29, 2024, https://www.cbc.ca/news/canada/nova-scotia/penny-bourdeau-prison-passes-permission-convicted-killing-daughter-1.7188432.
12. Both circumstances and personality determine our behavior, including whether we commit heinous crimes. One study of nearly a hundred women who committed murder found that some scored very high on the PCL-R test, while others scored very low or even zero. Ghitta Weizmann-Henelius,

Notes

Hanna Putkonen, Matti Grönroos, Nina Lindberg, Markku Eronen, and Helinä Häkkänen-Nyholm, "Examination of Psychopathy in Female Homicide Offenders—Confirmatory Factor Analysis of the PCL-R," *International Journal of Law and Psychiatry* 33, no. 3 (2010): 177–83.

13. Jon Meacham, "The Presidents on the Presidents: How They Judge One Another," *Time*, February 16, 2014, https://time.com/7801/the-presidents-on-the-presidents-how-they-judge-one-another/.
14. The Global Deception Research Team, "A World of Lies," *Journal of Cross-Cultural Psychology* 37, no. 1 (January 2006): 60–74.
15. Nixon himself admitted lying: James M. Naughton, "Nixon, Conceding He Lies, Says 'Let the American People Down,' Denies Any Crime on Watergate; 'Impeached Myself'; In TV Interview with Frost Former President Says Motives Were Political," *New York Times*, May 5, 1977, https://www.nytimes.com/1977/05/05/archives/nixon-conceding-he-lied-says-ilet-the-american-people-down-denies.html.
16. Bella M. DePaulo, James J. Lindsay, Brian E. Malone, Laura Muhlenbruck, Kelly Charlton, and Harris Cooper, "Cues to Deception," *Psychological Bulletin* 129, no. 1 (2003): 74–118.
17. Richard Bandler and John Grinder, *Frogs into Princes* (Moab, UT: Real People Press, 1979).
18. Richard Wiseman, Caroline Watt, Leanne ten Brinke, Stephen Porter, Sara-Louise Couper, and Calum Rankin, "The Eyes Don't Have It: Lie Detection and Neuro-Linguistic Programming," *PLOS One* 7, no. 7 (2012): e40259.
19. Samantha Mann, Aldert Vrij, and Ray Bull, "Detecting True Lies: Police Officers' Ability to Detect Suspects' Lies," *Journal of Applied Psychology* 89, no. 1 (February 2004): 137–49.
20. Vrij and Mann, "Who Killed My Relative?"; Jaume Masip and Carmen Herrero, "Police Detection of Deception: Beliefs About Behavioral Cues to Deception Are Strong Even Though Contextual Evidence Is More Useful," *Journal of Communication* 65, no. 1 (2015): 125–45.
21. Bruno Verschuere, Chu-Chien Lin, Sara Huismann, Bennett Kleinberg, Marleen Willemse, Emily Chong Jia Mei, Thierry van Goor, Leonie H. S. Löwy, Obed Kwame Appiah, and Ewout Meijer, "The Use-the-Best Heuristic Facilitates Deception Detection," *Nature Human Behaviour* 7 (May 2023): 718–28.
22. Aldert Vrij and Pär-Anders Granhag, "Eliciting Cues to Deception and Truth: What Matters Are the Questions Asked," *Journal of Applied Research in Memory and Cognition* 1, no. 2 (2012): 110–17; Aldert Vrij, Ronald P. Fisher, and Hartmut Blank, "A Cognitive Approach to Lie Detection: A Meta-Analysis," *Legal and Criminological Psychology* 22, no. 1 (2017): 1–21.

23. Vrij et al., "A Cognitive Approach to Lie Detection: A Meta-Analysis"; Aldert Vrij, Samantha A. Mann, Ronald P. Fisher, Sharon Leal, Rebecca Milne, and Ray Bull, "Increasing Cognitive Load to Facilitate Lie Detection: The Benefit of Recalling an Event in Reverse Order," *Law and Human Behavior* 32 (2008): 253–65.
24. "Lance Armstrong & Oprah Winfrey: Interview Transcript," *BBC Sport*, January 18, 2013, https://www.bbc.com/sport/cycling/21065539.
25. "United States Anti-Doping Agency v. Lance Armstrong: Reasoned Decision of the United States Anti-Doping Agency on Disqualification and Ineligibility," October 10, 2012, https://www.usada.org/wp-content/uploads/ReasonedDecision.pdf.
26. Sindri Eldon, "Why Iceland Swapping Out Its Prime Minister Won't Change Anything," *Vice*, April 13, 2016, https://www.vice.com/en/article/sigmundurdav-gunnlaugsson-iceland-sindri-eldon/.
27. You can watch part of that interview here: "Iceland PM Storms Out of Interview When Questioned Re. Tax Haven," interview, April 3, 2016, posted April 4, 2016, by Euronews, YouTube, 1 min., 59 sec., https://www.youtube.com/watch?v=fTdBGdFH8zc. See also Ryan Chittum, "Iceland Prime Minister Tenders Resignation Following Panama Papers Revelations," International Consortium of Investigative Journalists, April 5, 2016, https://www.icij.org/investigations/panama-papers/20160405-iceland-pm-resignation/.
28. DePaulo et al., "Cues to Deception."
29. Maria Hartwig, Pär-Anders Granhag, Leif A. Strömwall, and Ola Kronkvist, "Strategic Use of Evidence During Police Interviews: When Training to Detect Deception Works," *Law and Human Behavior* 30, no. 5 (2006): 603–19.
30. The Canadian Press, "Slain Girl's Mother Charged," *Toronto Star*, June 14, 2008, https://www.thestar.com/news/canada/slain-girls-mother-charged/article_a61d5d10-6efc-5a73-be15-6cb25a615c46.html.
31. Kim B. Serota and Timothy R. Levine, "A Few Prolific Liars: Variation in the Prevalence of Lying," *Journal of Language and Social Psychology* 34, no. 2 (2015): 138–57.
32. Peter K. Jonason, Minna Lyons, Holly M. Baughman, and Philip A. Vernon, "What a Tangled Web We Weave: The Dark Triad Traits and Deception," *Personality and Individual Differences* 70 (2014): 117–19.
33. Tobias Greitemeyer, Niklas Weiß, and Tobias Heuberger, "Are Everyday Sadists Specifically Attracted to Violent Video Games and Do They Emotionally Benefit from Playing Those Games?," *Aggressive Behavior* 45, no. 2 (2019): 206–13.
34. Cathy Spatz Widom, "A Methodology for Studying Noninstitutionalized Psychopaths," *Journal of Consulting and Clinical Psychology* 45, no. 4 (1977): 675.

Notes

35. Jonathan Gay, Scott B. Jackson, and Nicholas Seybert, "Seductive Language for Narcissists in Job Postings," *Management Science* 71, no. 5 (2024), https://doi.org/10.1287/mnsc.2024.05254.
36. Katherine A. Fowler, Scott O. Lilienfeld, and Christopher J. Patrick, "Detecting Psychopathy from Thin Slices of Behavior," *Psychological Assessment* 21, no. 1 (2009): 68–78.
37. Leanne ten Brinke, Stephen Porter, Natasha Korva, Katherine Fowler, Scott O. Lilienfeld, and Christopher J. Patrick, "An Examination of the Communication Styles Associated with Psychopathy and Their Influence on Observer Impressions," *Journal of Nonverbal Behavior* 41, no. 3 (2017): 269–87, https://www.healthline.com/health/duchenne-smile.
38. Christopher A. Gunderson, Thanh Viet Anh Vo, Benjamin Harriot, Chloe Kam, and Leanne ten Brinke, "In Search of Duping Delight," *Affective Science* 3, no. 3 (2022): 519–27.
39. It's not just you who benefits from some structure. Even trained clinicians—psychologists, psychiatrists, and the like—make better, more accurate judgments about the "dangerousness" of other people (i.e., risk assessments) if they have a set of guidelines to inform their decisions. William M. Grove and Paul E. Meehl, "Comparative Efficiency of Informal (Subjective, Impressionistic) and Formal (Mechanical, Algorithmic) Prediction Procedures: The Clinical–Statistical Controversy," *Psychology, Public Policy, and Law* 2, no. 2 (1996): 293–323; J. Monahan, "The Prediction of Violent Behavior," *American Journal of Psychiatry* 141, no. 1 (1984): 10–15.
40. David S. Kosson, Brian L. Steuerwald, Adelle E. Forth, and Katherine J. Kirkhart, "A New Method for Assessing the Interpersonal Behavior of Psychopathic Individuals: Preliminary Validation Studies," *Psychological Assessment* 9, no. 2 (1997): 89–101.
41. Dana R. Carney, C. Randall Colvin, and Judith A. Hall, "A Thin Slice Perspective on the Accuracy of First Impressions," *Journal of Research in Personality* 41 (2007): 1054–72; Peter Borkenau, Nadine Mauer, Rainer Riemann, Frank M. Spinath, and Alois Angleitner, "Thin Slices of Behavior as Cues of Personality and Intelligence," *Journal of Personality and Social Psychology* 86, no. 4 (2004): 599–614.
42. Delroy L. Paulhus, Erin E. Buckels, Paul D. Trapnell, and Daniel N. Jones, "Screening for Dark Personalities: The Short Dark Tetrad (SD4)," *European Journal of Psychological Assessment* 37 (2020): 208–22, https://doi.org/10.1027/1015-5759/a000602. Although this tool was created as a way for people to assess themselves, it turns out that self-ratings and ratings by close friends, family members, and romantic partners are in fact quite similar. You can approximate how other people would rate the darkness of their own personality,

presuming you know them pretty well. Marta Malesza Leuenberger and Magdalena Claudia Kaczmarek, "The Convergent Validity Between Self- and Peer-Ratings of the Dark Triad Personality," *Current Psychology* 39 (2020): 2166–73. Note that this research was completed before the addition of the fourth dark personality, sadism, but there is little reason to think that peer judgments of sadism would perform differently than the other three.

43. Hilary B. Bergsieker, Lisa M. Leslie, Vanessa S. Constantine, and Susan T. Fiske, "Stereotyping by Omission: Eliminate the Negative, Accentuate the Positive," *Journal of Personality and Social Psychology* 102, no. 6 (2012): 1214–38.

44. Alessandro Nai and Jürgen Maier, "Can Anyone Be Objective About Donald Trump? Assessing the Personality of Political Figures," *Journal of Elections, Public Opinion and Parties* 31, no. 3 (2021): 283–308; Aidan P. J. Smyth, Johanna Peetz, and Adrienne A. Capaldi, "Ex-appraisal Bias: Negative Illusions in Appraising Relationship Quality Retrospectively," *Journal of Social and Personal Relationships* 37, no. 5 (2020): 1673–80.

45. Rebecca Woods, "Ian Paterson: Surgeon was 'Psychopathic like Shipman,'" *BBC News*, April 28, 2017, https://www.bbc.com/news/uk-england-birmingham-39580765.

46. "Nottingham Crown Court Sentencing Remarks of Mr. Justice Jeremy Barker, R v. Ian Stuart Paterson," Judiciary of England and Wales, May 31, 2017, https://www.judiciary.uk/wp-content/uploads/2017/05/r-v-paterson-sentencing-remarks-mr-justice-jeremy-baker-20170531.pdf.

47. Dacher Keltner, Gerben A. Van Kleef, Serena Chen, and Michael W. Kraus, "A Reciprocal Influence Model of Social Power: Emerging Principles and Lines of Inquiry," *Advances in Experimental Social Psychology* 40 (2008): 151–92.

48. Alex Press, "It's Time to Weaponize the 'Whisper Network,'" *Vox*, October 17, 2017, https://www.vox.com/first-person/2017/10/16/16482800/harvey-weinstein-sexual-harassment-workplace.

49. Kosson et al., "A New Method for Assessing the Interpersonal Behavior."

50. Nathan Place, "Who Were the 'Ken and Barbie Killers'? The Shocking Crimes of Karla Homolka and Paul Bernardo," *Independent*, December 14, 2021, https://www.independent.co.uk/news/world/americas/ken-barbie-killers-homolka-bernardo-b1975492.html.

51. Christoph Klebl, Joshua J. Rhee, Katharine H. Greenaway, Yin Luo, and Brock Bastian, "Beauty Goes Down to the Core: Attractiveness Biases Moral Character Attributions," *Journal of Nonverbal Behavior* 46 (2022): 83–97; Alice H. Eagly, Richard D. Ashmore, Mona G. Makhijani, and Laura C. Longo, "What Is Beautiful Is Good, But . . . : A Meta-Analytic Review of Research on the Physical Attractiveness Stereotype," *Psychological Bulletin* 110, no. 1 (1991): 109–28.

52. Delroy L. Paulhus, "Interpersonal and Intrapsychic Adaptiveness of Trait Self-Enhancement: A Mixed Blessing," *Journal of Personality and Social Psychology* 74 (1998): 1197–1208; Mitja D. Back, Stefan C. Schmukle, and Boris Egloff, "Why Are Narcissists So Charming at First Sight? Decoding the Narcissism–Popularity Link at Zero Acquaintance," *Journal of Personality and Social Psychology* 98, no. 1 (2010): 132–45.

53. Kristoph J. Brazil and Adelle E. Forth, "Psychopathy and the Induction of Desire: Formulating and Testing an Evolutionary Hypothesis," *Evolutionary Psychological Science* 6, no. 1 (2020): 64–81; Liane J. Leedom, Emily Geslien, and Linda Hartoonian Almas, "'Did he ever love me?' A Qualitative Study of Life with a Psychopathic Husband," *Family and Intimate Partner Violence Quarterly* 5 (2012): 103–35.

54. Thomas L. Griffiths and Joshua B. Tenenbaum, "Optimal Predictions in Everyday Cognition," *Psychological Science* 17, no. 9 (2006): 767–73; Joyce E. Berg, Forrest D. Nelson, and Thomas A. Rietz, "Prediction Market Accuracy in the Long Run," *International Journal of Forecasting* 24, no. 2 (2008): 285–300.

55. Nadav Klein and Nicholas Epley, "Group Discussion Improves Lie Detection," *Proceedings of the National Academy of Sciences* 112, no. 24 (2015): 7460–5.

56. Andrew Beer, "Group Personality Judgments at Zero Acquaintance: Communication Among Judges Versus Aggregation of Independent Evaluations," *Journal of Research in Personality* 47, no. 4 (2013): 385–89.

5: Temporarily Terrible

1. Lee Ross, "The Intuitive Psychologist and His Shortcomings: Distortions in the Attribution Process," *Advances in Experimental Social Psychology* 10 (1977): 173–220.

2. Donald L. McCabe and Linda Klebe Treviño, "Academic Dishonesty: Honor Codes and Other Contextual Influences," *Journal of Higher Education* 64 (1993): 522–38.

3. Simon Gächter and Jonathan F. Schulz, "Intrinsic Honesty and the Prevalence of Rule Violations Across Societies," *Nature* 531, no. 7595 (2016): 496–99; Agne Kajackaite and Uri Gneezy, "Incentives and Cheating," *Games and Economic Behavior* 102 (2017): 433–44.

4. John Dollard, Leonard W. Doob, Neal E. Miller, Orval H. Mowrer, and Robert R. Sears, *Frustration and Aggression* (New Haven, CT: Yale University Press, 1939); Leonard Berkowitz, "Frustration-Aggression Hypothesis: Examination and Reformulation," *Psychological Bulletin* 106, no. 1 (1989): 59–73.

5. Johan Bjureberg and James J. Gross, "Regulating Road Rage," *Social and Personality Psychology Compass* 15 (2021): e12586.

6. Bjureberg and Gross, "Regulating Road Rage."
7. Clare Anderson and Charlotte R. Platten, "Sleep Deprivation Lowers Inhibition and Enhances Impulsivity to Negative Stimuli," *Behavioural Brain Research* 217, no. 2 (2011): 463–66.
8. Els van der Helm, Ninad Gujar, and Matthew P. Walker, "Sleep Deprivation Impairs the Accurate Recognition of Human Emotions," *Sleep* 33, no. 3 (2010): 335–42; Iris B. Mauss, Allison S. Troy, and Monique K. LeBourgeois, "Poorer Sleep Quality Is Associated with Lower Emotion-Regulation Ability in a Laboratory Paradigm," *Cognition & Emotion* 27, no. 3 (2013): 567–76.
9. Amie M. Gordon and Serena Chen, "The Role of Sleep in Interpersonal Conflict: Do Sleepless Nights Mean Worse Fights?," *Social Psychological and Personality Science* 5, no. 2 (2014): 168–75; Ellen T. Kahn-Greene, Erica L. Lipizzi, Amy K. Conrad, Gary H. Kamimori, William D.S. Killgore, "Sleep Deprivation Adversely Affects Interpersonal Responses to Frustration," *Personality and Individual Differences* 41, no. 8 (2006): 1433–43.
10. Michelle A. Short and Nathan Weber, "Sleep Duration and Risk-Taking in Adolescents: A Systematic Review and Meta-Analysis," *Sleep Medicine Reviews* 41 (2018): 185–96; Aimee K. Hildenbrand, Brian P. Daly, Elizabeth Nicholls, Stephanie Brooks-Holliday, and Jacqueline D. Kloss, "Increased Risk for School Violence-Related Behaviors Among Adolescents with Insufficient Sleep," *Journal of School Health* 83, no. 6 (2013): 408–14; Mary Grace Umlauf, John M. Bolland, and Brad E. Lian, "Sleep Disturbance and Risk Behaviors Among Inner-City African-American Adolescents," *Journal of Urban Health* 88 (2011): 1130–42; Meghan L. Royle, Eric J. Connolly, Sara Nowakowski, and Jeff R. Temple, "Sleep Duration, Sleep Quality, and Weapon Carrying in a Sample of Adolescents from Texas," *Preventive Medicine Reports* 35 (2023): 102385.
11. Brad Zuckerman, James Stevenson, and Veira Bailey, "Sleep Problems in Early Childhood: Continuities, Predictive Factors, and Behavioral Correlates," *Pediatrics* 80, no. 5 (1987): 664–71.
12. Rikuya Hosokawa, Riho Tomozawa, Megumi Fujimoto, Sumire Anzai, Mai Sato, Haruko Tazoe, and Toshiki Katsura, "Association Between Sleep Habits and Behavioral Problems in Early Adolescence: A Descriptive Study," *BMC Psychology* 10, no. 1 (2022): 1–11; Børge Sivertsen, Allison G. Harvey, Ted Reichborn-Kjennerud, Leila Torgersen, Eivind Ystrøm, and Mari Hysing, "Later Emotional and Behavioral Problems Associated with Sleep Problems in Toddlers: A Longitudinal Study," *JAMA Pediatrics* 169, no. 6 (2015): 575–82; Perri Klass, "Which Came First? The Behavior Problems, or the Poor Sleep," *New York Times*, October 17, 2016, https://www.nytimes.com/2016/10/17/well/family/which-came-first-the-behavior-problems-or-the-poor-sleep.html.

Notes

13. Viren Swami, Samantha Hochstöger, Erik Kargl, and Stefan Stieger, "Hangry in the Field: An Experience Sampling Study on the Impact of Hunger on Anger, Irritability, and Affect," *PLOS One* 17, no. 7 (2022): e0269629.
14. Jennifer K. MacCormack and Kristen A. Lindquist, "Feeling Hangry? When Hunger Is Conceptualized as Emotion," *Emotion* 19, no. 2 (2019): 301.
15. Catherine A. Anderson, "Temperature and Aggression: Ubiquitous Effects of Heat on Occurrence of Human Violence," *Psychological Bulletin* 106, no. 1 (1989): 74–96.
16. Leonard Berkowitz, "Pain and Aggression: Some Findings and Implications," *Motivation and Emotion* 17 (1993): 277–93; James Rotton and J. Frey, "Air Pollution, Weather, and Violent Crimes: Concomitant Time-Series Analysis of Archival Data," *Journal of Personality and Social Psychology* 49, no. 5 (1985): 1207–20.
17. Jenessa Sprague, Edelyn Verona, Will Kalkhoff, and Ashley Kilmer, "Moderators and Mediators of the Stress-Aggression Relationship: Executive Function and State Anger," *Emotion* 11, no. 1 (2011): 61–73.
18. Edelyn Verona, Naomi Sadeh, and John J. Curtin, "Stress-Induced Asymmetric Frontal Brain Activity and Aggression Risk," *Journal of Abnormal Psychology* 118, no. 1 (2009): 131.
19. Claude M. Steele and Lillian Southwick, "Alcohol and Social Behavior: I. The Psychology of Drunken Excess," *Journal of Personality and Social Psychology* 48, no. 1 (1985): 18–34.
20. Tim Newburn, "The Causes and Consequences of Urban Riot and Unrest," *Annual Review of Criminology* 4 (2021): 53–73; Matthew Radburn and Clifford Stott, "The Psychology of Riots—And Why It's Never Just Mindless Violence," *The Conversation*, November 15, 2019, https://theconversation.com/the-psychology-of-riots-and-why-its-never-just-mindless-violence-125676.
21. Michael Gerson, "There's a Reason Russian Soldiers Can't Look Their Victims in the Face," *Washington Post*, April 22, 2022, https://www.washingtonpost.com/opinions/2022/04/22/russia-ukraine-mass-killings-dehumanize-civilians/.
22. Thomas Gibbons-Neff, "'It Doesn't Count as a War Crime If You Had Fun': Inside the Minds of Some Russian Soldiers," *New York Times*, June 14, 2023, https://www.nytimes.com/2023/06/14/world/europe/ukraine-russia-war-occupied-village.html; Gerson, "There's a Reason."
23. Mina Cikara and Susan T. Fiske, "Their Pain, Our Pleasure: Stereotype Content and Schadenfreude," *Annals of the New York Academy of Sciences* 1299 (2013): 52–59; Mina Cikara, Matthew M. Botvinick, and S. T. Fiske, "Us Versus Them: Social Identity Shapes Neural Responses to Intergroup Competition and Harm," *Psychological Science* 22, no. 3 (2011): 306–13.

24. Russell Spears, "Social Influence and Group Identity," *Annual Review of Psychology* 72 (2021): 367–90; Tom Postmes and Russell Spears, "Deindividuation and Antinormative Behavior: A Meta-Analysis," *Psychological Bulletin* 123, no. 3 (1998): 238–59.
25. *Regina v. Jonathan Mahoney*, "Excerpts from the Proceedings Reasons for Sentence of the Honourable Judge D. St. Pierre," Vancouver, British Columbia, August 15, 2013.
26. *Regina v. Timothy Tin-Chew Kwong*, January 3, 2013, https://www.canlii.org/en/bc/bcpc/doc/2013/2013bcpc8/2013bcpc8.html.
27. *R. v. Kwong*, 2013.
28. Julia Davidson, Mary P. Aiken, Kirsty Phillips, and Ruby Farr, "European Youth Cybercrime, Online Harm and Online Risk Taking: 2022 Research Report," Institute for Connected Communities, University of East London, 2022, https://www.researchgate.net/publication/366016611_European_Youth_Cybercrime_Online_Harm_and_Online_Risk_Taking_2022_Research_Report.
29. Joseph Henrich and Michael Muthukrishna, "The Origins and Psychology of Human Cooperation," *Annual Review of Psychology* 72 (2021): 207–40; Martin Daly and Margo I. Wilson, "Violence Against Stepchildren," *Current Directions in Psychological Science* 5, no. 3 (1996): 77–80; Lisa M. DeBruine, "Facial Resemblance Enhances Trust," *Proceedings of the Royal Society B: Biological Sciences* 269, no. 1498 (2002): 1307–12; Lisa M. DeBruine, "Trustworthy but Not Lust-Worthy: Context-Specific Effects of Facial Resemblance," *Proceedings of the Royal Society B: Biological Sciences* 272, no. 1566 (2005): 919–22.
30. Charlotte S. L. Rossetti and Christian Hilbe, "Direct Reciprocity Among Humans," *Ethology* 130 (2024): e13407, https://doi.org/10.1111/eth.13407.
31. Henrich and Muthukrishna, "The Origins and Psychology of Human Cooperation."
32. Joanna M. Berg, Scott O. Lilienfeld, and Irwin D. Waldman, "Bargaining with the Devil: Using Economic Decision-Making Tasks to Examine the Heterogeneity of Psychopathic Traits," *Journal of Research in Personality* 47, no. 5 (2013): 472–82.
33. Eryk Krysowski and James Tremewan, "Why Does Anonymity Make Us Misbehave: Different Norms or Less Compliance?," *Economic Inquiry* 59, no. 2 (April 2021): 776–89.
34. Edward Diener, Scott C. Fraser, Arthur L. Beaman, and Roger T. Kelem, "Effects of Deindividuation Variables on Stealing Among Halloween Trick-or-Treaters," *Journal of Personality and Social Psychology* 33, no. 2 (1976): 178–83.
35. Anuj K. Shah and Michael LaForest, "Knowledge About Others Reduces One's Own Sense of Anonymity," *Nature* 603, no. 7900 (2022): 297–301.

36. One study of soccer players found that they were penalized more for bad behavior when they were playing rival teams. Gavin J. Kilduff, Adam D. Galinsky, Edoardo Gallo, and J. James Reade, "Whatever It Takes to Win: Rivalry Increases Unethical Behavior," *Academy of Management Journal* 59, no. 5 (2016): 1508–34.
37. Muzafer Sherif, "Experiments in Group Conflict," *Scientific American* 195, no. 5 (1956): 54–59.
38. Samuel L. Gaertner, John F. Dovidio, Brenda S. Banker, Missy Houlette, Kelly M. Johnson, and Elizabeth A. McGlynn, "Reducing Intergroup Conflict: From Superordinate Goals to Decategorization, Recategorization, and Mutual Differentiation," *Group Dynamics: Theory, Research, and Practice* 4, no. 1 (2000): 98–114.
39. Todd Ashker, "Summary: Todd's Short Bio," *Todd Ashker* (blog), August 2015, https://toddashker.wordpress.com/bio/.
40. Tom Gilovich, Dacher Keltner, Serena Chen, and Richard E. Nisbett, *Social Psychology* (New York: W. W. Norton, 2018), 409–10.
41. Inmates in solitary confinement commonly show signs of an imminent nervous breakdown and experience hallucinations. They think about suicide as a way to escape their confinement. Craig Haney, "Restricting the Use of Solitary Confinement," *Annual Review of Criminology* 1, no. 1 (2018): 285–310.
42. M. Alex Johnson, "Almost 30,000 California Inmates in Second Day of Hunger Strike," *NBC News*, July 9, 2013, https://www.nbcnews.com/news/us-news/almost-30-000-california-inmates-second-day-hunger-strike-flna6c10587665.
43. Robyn K. Mallett, Timothy D. Wilson, and Daniel T. Gilbert, "Expect the Unexpected: Failure to Anticipate Similarities Leads to an Intergroup Forecasting Error," *Journal of Personality and Social Psychology* 94, no. 2 (2008): 265–77.
44. Morton Deutsch and Mary Evans Collins, *Interracial Housing: A Psychological Evaluation of a Social Experiment* (Minneapolis: University of Minnesota Press, 1951); Ernest Works, "The Prejudice-Interaction Hypothesis from the Point of View of the Negro Minority Group," *American Journal of Sociology* 67, no. 1 (1961): 47–52; Thomas F. Pettigrew and Linda R. Tropp, "A Meta-Analytic Test of Intergroup Contact Theory," *Journal of Personality and Social Psychology* 90, no. 5 (2006): 751.
45. Sarah E. Gaither and Samuel R. Sommers, "Living with an Other-Race Roommate Shapes Whites' Behavior in Subsequent Diverse Settings," *Journal of Experimental Social Psychology* 49, no. 2 (2013): 272–76.
46. Emile Bruneau, Boaz Hameiri, Samantha L. Moore-Berg, and Nour Kteily, "Intergroup Contact Reduces Dehumanization and Meta-Dehumanization:

Cross-Sectional, Longitudinal, and Quasi-Experimental Evidence from 16 Samples in Five Countries," *Personality and Social Psychology Bulletin* 47, no. 6 (2021): 906–20.

47. Karen Huang, Michael Yeomans, Alison Wood Brooks, Julia Minson, and Francesca Gino, "It Doesn't Hurt to Ask: Question-Asking Increases Liking," *Journal of Personality and Social Psychology* 113, no. 3 (2017): 430–52.

48. M. Audrey Korsgaard, David M. Schweiger, and Harry J. Sapienza, "Building Commitment, Attachment, and Trust in Strategic Decision-Making Teams: The Role of Procedural Justice," *Academy of Management Journal* 38, no. 1 (1995): 60–84.

49. Jillian D. Chown and Christopher C. Liu, "Geography and Power in an Organizational Forum: Evidence from the US Senate Chamber," *Strategic Management Journal* 36, no. 2 (2015): 177–96; Christopher C. Liu and Sameer B. Srivastava, "Pulling Closer and Moving Apart: Interaction, Identity, and Influence in the US Senate, 1973 to 2009," *American Sociological Review* 80, no. 1 (2015): 192–217.

50. B. Ann Bettencourt and Norman Miller, "Gender Differences in Aggression as a Function of Provocation: A Meta-Analysis," *Psychological Bulletin* 119, no. 3 (1996): 422–47.

51. Katherine A. DeCelles, D. Scott DeRue, Joshua D. Margolis, and Tara L. Ceranic, "Does Power Corrupt or Enable? When and Why Power Facilitates Self-Interested Behavior," *Journal of Applied Psychology* 97, no. 3 (2012): 681–89.

52. Solomon E. Asch, "Studies of Independence and Conformity: I. A Minority of One Against a Unanimous Majority," *Psychological Monographs: General and Applied* 70, no. 9 (1956): 1–70. In Asch's conformity studies, participants were much more likely to disagree with the group (and answer the question correctly) if just one other person broke the ice. That is, if another person dissented from the larger group—even if they were also incorrect—the participant was less likely to conform to group pressure. Brett Beasley, "Breaking Conformity: The Power of One Lone Voice," Notre Dame Deloitte Center for Ethical Leadership, accessed July 20, 2025, https://ethicalleadership.nd.edu/news/the-power-of-one-how-a-lone-dissenter-really-can-make-a-difference/.

53. Carl Elliott, "Tuskegee Truth Teller," *American Scholar*, December 4, 2017, https://theamericanscholar.org/tuskegee-truth-teller/.

54. "Remarks by the President in Apology for Study Done in Tuskegee," White House Office of the Press Secretary, May 16, 1997, https://clintonwhitehouse4.archives.gov/New/Remarks/Fri/19970516-898.html.

55. Kimberly Paterson, "Tapping into the Power of Dissent," *Leader's Edge*, April

Notes

30, 2023, https://www.leadersedge.com/brokerage-ops/tapping-into-the-power-of-dissent.

6: Should I Stay or Should I Go?

1. Samantha Joel, Geoff MacDonald, and Elizabeth Page-Gould, "Wanting to Stay and Wanting to Go: Unpacking the Content and Structure of Relationship Stay/Leave Decision Processes," *Social Psychological and Personality Science* 9, no. 6 (2018): 631–44.
2. John Angus D. Hildreth and Cameron Anderson, "Does Loyalty Trump Honesty? Moral Judgments of Loyalty-Driven Deceit," *Journal of Experimental Social Psychology* 79 (2018): 87–94.
3. Dan Pilat and Sekoul Krastev, "Why Do People Support Their Past Ideas, Even When Presented with Evidence That They're Wrong?," *The Decision Lab*, accessed July 20, 2025, https://thedecisionlab.com/biases/commitment-bias.
4. Wendy D. Manning and Pamela J. Smock, "Measuring and Modeling Cohabitation: New Perspectives from Qualitative Data," *Journal of Marriage and Family* 67 (2005): 989–1002; Samantha Joel and Geoff MacDonald, "We're Not That Choosy: Emerging Evidence of a Progression Bias in Romantic Relationships," *Personality and Social Psychology Review* 25, no. 4 (2021): 317–43.
5. Bella M. DePaulo and Wendy L. Morris, "Singles in Society and in Science," *Psychological Inquiry* 16, nos. 2–3 (2005): 57–83.
6. Joel and MacDonald, "We're Not That Choosy."
7. Ingo S. Seifert, Julia M. Rohrer, and Stefan C. Schmukle, "Using Within-Person Change in Three Large Panel Studies to Estimate Personality Age Trajectories," *Journal of Personality and Social Psychology* 126, no. 1 (2023): 150–74; Mark E. Olver and Stephen C. P. Wong, "Short- and Long-Term Recidivism Prediction of the PCL-R and the Effects of Age: A 24-Year Follow-Up," *Personality Disorders: Theory, Research, and Treatment* 6, no. 1 (2015): 97–105.
8. Donna M. Andersen, Emma Veltman, and Martin Sellbom, "Surviving Senior Psychopathy: Informant Reports of Deceit and Antisocial Behavior in Multiple Types of Relationships," *International Journal of Offender Therapy and Comparative Criminology* 66, no. 15 (2022): 1703–25.
9. Robert D. Hare, Danny Clark, Martin Grann, and David Thornton, "Psychopathy and the Predictive Validity of the PCL-R: An International Perspective," *Behavioral Sciences & the Law* 18, no. 5 (2000): 638. Similarly, research finds that treatment in "therapeutic communities" may increase the likelihood of violent reoffending, for offenders with psychopathy: Marnie E. Rice, Grant T. Harris, and Catherine A. Cormier, "An Evaluation of a Maximum Security Therapeutic Community for Psychopaths and Other

Mentally Disordered Offenders," *Law and Human Behavior* 16, no. 4 (1992): 399–412.

10. Mark E. Olver, "Treatment of Psychopathic Offenders: Evidence, Issues, and Controversies," *Journal of Community Safety and Well-Being* 1, no. 3 (2016): 75–82.

11. Georgette E. Fleming, Bryan Neo, Nancy E. Briggs, Silvana Kaouar, Paul J. Frick, and Eva R. Kimonis, "Parent Training Adapted to the Needs of Children with Callous–Unemotional Traits: A Randomized Controlled Trial," *Behavior Therapy* 53, no. 6 (2022): 1265–81.

12. Sara Rego, Joana Arantes, and Paula Magalhães, "Is There a Sunk Cost Effect in Committed Relationships?," *Current Psychology* 37 (2018): 508–19. We also have a status quo bias in that "when it comes to matters of the heart, we tend to love what we currently have." Gul Gunaydin, Emre Selcuk, Cansu Yilmaz, and Cindy Hazan, "I Have, Therefore I Love: Status Quo Preference in Mate Choice," *Personality and Social Psychology Bulletin* 44, no. 4 (2017): 1–12.

13. Zacchariah I. Hamzagic, Daniel G. Derksen, M. Kyle Matsuba, André Aßfalg, and Daniel M. Bernstein, "Harm to Others Reduces the Sunk-Cost Effect," *Memory & Cognition* 49 (2021): 544–56.

14. Giles Harvey, "What Alice Munro Knew," *New York Times*, December 8, 2024, https://www.nytimes.com/2024/12/08/magazine/alice-munro-andrea-skinner-abuse.html.

15. Andrea Robin Skinner, "My Stepfather Sexually Abused Me When I Was a Child. My Mother, Alice Munro, Chose to Stay with Him," *Toronto Star*, July 7, 2024, https://www.thestar.com/opinion/contributors/my-stepfather-sexually-abused-me-when-i-was-a-child-my-mother-alice-munro-chose/article_8415ba7c-3ae0-11ef-83f5-2369a808ea37.html.

16. Ekin Ok, Yi Qian, Brendan Strejcek, and Karl Aquino, "Signaling Virtuous Victimhood as Indicators of Dark Triad Personalities," *Journal of Personality and Social Psychology* 120, no. 6 (2021): 1634–61.

17. Evita March, Cameron S. Kay, Bojana M. Dinić, Danielle Wagstaff, Beáta Grabovac, and Peter K. Jonason, "'It's All in Your Head': Personality Traits and Gaslighting Tactics in Intimate Relationships," *Journal of Family Violence* 40, no. 2 (June 2023): 259–68.

18. Kristoph J. Brazil, Chantelle J. Dias, and Adelle E. Forth, "Successful and Selective Exploitation in Psychopathy: Convincing Others and Gaining Trust," *Personality and Individual Differences* 170 (2021): 110394.

19. Courtney Humeny, Adelle E. Forth, and John Logan, "Psychopathic Traits Predict Survivors' Experiences of Domestic Abuse," *Personality and Individual Differences* 171 (2021): 110497.

20. Paul Babiak, Craig S. Neumann, and Robert D. Hare, "Corporate

Psychopathy: Talking the Walk," *Behavioral Sciences & the Law* 28, no. 2 (2010): 174–93.

21. Mitja D. Back, Stefan C. Schmukle, and Boris Egloff, "Why Are Narcissists So Charming at First Sight? Decoding the Narcissism-Popularity Link at Zero Acquaintance," *Journal of Personality and Social Psychology* 98, no. 1 (2010): 132–45.

22. Angela Book, Kimberly Costello, and Joseph A. Camilleri, "Psychopathy and Victim Selection: The Use of Gait as a Cue to Vulnerability," *Journal of Interpersonal Violence* 28, no. 11 (2013): 2368–83.

23. Donald G. Dutton and Susan Painter, "Emotional Attachments in Abusive Relationships: A Test of Traumatic Bonding Theory," *Violence and Victims* 8, no. 2 (1993): 105–20.

24. The impact doesn't seem severe over the short term, although the consequences might become more apparent as children in divorced families reach their teenage and young adult years, when they might struggle more psychologically, financially, and socially. Paul R. Amato and Bruce Keith, "Parental Divorce and the Well-Being of Children: A Meta-Analysis," *Psychological Bulletin* 110, no. 1 (1991): 26–46.

25. Cheryl Buehler, Christine Anthony, Ambika Krishnakumar, Gaye Stone, Jean Gerard, and Sharon Pemberton, "Interparental Conflict and Youth Problem Behaviors: A Meta-Analysis," *Journal of Child and Family Studies* 6 (1997): 233–47; Joan B. Kelly, "Children's Adjustment in Conflicted Marriage and Divorce: A Decade Review of Research," *Journal of the American Academy of Child & Adolescent Psychiatry* 39, no. 8 (2000): 963–73.

26. Liane J. Leedom, "The Impact of Psychopathy on the Family," in *Psychopathy: New Updates on an Old Phenomenon*, ed. Federico Durbano (Rijeka, Croatia: InTech, 2017), 139–67.

27. Salar Mesdaghinia, "Why Moral Followers Quit: Examining the Role of Leader Bottom-Line Mentality and Unethical Pro-Leader Behavior," *Journal of Business Ethics* 159 (2019): 491–505.

28. Oluremi B. Ayoko, Victor J. Callan, and Charmine E. J. Härtel, "Workplace Conflict, Bullying, and Counterproductive Behaviors," *International Journal of Organizational Analysis* 11, no. 4 (2003): 283–301.

29. Mark E. Olver, "Treatment of Psychopathic Offenders: A Review of Research, Past, and Current Practice," in *Psychopathy and Criminal Behavior: Current Trends and Challenges*, eds. Paulo Barbosa Marques, Mauro Paulino, and Laura Alho (London: Academic Press, 2021), 469–81.

30. Other therapies that rely on similar mechanisms of change—that is, transforming maladaptive thinking and behavioral patterns, including those that originate in childhood—may also prove effective. Violent criminal offenders,

over half of whom had PCL-R scores of 25 or greater, showed a reduction in risk for reoffending and improved temperament after eighteen months of intensive work in a modality called "schema therapy." Farid Chakhssi, Truus Kersten, Corine de Ruiter, and David P. Bernstein, "Treating the Untreatable: A Single Case Study of a Psychopathic Inpatient Treated with Schema Therapy," *Psychotherapy* 51, no. 3 (2014): 447.

31. Jennifer L. Skeem, John Monahan, and Edward P. Mulvey, "Psychopathy, Treatment Involvement, and Subsequent Violence Among Civil Psychiatric Patients," *Law and Human Behavior* 26 (2002): 577–603.
32. James R. P. Ogloff, Stephen Wong, and Anthony Greenwood, "Treating Criminal Psychopaths in a Therapeutic Community Program," *Behavioral Sciences & the Law* 8, no. 2 (1990): 181–90.
33. James F. Hemphill and Stephen D. Hart, "Motivating the Unmotivated: Psychopathy, Treatment, and Change," in *Motivating Offenders to Change: A Guide to Enhancing Engagement in Therapy*, ed. Mary McMurran (Chichester, UK: John Wiley & Sons, 2002), 193–219.
34. Hemphill and Hart, "Motivating the Unmotivated."
35. Mark E. Olver, "Treatment of Psychopathic Offenders: Evidence, Issues, and Controversies," *Journal of Community Safety and Well-Being* 1, no. 3 (2016): 75–82.
36. Eva R. Kimonis, Paul J. Frick, Neil W. Boris, Anna T. Smyke, Amy H. Cornell, Jamie M. Farrell, and Charles H. Zeanah, "Callous-Unemotional Features, Behavioral Inhibition, and Parenting: Independent Predictors of Aggression in a High-Risk Preschool Sample," *Journal of Child and Family Studies* 15, no. 6 (2006): 745–56.
37. Eva R. Kimonis, Georgette Fleming, Nancy Briggs, Lauren Brouwer-French, Paul J. Frick, David J. Hawes, Daniel M. Bagner, Rae Thomas, and Mark Dadds, "Parent-Child Interaction Therapy Adapted for Preschoolers with Callous-Unemotional Traits: An Open Trial Pilot Study," *Journal of Clinical Child & Adolescent Psychology* 48, sup 1 (2019): S347–61.
38. Dr. Daniel Waschbusch (professor at Pennsylvania State University), interview with the author, February 16, 2024.
39. Jacquelyn C. Campbell, Daniel Webster, Jane Koziol-McLain, Carolyn Rebecca Block, Doris Campbell, Mary Ann Curry, Faye Gary, Nancy Glass, Judith McFarlane, Carolyn Sachs, Phyllis Sharps, Yvonne Ulrich, Susan A. Wilt, Jennifer Manganello, Xiao Xu, Janet Schollenberger, Victoria Frye, and Kathryn Laughon, "Risk Factors for Femicide in Abusive Relationships: Results from a Multisite Case Control Study," *American Journal of Public Health* 93, no. 7 (2003): 1089–97.
40. Marcus Juodis, Andrew Starzomski, Stephen Porter, and Michael Woodworth,

Notes

"A Comparison of Domestic and Non-domestic Homicides: Further Evidence for Distinct Dynamics and Heterogeneity of Domestic Homicide Perpetrators," *Journal of Family Violence* 29 (2014): 299–313.

41. "How to Plan for Your Safety if You Are in an Abusive Relationship," Government of Canada, accessed July 20, 2025, https://www.canada.ca/en/public-health/services/health-promotion/stop-family-violence/plan-your-safety.html.
42. Ava Green and Kathy Charles, "Voicing the Victims of Narcissistic Partners: A Qualitative Analysis of Responses to Narcissistic Injury and Self-Esteem Regulation," *Sage Open* 9, no. 2 (2019), https://doi.org/10.1177/2158244019846693.
43. Daniel N. Jones and Delroy L. Paulhus, "Different Provocations Trigger Aggression in Narcissists and Psychopaths," *Social Psychological and Personality Science* 1, no. 1 (2010): 12–18.
44. Justin K. Mogilski and Lisa L. M. Welling, "Staying Friends with an Ex: Sex and Dark Personality Traits Predict Motivations for Post-relationship Friendship," *Personality and Individual Differences* 115 (2017): 114–9.
45. Courtney Humeny, Adelle Forth, and John Logan, "Psychopathic Traits Predict Survivors' Experiences of Domestic Abuse," *Personality and Individual Differences* 171 (2021): 110497.
46. Juodis et al., "A Comparison of Domestic and Non-domestic Homicides."

7: Seven Rules for Managing Poisonous People

1. Marsha M. Linehan, *DBT Skills Training Manual* (New York: Guilford Press, 2014).
2. M. E. Thomas, *Confessions of a Sociopath: A Life Spent Hiding in Plain Sight* (New York: Crown, 2013), 164.
3. L. Maxim Laurijssen, Barbara Wisse, Stacey Sanders, and Ed Sleebos, "How to Neutralize Primary Psychopathic Leaders' Damaging Impact: Rules, Sanctions, and Transparency," *Journal of Business Ethics* 189 (February 2024): 365–83. Originally published February 16, 2023.
4. Amy B. Brunell, William A. Gentry, W. Keith Campbell, Brian J. Hoffman, Karl W. Kuhnert, and Kenneth G. DeMarree, "Leader Emergence: The Case of the Narcissistic Leader," *Personality and Social Psychology Bulletin* 34, no. 12 (2008): 1663–76.
5. Dr. Stephen Wong gave such advice to psychologists working with criminal offenders with psychopathy; even trained professionals benefit from the buddy system. Stephen C. Wong, "A Treatment Framework for Violent Offenders with Psychopathic Traits," in *Handbook of Personality Disorders*, 2nd ed., eds. W. John Livesley and Roseann Larstone (New York: Guilford Press, 2018), 629–44.

6. Anne Lamott, *Crooked Little Heart: A Novel* (New York: Anchor, 2011), 185.
7. Adam Grant, "Anne Lamott's Thoughts on Love, Writing, and Being Judgy," in *ReThinking with Adam Grant*, produced by TED, April 16, 2024, https://www.ted.com/podcasts/rethinking-with-adam-grant/anne-lamott-love-writing-and-being-judgy-transcript; personal communication with E. Svetieva (March 2, 2024).
8. Katherine A. DeCelles, D. Scott DeRue, Joshua D. Margolis, and Tara L. Ceranic, "Does Power Corrupt or Enable? When and Why Power Facilitates Self-Interested Behavior," *Journal of Applied Psychology* 97, no. 3 (2012): 681–89.
9. Ana Guinote, "How Power Affects People: Activating, Wanting, and Goal Seeking," *Annual Review of Psychology* 68 (2017): 353–81.
10. Andrea L. Glenn, Leah M. Efferson, Ravi Iyer, and Jesse Graham, "Values, Goals, and Motivations Associated with Psychopathy," *Journal of Social and Clinical Psychology* 36, no. 2 (2017): 108–25.
11. "New EY US Consulting Study: Employees Overwhelmingly Expect Empathy in the Workplace, but Many Say it Feels Disingenuous," Ernst & Young, March 30, 2023, https://www.ey.com/en_us/newsroom/2023/03/new-ey-us-consulting-study#:~:text=The%20survey%20follows%20the%20initial,even%20company%20revenue%20(83%25).
12. Thomas, *Confessions of a Sociopath*.
13. Max H. Bazerman, "The Mind of the Negotiator: The Mythical Fixed Pie," *Negotiation* 1, no. 1 (November 2003).
14. Leanne ten Brinke, Pamela J. Black, Stephen Porter, Dana R. Carney, "Psychopathic Personality Traits Predict Competitive Wins and Cooperative Losses in Negotiation," *Personality and Individual Differences* 79 (2015): 116–22.
15. Glenn et al., "Values, Goals, and Motivations Associated with Psychopathy."
16. Rodney Perkins, "Klaus Kinski's Legacy Lives on in Jesus Christus Erlöser," Screen Anarchy, July 2, 2008, https://screenanarchy.com/2008/07/klaus-kinski-jesus-christus-erloser.html.
17. Harry de Quetteville, "Widow of German Actor Klaus Kinski Sues Lunatic Asylum," *The Telegraph*, July 30, 2008, https://www.telegraph.co.uk/news/worldnews/europe/germany/2475233/Widow-of-German-actor-Klaus-Kinski-sues-lunatic-asylum.html.
18. *My Best Fiend*, Werner Herzog Filmproduktion, 1999, https://www.youtube.com/watch?v=rB0r8Ol0Hyk.
19. R. James R. Blair, "Neurobiological Basis of Psychopathy," *British Journal of Psychiatry* 182, no. 1 (2003): 5–7.
20. R. James R. Blair, Derek G. V. Mitchell, Alan Leonard, Salima Budhani, Karina S. Peschardt and Craig Newman, "Punishment Avoidance Learning in

Notes

Individuals with Psychopathy: Modulation by Reward but Not by Punishment," *Personality and Individual Differences* 37 (2004): 1179–92.

21. Joseph P. Newman, John J. Curtin, Jeremy D. Bertsch, and Arielle R. Baskin-Sommers, "Attention Moderates the Fearlessness of Psychopathic Offenders," *Biological Psychiatry* 67, no. 1 (2010): 66–70.
22. Kinneret Teodorescu, Ori Plonsky, Shahar Ayal, and Rachel Barkan, "Frequency of Enforcement Is More Important than the Severity of Punishment in Reducing Violation Behaviors," *Proceedings of the National Academy of Sciences* 118, no. 42 (2021): e2108507118.
23. Daniel A. Waschbusch, Michael T. Willoughby, Sarah M. Haas, Ty Ridenour, Sarah Helseth, Kathleen I. Crum, Amy R. Altszuler, J. Megan Ross, Erika K. Coles and William E. Pelham Jr., "Effects of Behavioral Treatment Modified to Fit Children with Conduct Problems and Callous-Unemotional (CU) Traits," *Journal of Clinical Child & Adolescent Psychology* 49, no. 5 (2019): 639–50.
24. Dr. Pevitr Bansal (assistant professor at Montclair State University), interview with the author, February 23, 2024.
25. Tara C. Moore Partin, Rachel E. Robertson, Daniel M. Maggin, Regina M. Oliver, and Joseph H. Wehby, "Using Teacher Praise and Opportunities to Respond to Promote Appropriate Student Behavior," *Preventing School Failure: Alternative Education for Children and Youth* 54, no. 3 (2009): 172–78.
26. Chak Fu Lam, Alexander C. Romney, Daniel W. Newton, and Wen Wu, "Challenging the Status Quo in a Non-Challenging Way: A Dominance Complementarity View of Voice Inquiry," *Personnel Psychology* 77, no. 3 (2024): 1235–64.
27. Mark Olver (professor at the University of Saskatchewan), interview with the author, March 18, 2024.
28. Nathan L. Arbuckle and William A. Cunningham, "Understanding Everyday Psychopathy: Shared Group Identity Leads to Increased Concern for Others Among Undergraduates Higher in Psychopathy," *Social Cognition* 30, no. 5 (2012): 564–83.
29. Daniel N. Jones and Delroy L. Paulhus, "Different Provocations Trigger Aggression in Narcissists and Psychopaths," *Social Psychological and Personality Science* 1, no. 1 (2010): 12–18.
30. Sara Konrath, Brad J. Bushman, and W. Keith Campbell, "Attenuating the Link Between Threatened Egotism and Aggression," *Psychological Science* 17, no. 11 (2006): 995–1001.
31. Eric Novotny, Zachary Carr, Mark G. Frank, S. B. Dietrich, Timothy Shaddock, Megan Cardwell, and Andrea Decker, "How People Really Suspect and Discover Lies," *Journal of Nonverbal Behavior* 42 (2018): 41–52, https://doi

.org/10.1007/s10919-017-0263-2; Hee Sun Park, Timothy Levine, Steven McCornack, Kelly Morrison, and Merissa Ferrara, "How People Really Detect Lies," *Communication Monographs* 69, no. 2 (2010): 144–57, https://doi.org/10.1080/714041710.
32. Paul Babiak, Craig S. Neumann, and Robert D. Hare, "Corporate Psychopathy: Talking the Walk," *Behavioral Sciences & the Law* 28, no. 2 (2010): 174–93.
33. Ruth Beer, Ignacio Rios, and Daniela Saban, "Increased Transparency in Procurement: The Role of Peer Effects," *Management Science* 67, no. 12 (2021): 7511–34.
34. Steven M. Norman, Bruce J. Avolio, and Fred Luthans, "The Impact of Positivity and Transparency on Trust in Leaders and Their Perceived Effectiveness," *The Leadership Quarterly* 21, no. 3 (2010): 350–64; Francis J. Flynn and Chelsea R. Lide, "Communication Miscalibration: The Price Leaders Pay for Not Sharing Enough," *Academy of Management Journal* 66, no. 4 (2023): 1102–22.
35. Stephen Porter, Leanne ten Brinke, and Kevin Wilson, "Crime Profiles and Conditional Release Performance of Psychopathic and Non-psychopathic Sexual Offenders," *Legal and Criminological Psychology* 14, no. 1 (2009): 109–18.
36. Lisa Crossley, Michael Woodworth, Pamela J. Black, and Robert Hare, "The Dark Side of Negotiation: Examining the Outcomes of Face-to-Face and Computer-Mediated Negotiations among Dark Personalities," *Personality and Individual Differences* 91 (2016): 47–51.
37. Dr. Michael Woodworth (professor at the University of British Columbia Okanagan), interview with the author, November 14, 2024.
38. Lyn M. Van Swol, Michael T. Braun, and Miranda R. Kolb, "Deception, Detection, Demeanor, and Truth Bias in Face-to-Face and Computer-Mediated Communication," *Communication Research* 42, no. 8 (2015): 1116–42.
39. Rebecca Onion, "The CIA's 1961 'Personality Sketch' of Nikita Khrushchev," *Slate*, February 21, 2014, https://slate.com/human-interest/2014/02/nikita-khrushchev-the-central-intelligence-agency-s-assessment-of-the-leader-s-personality.html.

8: I'm the Problem, It's Me

1. Yiyi Wang, Paul L. Harris, Meng Pei, and Yanjie Su, "Do Bad People Deserve Empathy? Selective Empathy Based on Targets' Moral Characteristics," *Affective Science* 4, no. 2 (2023): 413–28; Stephen Anderson and C. Daryl Cameron, "How the Self Guides Empathy Choice," *Journal of Experimental Social Psychology* 106 (May 2023): 104444.
2. Keegan D. Greenier, "The Roles of Disliking, Deservingness, and Envy in Predicting Schadenfreude," *Psychological Reports* 124, no. 3 (2021): 1220–36.

Notes

3. Wang et al., "Do Bad People Deserve Empathy?"
4. Dr. Abigail Marsh (professor at Georgetown University), interview with the author, February 15, 2024.
5. Hemant Kakkar and Niro Sivanathan, "The Impact of Leader Dominance on Employees' Zero-Sum Mindset and Helping Behavior," *Journal of Applied Psychology* 107, no. 10 (2022): 1706–24.
6. Nathan W. Hudson, Daniel A. Briley, William J. Chopik, and Jaime Derringer, "You Have to Follow Through: Attaining Behavioral Change Goals Predicts Volitional Personality Change," *Journal of Personality and Social Psychology* 117, no. 4 (2019): 839–57.
7. Nathan W. Hudson, "Lighten the Darkness: Personality Interventions Targeting Agreeableness Also Reduce Participants' Levels of the Dark Triad," *Journal of Personality* 91, no. 4 (2023): 901–16.
8. Bella M. DePaulo, Deborah A. Kashy, Susan E. Kirkendol, Melissa M. Wyer, and Jennifer A. Epstein, "Lying in Everyday Life," *Journal of Personality and Social Psychology* 70, no. 5 (1996): 979–95.
9. Kim B. Serota and Timothy R. Levine, "A Few Prolific Liars: Variation in the Prevalence of Lying," *Journal of Language and Social Psychology* 34, no. 2 (2015), 138–57.
10. Samantha Sprigings, Cameo J. Brown, and Leanne ten Brinke, "Deception Is Associated with Reduced Social Connection," *Communications Psychology* 1, no. 1 (2023): 19. See also our discussion in Elena Svetieva and Leanne ten Brinke, "Be Honest: Little White Lies Are More Harmful Than You Think," *Psyche*, May 10, 2023, https://psyche.co/ideas/be-honest-little-white-lies-are-more-harmful-than-you-think.
11. Elizabeth W. Dunn, Lara B. Aknin, and Michael I. Norton, "Prosocial Spending and Happiness: Using Money to Benefit Others Pays Off," *Current Directions in Psychological Science* 23, no. 1 (2014): 41–47.
12. Nicholas Epley and Juliana Schroeder, "Mistakenly Seeking Solitude," *Journal of Experimental Psychology: General* 143, no. 5 (2014): 1980–99.
13. Amit Kumar and Nicholas Epley, "Undervaluing Gratitude: Expressers Misunderstand the Consequences of Showing Appreciation," *Psychological Science* 29, no. 9 (2018): 1423–35.
14. Teddy Amenabar, "Can You Apologize Too Much? Sorry, But Read This to Find Out," *Washington Post*, April 6, 2023, https://www.washingtonpost.com/wellness/2023/04/06/saying-sorry-apologize-too-much/; Alison Wood Brooks, Hengchen Dai and Maurice E. Schweitzer, "I'm Sorry About the Rain! Superfluous Apologies Demonstrate Empathic Concern and Increase Trust," *Social Psychological and Personality Science* 5, no. 4 (2014): 467–74.
15. Joost M. Leunissen, David De Cremer, Marius van Dijke, and Christopher

P. Reinders Folmer, "Forecasting Errors in the Averseness of Apologizing," *Social Justice Research* 27 (2014): 322–39.

16. Michael E. McCullough, Everett L. Worthington Jr., and Kenneth C. Rachal, "Interpersonal Forgiving in Close Relationships," *Journal of Personality and Social Psychology* 73, no. 2 (1997): 321–36; Ryan Fehr, Michele J. Gelfand, and Monisha Nag, "The Road to Forgiveness: A Meta-Analytic Synthesis of Its Situational and Dispositional Correlates," *Psychological Bulletin* 136, no. 5 (2010): 894–914.

17. Dr. Gabrielle Adams now works at the University of Virginia's Darden School of Business. Leanne ten Brinke and Gabrielle S. Adams, "Saving Face? When Emotion Displays During Public Apologies Mitigate Damage to Organizational Performance," *Organizational Behavior and Human Decision Processes* 130 (2015): 1–12.

18. Adam M. Grant and Francesca Gino, "A Little Thanks Goes a Long Way: Explaining Why Gratitude Expressions Motivate Prosocial Behavior," *Journal of Personality and Social Psychology* 98, no. 6 (2010): 946–55.

19. Bruce Rind and Prashant Bordia, "Effect of Server's 'Thank You' and Personalization on Restaurant Tipping," *Journal of Applied Social Psychology* 25 (1995): 745–51.

20. Grant and Gino, "A Little Thanks Goes a Long Way"; Lawrence K. Ma, Richard J. Tunney, and Eamonn Ferguson, "Does Gratitude Enhance Prosociality?: A Meta-Analytic Review," *Psychological Bulletin* 143, no. 6 (2017): 601–35.

21. Erik C. Nook, Desmond C. Ong, Sylvia A. Morelli, Jason P. Mitchell, and Jamil Zaki, "Prosocial Conformity: Prosocial Norms Generalize Across Behavior and Empathy," *Personality and Social Psychology Bulletin* 42, no. 8 (2016): 1045–62; James H. Fowler and Nicholas A. Christakis, "Cooperative Behavior Cascades in Human Social Networks," *Proceedings of the National Academy of Sciences* 107, no. 12 (March 23, 2010).

22. Martin L. Hoffman, "Altruistic Behavior and the Parent-Child Relationship," *Journal of Personality and Social Psychology* 31, no. 5 (1975): 937–43, https://doi.org/10.1037/h0076825.

23. J. Stuart Ablon (psychologist at Harvard Medical School), interview with the author, September 5, 2023.

24. Kathleen I. Crum, Daniel A. Waschbusch, Daniel M. Bagner, and Stefany Coxe, "Effects of Callous–Unemotional Traits on the Association Between Parenting and Child Conduct Problems," *Child Psychiatry & Human Development* 46 (2015): 967–80.

25. Larissa N. Niec, ed., *Handbook of Parent-Child Interaction Therapy: Innovations and Applications for Research and Practice* (Cham, Switzerland: Springer, 2018).

Notes

26. Corey C. Lieneman, Laurel A. Brabson, April Highlander, Nancy M. Wallace, and Cheryl B. McNeil, "Parent-Child Interaction Therapy: Current Perspectives," *Psychology Research and Behavior Management* 10 (2017): 239–56; Eva R. Kimonis, Georgette Fleming, Nancy Briggs, Lauren Brouwer-French, Paul J. Frick, David J. Hawes, Daniel M. Bagner, Rae Thomas, and Mark Dadds, "Parent-Child Interaction Therapy Adapted for Preschoolers with Callous-Unemotional Traits: An Open Trial Pilot Study," *Journal of Clinical Child & Adolescent Psychology* 48, sup 1 (2019): S347–361.

27. Sheila M. Eyberg, Beverly W. Funderburk, Toni L. Hembree-Kigin, Cheryl B. McNeil, Jane G. Querido, and Korey K. Hood, "Parent-Child Interaction Therapy with Behavior Problem Children: One and Two Year Maintenance of Treatment Effects in the Family," *Child & Family Behavior Therapy* 23, no. 4 (2001). Other treatment programs use similar strategies (modeling, operant conditioning) to encourage positive behavioral change: Amy Datyner, Eva R. Kimonis, Elizabeth Hunt, and Kathleen Armstrong, "Using a Novel Emotional Skills Module to Enhance Empathic Responding for a Child with Conduct Disorder with Limited Prosocial Emotions," *Clinical Case Studies* 15, no. 1 (2016): 35–52; Daniel A. Waschbusch, Michael T. Willoughby, Sarah M. Haas, Ty Ridenour, Sarah Helseth, Kathleen I. Crum, Amy R. Altszuler, J. Megan Ross, Erika K. Coles, and William E. Pelham Jr., "Effects of Behavioral Treatment Modified to Fit Children with Conduct Problems and Callous-Unemotional (CU) Traits," *Journal of Clinical Child & Adolescent Psychology* 49, no. 5 (2019): 639–50.

28. Lieneman et al., "Parent-Child Interaction Therapy."

29. Ben Karpman, "Conscience in the Psychopath: Another Version," *American Journal of Orthopsychiatry* 18 (1948): 455–91; Norman G. Poythress, John F. Edens, Jennifer L. Skeem, Scott O. Lilienfeld, Kevin S. Douglas, Paul J. Frick, Christopher J. Patrick, Monica Epstein, and Tao Wang, "Identifying Subtypes Among Offenders with Antisocial Personality Disorder: A Cluster-Analytic Study," *Journal of Abnormal Psychology* 119 (2010): 389–400; Jennifer L. Skeem, Devon L. Polaschek, Christopher J. Patrick, and Scott O. Lilienfeld, "Psychopathic Personality: Bridging the Gap Between Scientific Evidence and Public Policy," *Psychological Science in the Public Interest* 12, no. 3 (2011): 95–162; Irwin D. Waldman and Seunghyeon Rhee, "Genetic and Environmental Influences on Psychopathy and Antisocial Behavior," in *Handbook of Psychopathy*, ed. Christopher J. Patrick (New York: Guilford Press, 2006), 205–28.

30. Ben Phillips, "'They're Not True Humans': Beliefs About Moral Character Drive Denials of Humanity," *Cognitive Science* 46, no. 2 (2022): e13089.

31. Dr. Mark Olver (professor at the University of Saskatchewan), interview with the author, March 18, 2024.

32. Andrew H. Hales, Matthew P. Kassner, Kipling D. Williams, and William G. Graziano, "Disagreeableness as a Cause and Consequence of Ostracism," *Personality and Social Psychology Bulletin* 42, no. 6 (2016): 782–97.
33. Dr. Mark Olver, interview with the author, March 18, 2024.
34. "Story from David," PsychopathyIs, April 14, 2022, https://psychopathyis.org/personal-stories/story-from-david/.
35. Heidi K. Gardner and Mark Mortenson, "Managers Are Trapped in a Performance-Compassion Dilemma," *Harvard Business Review*, April 7, 2022, https://hbr.org/2022/04/managers-are-trapped-in-a-performance-compassion-dilemma.
36. Rune Stubager, Henrik Bech Seeberg, and Florence So, "One Size Doesn't Fit All: Voter Decision Criteria Heterogeneity and Vote Choice," *Electoral Studies* 52 (2018): 1–10.
37. Tal Axelrod, "Why Some in New Poll Still Want Trump in 2024 Even If He's Criminally Charged," *ABC News*, May 10, 2023, https://abcnews.go.com/Politics/new-poll-trump-2024-criminally-charged/story?id=99201832.
38. Nicholas Coccoma, "The Case for Abolishing Elections," *Boston Review*, November 7, 2022, https://www.bostonreview.net/articles/the-case-for-abolishing-elections/; Adam Grant, "The Worst People Run for Office. It's Time for a Better Way," *New York Times*, August 21, 2023, https://www.nytimes.com/2023/08/21/opinion/elections-democracy.html.
39. Gabriel Adeleye, "The Purpose of Dokimasia," *Greek, Roman, and Byzantine Studies* 24, no. 4 (1983): 295–306.
40. Grant, "The Worst People Run for Office."
41. S. Alexander Haslam, Craig McGarty, Patricia M. Brown, Rachael A. Eggins, Brenda E. Morrison, and Katherine J. Reynolds, "Inspecting the Emperor's Clothes: Evidence That Random Selection of Leaders Can Enhance Group Performance," *Group Dynamics: Theory, Research, and Practice* 2, no. 3 (1998): 168–84.
42. Joël Berger, "How to Prevent Leadership Hubris? Comparing Competitive Selections, Lotteries, and Their Combination," *The Leadership Quarterly* 31 (2020): 101388.
43. Joël Berger, Margit Osterloh, and Katja Rost, "Focal Random Selection Closes the Gender Gap in Competitiveness," *Science Advances* 6, no. 47 (November 2020), https:// doi.org/10.1126/sciadv.abb2142.
44. Johanna Hartung, Martina Bader, Morten Moshagen, and Oliver Wilhelm, "Age and Gender Differences in Socially Aversive ('Dark') Personality Traits," *European Journal of Personality* 36, no. 1 (2022): 3–23.
45. James N. Druckman, Martin J. Kifer, and Michael Parkin, "Timeless Strategy Meets New Medium: Going Negative on Congressional Campaign Web Sites, 2002–2006," *Political Communication* 27, no. 1 (2010): 88–103.

Notes

46. Leslie Graves, "The Pathfinder: Ranked-Choice Voting Coming to More Statewide Ballots in 2024," PBS, December 18, 2023, https://www.pbs.org/wnet/preserving-democracy/2023/12/18/ranked-choice-voting-coming-to-more-statewide-ballots-in-2024/.
47. "Where Is RCV Used?," Ranked Choice Voting Resource Center, accessed July 20, 2025, https://www.rcvresources.org/where-is-rcv-used; "Research and Data on RCV in Practice," FairVote, accessed July 20, 2025, https://fairvote.org/resources/data-on-rcv/.
48. Cynthia Mathieu, Robert D. Hare, Daniel N. Jones, Paul Babiak, and Craig S. Neumann, "Factor Structure of the B-Scan 360: A Measure of Corporate Psychopathy," *Psychological Assessment* 25, no. 1 (2013): 288–93.
49. Leanne ten Brinke, Aimee Kish, and Dacher Keltner, "Hedge Fund Managers with Psychopathic Tendencies Make for Worse Investors," *Personality and Social Psychology Bulletin* 44, no. 2 (2018): 214–23.
50. Andrew B. Blake, Vivian H. Luu, Oleg V. Petrenko, William L. Gardner, Kristie J. N. Moergen, and Maira E. Ezerins, "Let's Agree About Nice Leaders: A Literature Review and Meta-Analysis of Agreeableness and Its Relationship with Leadership Outcomes," *The Leadership Quarterly* 33, no. 1 (2022): 101593.
51. Kevin Freiberg and Jackie Freiberg, "20 Reasons Why Herb Kelleher Was One of the Most Beloved Leaders of Our Time," *Forbes*, January 4, 2019, https://www.forbes.com/sites/kevinandjackiefreiberg/2019/01/04/20-reasons-why-herb-kelleher-was-one-of-the-most-beloved-leaders-of-our-time/.
52. Jane Whitney Gibson and Charles W. Blackwell, "Flying High with Herb Kelleher: A Profile in Charismatic Leadership," *Journal of Leadership Studies* 6, nos. 3–4 (1999): 120–37, 131.
53. Accenture, 2024 annual report, 8.
54. "Accenture CEO Julie Sweet Accepts ADL's Prestigious 2024 Courage Against Hate Award," ADL, March 11, 2024, https://www.adl.org/resources/press-release/accenture-ceo-julie-sweet-accepts-adls-prestigious-2024-courage-against.
55. Accenture 2010–2025, Macrotrends, accessed April 2, 2025, https://www.macrotrends.net/stocks/charts/ACN/accenture/gross-profit.
56. Rebecca L. Schaumberg and Francis J. Flynn, "Uneasy Lies the Head That Wears the Crown: The Link Between Guilt Proneness and Leadership," *Journal of Personality and Social Psychology* 103, no. 2 (2012): 327–42.

Epilogue: The Ultimate Arms Race

1. "Democracy Index 2022," Economist Intelligence Unit, accessed July 20, 2025, https://www.eiu.com/n/campaigns/democracy-index-2022/; "Freedom

Notes

in the World 2023," Freedom House, March 2023, https://freedomhouse.org/sites/default/files/2023-03/FIW_World_2023_DigtalPDF.pdf.

2. Hemant Kakkar and Niro Sivanathan, "The Impact of Leader Dominance on Employees' Zero-Sum Mindset and Helping Behavior," *Journal of Applied Psychology* 107, no. 10 (2022): 1706–24; C. R. Hasty and J. K. Maner, "Dominance, Prestige, and Intergroup Conflict: How and Why Leadership Preferences Change in Response to Social Context," *Evolutionary Behavioral Sciences* 19, no. 1 (2025): 85–113.

3. Henri C. Santos, Michael E. Varnum, and Igor Grossmann, "Global Increases in Individualism," *Psychological Science* 28, no. 9 (2017): 1228–39.

4. Aidan Connaughton and J. J. Moncus, "Around the World, People Who Trust Others Are More Supportive of International Cooperation," Pew Research Center, December 15, 2020, https://www.pewresearch.org/short-reads/2020/12/15/around-the-world-people-who-trust-others-are-more-supportive-of-international-cooperation/; Jean M. Twenge, W. Keith Campbell, and Nathan T. Carter, "Declines in Trust in Others and Confidence in Institutions Among American Adults and Late Adolescents, 1972–2012," *Psychological Science* 25, no. 10 (2014): 1914–23.

5. Hemant Kakkar and Niro Sivanathan, "When the Appeal of a Dominant Leader Is Greater than a Prestige Leader," *Proceedings of the National Academy of Sciences* 114, no. 26 (2017): 6734–39.

6. Jacob Dye and E. Solomon, "Problem of Cheating," in *Encyclopedia of Evolutionary Psychological Science*, eds. Todd K. Shackelford and Viviana A. Shackelford (Springer Nature Switzerland, 2021), https://doi.org/10.1007/978-3-319-19650-3_1210.

7. Camille Bonneaud, Luc Tardy, Mathieu Giraudeau, Geoffrey E. Hill, Kevin J. McGraw, and Alastair J. Wilson, "Evolution of Both Host Resistance and Tolerance to an Emerging Bacterial Pathogen," *Evolution Letters* 3, no. 5 (2019): 544–54.

Index

Ablon, J. Stuart, 189
abuse
   in childhood, 144, 191, 227n53
   domestic violence, 149, 150
   trauma bonding and, 143
Accenture, 204–5
Adams, Gabrielle, 187–88
agreeableness, 33, 99, 135
   challenges, 186
   in leaders, 204
aggression, 114–15, 126
   driving and, 113–16
Aguirre, the Wrath of God, 163, 164
Allison, 150–51
Alsop, Joseph, 175
altruism, 10–11, 48, 189
   identity and, 120
American Psychiatric Association, 38, 221n6
American Psychological Association, 222n23
amygdala, 165
Anderson, Craig, 115
anger, 81, 97, 126
anonymity, 117–22, 125
antagonism, 33–34
Anti-Defamation League, 204
antisociality (bucket 4), 31–34, 39, 47, 48, 53, 61, 112, 206–7, 229n14
   in oneself, 185
antisocial personality disorder (ASPD), 38–39, 226nn52–53
Antisocial Process Screening Device, 233n49
apologizing, 187–88, 191
approach motivation, 115
Armstrong, Lance, 91–92
Aryan Brotherhood, 123–24

Asch, Solomon E., 251n52
Ashker, Todd, 123–24
Athens, 196–97
athletes, 71–72
authoritarianism, 36, 73, 207

Baltimore Orioles, 117
Bandura, Albert, 79
Bankman-Fried, Sam, 80
Bansal, Pevitr, 166
Belmont Report, 129
Bergman, Sven, 92
Bernardo, Paul, 106–7
Biden, Joe, 74
Big Five traits, 99
blood glucose, 114
Bolsonaro, Jair, 51, 53
Bonds, Barry, 71–72
borderline personality disorder, 39
bosses, 138, 154–55, 167, 171
   damages caused by bad behavior in, 62, 79, 81, 137, 145–46
   employee departures due to, 46, 133, 137, 150
   fears about firing, 145–46
   overseeing "bad apple" employees, 162–63, 175
   questions asked by, 125
   rules and, 157
Boston Bruins, 117–18, 126–27
Boston Red Sox, 117
Boudreau, Karissa, 85–88, 93
Boudreau, Penny, 85–89, 93
boundaries, 156–59
Boutilier, Clive Michael, 1–4
Boutilier v. Immigration and Naturalization Service, 2–3

Index

brain
  amygdala in, 165
  rivals and, 117
  stress and, 115
Brian (father of Charlie), 144–45, 176–77
Brooks, Alison Wood, 187
bucket 1 traits (relating to others), 26–27, 32, 34, 37, 39, 45, 47, 60, 229n14
  in oneself, 184
bucket 2 traits (emotions), 27–29, 32, 34, 36, 37, 39, 47, 60, 229n14
  in oneself, 184
bucket 3 traits (risk-taking and impulsiveness), 29–32, 34, 39, 40, 53, 60–61, 81, 229n14
  in oneself, 185
bucket 4 traits (social rules and conventions), 31–34, 39, 47, 48, 53, 112, 206–7, 229n14
  in oneself, 185
Bundy, Ted, 22, 23, 25
Buxtun, Peter, 128–29

callous-unemotional traits and protopsychopathy in children, 8, 56–59, 82, 136, 148, 166, 190, 192, 232n35
  Antisocial Process Screening Device for, 233n49
canceling people, 191–92
Central Intelligence Agency (CIA), 174, 175
CEOs, 133–34, 154, 188, 193, 200–204
Charlie, 144–45, 176–77
charm and charisma, 23, 26, 45, 62–63, 142, 198
Chatelaine, 75
cheating, 91, 121, 208
  academic, 112, 121, 239n44
Chelsea, 154–55
children
  abuse and adverse experiences of, 36, 144, 191, 227n53
  behavioral issues in, 189–90
  callous-unemotional traits and protopsychopathy in, 8, 56–59, 82, 136, 148, 166, 190, 192, 232n35
    Antisocial Process Screening Device for, 233n49
  conduct disorder in, 58–59, 232n35
    Children's Symptom Inventory-4 screening for, 233n49
  empathy and altruism in, 11, 136, 148, 189, 190

lying by, 171
parents' conflicts and divorce and, 143–44, 254n24
playmates for, 128
situational psychopathy and, 121
chimpanzees, 69, 72
Chip, 194
CIA (Central Intelligence Agency), 174, 175
Clark, 130–33, 152
Cleaver, Eldridge, 4
Clinton, Bill, 129
Clinton, Hillary, 51
Cluster B personality disorder, 39
cognitive behavioral therapies, 146
Collaborative Problem Solving, 189
collective wisdom, 108–9
commitment bias, 134
compassion, 15, 22, 190–93
competition, 82, 125
  out-groups and, 117, 122–23
conduct disorder, 58–59, 232n35
  Children's Symptom Inventory-4 screening for, 233n49
Constitution, U.S., 124
cooperative behaviors, 10–11, 208, 209
cortisol, 114
COVID-19 pandemic, 24, 32, 209
Craig, 54–55
credulity, 73–76
crime, criminals, 6–8, 12, 23, 48–51, 135, 192, 241n12
  murder, 6, 7, 22–23, 115, 149, 150, 230n17, 241n12
  reoffending and, 7, 135, 173
  sex, 21–22, 115, 220n1
  societal costs of, 48–51
  solitary confinement and, 124
  therapy and, 146, 147, 167, 206, 254n30
  Trump and, 33
  vulnerable people and, 66, 235n6
CU (callous-unemotional) traits and protopsychopathy in children, 8, 56–59, 82, 136, 148, 166, 190, 192, 232n35
  Antisocial Process Screening Device for, 233n49

dark personalities (poisonous people), 6, 9, 11–16
  detecting, 11–12, 15, 84, 85–109, 210
    in casual acquaintances, 100–104
    Dark Behavior Scanner for, 101–6, 183

Index

first impressions and, 94–100, 106–9, 142
  friends' help in, 107–9
  lying and, 73, 74, 80, 88–94
  Short Dark Tetrad tool for, 100–101, 244n42
  structured approach to, 97–98, 244n39
  verbal and nonverbal cues in, 98–99
  when to steer clear of a colleague or acquaintance, 106
embrace of, 42
harm caused by, 8, 9, 11, 39–40, 42, 43–63, 78–79, 191
resistance and tolerance to, 210–11
rules for managing, 154–78
  avoid face-to-face negotiations, 173–75
  become a detective, 170–73
  don't hand them power over others, 159–60
  emphasize your common identity, 168–70
  establish clear boundaries, 156–59
  look for win-wins, 160–64, 173, 183
  realistic expectations and, 175–78
  use the carrot, not the stick, 164–68
treatment for, 135–36, 146–48
unchanging behavior in, 135–36
understanding, 21–23
see also psychopathy
dark traits, 3, 6, 9, 13, 15, 23, 37
  admiration of, 41–42
  Dark Tetrad of, 37–39, 98
  Machiavellianism, 3, 37–38, 45, 52, 65, 77, 98, 101–2, 186
  narcissism, 3, 6, 37–39, 45, 48, 52, 53, 71, 72, 98, 102, 107, 142, 149, 158, 169, 186, 228n3
  in oneself, 12, 15, 121, 179–205
  sadism, 3, 6, 37, 38, 98, 102–3, 116
  spread of, 64–84, 146, 195
  see also psychopathy
dating, 75, 90, 100, 107, 134
David, 192–93
deception, *see* lying and deception
dehumanization, 116
democracy, 36, 51–53, 73, 83, 207
desegregation, 124–25

Diagnostic and Statistical Manual of Mental Disorders (DSM-5), 221n6
Diana, 76–78, 83, 84
dictator game, 120, 127–28
Dirk, 66–68
domestic violence, 149, 150
dominating behavior, 65–66, 68–70, 73
  fear caused by, 81–82
  pissing contests and, 72, 73
Douglas, William O., 2–6, 8, 26, 29–32
Drexel University, 79
driving, aggressive, 113–16
duping delight, 75
Dworkin, Ronald, 3

Emory University, 95
emotional intelligence (EQ), 160
emotions, 183, 191, 192
  in assessment of others, 105–6
  in bucket 2, 27–29, 32, 34, 36, 37, 39, 47, 60, 184, 229n14
    in oneself, 184
  de-escalating, 125–26
  facial expressions and, 86
  sleep and, 114
empathy, 11, 15, 22, 27, 32, 36, 38, 162, 180, 189, 191, 192
  in children, 11, 136, 148, 189, 190
  for dark personalities, 190–93
  in leaders, 71
  out-groups and, 116
  sleep and, 114
  striving for, 186
environment, 36–37, 115, 225n37, 225n42
Erdoğan, Recep Tayyip, 53
ethics, *see* morality
Eugene, OR, 34, 36
evolution, 40, 80–81, 119, 208, 209
  romantic relationships and, 134–35
expectations, 158–59, 175–78
eye contact, 89

facial expressions
  apologies and, 188
  emotions and, 86
  lying and, 86–89
  smiling, 97
family, 36, 58, 72, 119
  work and, 81
  see also children; parents
fatigue, 114
FBI, 59–61

Index

fear, 81–82, 192
field theory, 225n42
finance industry, 43–46
finches, 209–10
first impressions, 94–100, 142
    updating, 106–9
first responders, 47–48, 53
fixed pie myth, 161
Forbes, 80, 204
Frank, 154–55
Frankfurter, Felix, 4
Freiberg, Kevin and Jackie, 204
Fremlin, Gerald, 137–38
Frey, James, 74
frustration, 113
fundamental attribution error, 112, 121
Fyre Festival, 74

Gacy, John Wayne, 22
games
    dictator, 120, 127–28
    points, 64–65, 234n2
gaslighting, 141–42
gaze, 89, 174
Gene, 181–82
genes, 36, 40, 82, 119, 134–35, 208, 224n37, 227n53
genocides, 116
Georgetown University, 181
Ginny, 30
Gloria, 126
goals, 94, 113
    power and, 159
    shared, 125, 163–64
Goldwater rule, 222n23
good and evil, 206
goodness, 186–90
gossip, 105
Grant, Adam, 197–98
gratitude, 187, 188
Greece, ancient, 196–97
groups
    anonymity in, 117–22, 125
    insider and outsider, 116–17, 122–25, 168, 183
        common identity and, 168–70
guilt, 71, 74, 120, 142, 192
Guinote, Ana, 159
gullibility, 73–76
Gunderson, Chris, 74
Gunnlaugsson, Sigmundur Davíð, 92

Halifax, Nova Scotia, 21, 85
Halloween, 122
Hanssen, Robert, 59–62
Hare, Robert, 25
Harvard University, 90, 95
heat, 115
hedge fund managers, 43–46, 228n3
heroism, 48
Herzog, Werner, 163, 164
Hitler, Adolf, 22
Hobbes, Thomas, 9–10
Hollywood Reporter, 79
Holmes, Elizabeth, 80
Homolka, Karla, 106–7
hostage negotiations, 162
hot weather, 115
Hudson, Nathan, 186
human nature, 9–10, 206
hunger, 114–15
Hunter, Tricia, 17–21, 23, 29, 31, 40–42

Iceland, 92
Immigration and Nationality Act (1952), 2, 3n
Immigration and Naturalization Service (INS), 2
impulsiveness and risk-taking (bucket 3), 29–32, 34, 39, 40, 53, 60–61, 81, 229n14
    in oneself, 185
individualism, 207
in-groups and out-groups, 116–17, 122–25, 168, 183
    common identity and, 168–70
internet, 53
    social media, 82, 207
Interpersonal Measure of Psychopathy (IM-P), 98
interpersonal traits (bucket 1), 26–27, 32, 34, 37, 39, 45, 47, 60, 229n14
    in oneself, 184
investment managers, 43–46, 228n3

job candidates, 91, 95, 100, 193, 194
Jobs, Steve, 42
Jodi, 75, 238n37

Kalanick, Travis, 81
Kelleher, Herb, 204
Kelly, 18–21, 23, 26, 29, 31, 40–41
Keltner, Dacher, 43–45, 52, 228n3
Kendra, 76–78, 83, 84

Index

Kennedy, John F., 174
Kevin, 28–29
Khrushchev, Nikita, 174–75
kindness, 8, 84, 180–81, 186–90, 205
Kinski, Klaus, 163–64
Kwong, Timothy, 117–18

Lamott, Anne, 158
law enforcement
   elite agency for, 110–12, 127
   police officers in, 47
leaders, 7–8, 12–13, 42, 69–72, 207
   agreeable, 204
   bosses, 138, 154–55, 167, 171
      damages caused by bad behavior in, 62, 79, 81, 137, 145–46
      employee departures due to, 46, 133, 137, 150
      fears about firing, 145–46
      overseeing "bad apple" employees, 162–63, 175
      questions asked by, 125
      rules and, 157
   CEOs, 133–34, 154, 188, 193, 200–204
   choosing, 193–200
   empathy in, 71
   Machiavellianism and, 37–38, 65
   personality of, 194, 196
   political, 51–53, 73, 76, 82, 83, 91, 134, 138
      election of, 193–200
   success and, 200–205
   threats to status of, 72
Leedom, Liane, 58
Leviathan (Hobbes), 9–10
Leviev, Simon, 74
Lewin, Kurt, 36, 225n42
life space, 225n42
Lilienfeld, Scott, 223n23
Lincoln, Abraham, 198
Liu, Chris, 125
London Business School, 187–88
love bombing, 65, 142
loyalty, 134
Luke, 56–57
lying and deception, 26–27, 32, 74–76, 80, 141–42, 186–87
   detecting, 73, 74, 80, 88–94, 108–9, 122, 170–72, 174
      facial expressions and, 86–89
      fidgeting and, 89, 174
      verbal cues and, 90

   gaslighting, 141–42
   goals and, 94
   therapy and, 136
   white lies, 94, 186–87

Machiavelli, Niccolò, 37–38, 65
Machiavellianism, 3, 37–38, 45, 52, 65, 77, 98, 101–2, 186
Macron, Emmanuel, 51
Madoff, Bernie, 48–49
managers, *see* bosses
manipulation, 26, 37–38, 52, 62, 81, 136, 142, 150
Mann, Samantha, 86–87
Manson, Charles, 6, 25
manspreading, 68–69
Marsh, Abigail, 181
Martin, 110–11, 127
Marty, 30–32
Mawritz, Mary Bardes, 79
Maya, 27–29
McFarland, Billy, 74
Meghan, 150–52
Melissa, 139–41
Mencius, 10
Merkel, Angela, 51
Million Little Pieces, A (Frey), 74
missing persons, 74, 86–87
   Karissa Boudreau, 85–88, 93
Modi, Narendra, 53
morality, 10–11, 22, 119, 162
   law enforcement agents and, 110–12, 127
   moral identity, 128, 129, 159
   moral superiority, 181
Mortenson, Greg, 74
Munro, Alice, 137–38
murder, 6, 7, 22–23, 115, 149, 150, 230n17, 241n12
Murphy, Bruce Allen, 26

narcissism, 3, 6, 37–39, 45, 48, 52, 53, 71, 72, 98, 102, 107, 142, 149, 158, 169, 186, 228n3
nature and nurture, 36
negative information, noticing of, 80–82
negotiations, 161–62
   face-to-face, 173–75
   hostage, 162
Netanyahu, Benjamin, 53
Neumann, Craig, 35
New York Magazine, 79

Index

New York Times, 57, 61, 81, 198
New York Yankees, 117
Nicholas, 130–33, 138, 152
Nixon, Richard, 89
norms, 80, 81, 112, 127, 129, 157–58, 208

Olver, Mark, 167, 168, 191, 192
Orbán, Viktor, 53
out-groups and in-groups, 116–17, 122–25, 168, 183
    common identity and, 168–70

Panama Papers, 92
parents, 36, 56–59, 82, 121
    conflicts and divorce of, 143–44, 254n24
    empathy and, 189, 190
    Parent-Child Interaction Therapy for, 190
    psychopathic, 144–45
    teenagers and, 171
passive avoidance, 165
Paterson, Ian, 103–4
Paul, 66–68
Paulhus, Delroy L., 100
Pearlman, Jeff, 71
Pennsylvania State University, 148
personality
    development of, 36
    disorders, 24–25
        defined, 221n6
        psychopathy and, 38–39
    of leaders, 194, 196
    as pattern of behavior, 100, 104–5
personality traits, 206
    Big Five, 99
    dark, 3, 6, 9, 13, 15, 23, 37
        admiration of, 41–42
        Dark Tetrad of, 37–39, 98
        Machiavellianism, 3, 37–38, 45, 52, 65, 77, 98, 101–2, 186
        narcissism, 3, 6, 37–39, 45, 48, 52, 53, 71, 72, 98, 102, 107, 142, 149, 158, 169, 186, 228n3
        in oneself, 12, 15, 121, 179–205
        sadism, 3, 6, 37, 38, 98, 102–3, 116
        spread of, 64–84, 146, 195
        see also dark personalities; psychopathy

as enduring, 135
    normal, psychopathic traits linked to, 33–34
pessimists, 9–10
phishing attacks, 74
pissing contests, 72, 73
poisonous people, *see* dark personalities
police officers, 47
politics, 51–53, 73, 76, 82, 83, 91, 134, 138
    candidates and elections in, 193–200
populists, 52–53
posture, 68–69
Powe, Lucas, 29
power, 12, 13, 15, 37–38, 65, 70–71, 79, 127, 198
    corruption and, 159
    goals and, 159
    moral identity and, 128, 159
    threats to, 72
predatory behavior, 66, 108
presidents, U.S., 53
Prince, The (Machiavelli), 37
prosociality, 48, 80, 109, 167, 168, 189, 190, 192, 193, 205, 206–8
psychopathy, 6–7, 13
    callous-unemotional traits and proto-psychopathy in children, 8, 56–59, 82, 136, 148, 166, 190, 192, 232n35
        Antisocial Process Screening Device for, 233n49
    cholesterol theory of, 24–25
    as continuum, 25, 35
    in Dark Behavior Scanner, 101
    in Dark Tetrad, 37
    evolution of, 40
    nature and nurture in, 36
    normal personality traits linked to, 33–34
    personality disorders and, 38–39
    prevalence of, 34–37, 39
    research on, 3, 7, 9, 11
    situational, 36–37, 109, 110–29, 183
        awareness of, 120–21
        driving and, 113–16
        groups and anonymity and, 117–22, 125
        out-groups and, 116–17, 122–25
    sociopathy as synonym for, 226n53

Index

see also dark personalities; dark traits
psychopathy, defining, 2–3, 6, 24–34
  bucket 1 traits (relating to others), 26–27, 32, 34, 37, 39, 45, 47, 60, 229n14
    in oneself, 184
  bucket 2 traits (emotions), 27–29, 32, 34, 36, 37, 39, 47, 60, 229n14
    in oneself, 184
  bucket 3 traits (risk-taking and impulsiveness), 29–32, 34, 39, 40, 53, 60–61, 81, 229n14
    in oneself, 185
  bucket 4 traits (social rules and conventions), 31–34, 39, 47, 48, 53, 61, 112, 206–7, 229n14
    in oneself, 185
  Interpersonal Measure of Psychopathy (IM-P), 98
  Psychopathy Checklist-Revised (PCL-R), 23, 25, 30, 34, 47, 49, 88, 96, 98, 105, 146, 200, 220n1, 232n35, 241n12, 255n30
  Psychopathy Checklist-Screening Version (PCL-SV), 23, 32
  triarchic model for, 221n10
punishment, 94, 117, 147, 164–68, 191–93
Putin, Vladimir, 51, 53

racial segregation, 124–25
ranked-choice voting, 199–200
reframing, 146
relating to others (bucket 1 traits), 26–27, 32, 34, 37, 39, 45, 47, 60, 229n14
  in oneself, 184
relationships, 11–12, 14–15, 54–56, 65, 107, 130–53
  commitment bias in, 134
  conflicted feelings about ending, 133–35
  dating, 75, 90, 100, 107, 134
  evolution and, 134–35
  hard truths about, 133–52
  isolation and, 72
  love bombing in, 65, 142
  making a clean break from, 150, 152
  opportunity costs and, 138
  others affected by, 143–46
  and persistence of dark traits, 135–36
  responsibility for problems in, 141–43
  risks involved in leaving, 149–52
  rules in, 158
  sunk cost fallacy and, 136–38
  therapy and, 146–48
  warning signs in, 139
remorse, 27, 29, 37, 60, 118, 142, 150, 191
reputation, 119–20
resentment, 158–59
rewarding good behavior, 147, 164–68
riots, 115, 116, 118, 126
risk-taking and impulsiveness (bucket 3 traits), 29–32, 34, 39, 40, 53, 60–61, 81, 229n14
  in oneself, 185
road rage, 113–16
Robbers Cave State Park, 123
Rousseau, Jean-Jacques, 10
Rudin, Scott, 79–80
rules, 156–58, 166
rumors, 105, 106
Russia, 32
  Soviet Union, 59–61, 174
  Ukraine and, 116

sadism, 3, 6, 37, 38, 98, 102–3, 116
schadenfreude, 180
scientific research
  on ethical behavior, 10
  on psychopathy, 3, 7, 9, 11
segregation, 124–25
Senate, U.S., 52, 125
sex crimes, 21–22, 115, 220n1
sexual exploitation hypothesis, 75
shame, 120, 191
Shannon, Elaine, 62
sharing, 64–65
Shea, Courtney, 75
Shkreli, Martin, 80
Short Dark Tetrad (SD4), 100–101, 244n42
situational psychopathy, 36–37, 109, 110–29, 183
  awareness of, 120–21
  driving and, 113–16
  groups and anonymity and, 117–22, 125
  out-groups and, 116–17, 122–25
Skinner, Andrea, 137–38
sleep, 114
smiling, 97
social hierarchy, 69
social media, 82, 207

Index

social rules and conventions (bucket 4 traits), 31–34, 39, 47, 48, 53, 61, 112, 206–7, 229n14
    in oneself, 185
social value orientations (SVOs), 64–65
sociopathy, 226n53
solitary confinement, 124
Sorokin, Anna "Delvey," 73–74
Southwest Airlines, 204
Soviet Union, 59–61, 174
Spivey, Ludd, 38
sports
    athletes, 71–72
    rivalry and fan violence, 117–18, 126–27
Srivastava, Sameer, 125
Staci, 54–55
status quo bias, 253n12
Stella, 30–31
Steve, 132–33
stress, 114–15
success
    psychopaths and, 43–48, 227n1
    rethinking, 200–205
sunk cost fallacy, 136–38
Supreme Court, U.S., 2–6, 30–32
Svetieva, Elena, 158–59
Sweet, Julie, 204
syphilis, 128

technology, 208
therapy, 135–36
    criminals and, 146, 147, 167, 206, 254n30
    relationships and, 146–48
    workplace and, 147
Thomas, M. E., 156, 160
Three Cups of Tea (Mortenson), 74
360-degree reviews, 171
Tim, 30
Time, 62
Tinder, 74
Tom, 151–52
Tonia, 126, 172
transparency, 172–73
trauma bonding, 143
Tricia, 17–21, 23, 29, 31, 40–42
Truman, Harry S., 89
Trump, Donald, 32–33, 51, 53, 74, 83, 195, 222n23, 224n30
trust, 73, 119, 170–73, 207, 209

truth-default, 73, 76
Tuskegee Experiment, 128–29
twin studies, 36, 224n37
Twitter, 53

Uber, 81
Ukraine, 116
University of Amsterdam, 90
University of British Columbia, 100, 174
University of California, Berkeley, 5, 7, 43, 161
University of Denver, 50
University of Minnesota, 95
University of North Texas, 35
University of Portsmouth, 86
University of Saskatchewan, 167

Vancouver Canucks, 117–18, 126–27
Vande Velde, Christian, 91
Vautour, Marcel Andre, 75–76, 238n37
Verschuere, Bruno, 90
victimhood, 141
Vince, 139–41
Vise, David, 60
voting, ranked-choice, 199–200
Vrij, Aldert, 86–87
vulnerability, 66, 68, 73, 143, 235n6

war, 116, 117
Waschbusch, Daniel, 148
Washington, George, 53
Washington Post, 32, 187
Welch, Jack, 42
Westen, Peter Kay, 4–6, 8
whisper networks, 105
Widom, Cathy, 95
Winfrey, Oprah, 91, 227n1
Wintris, 92
win-win situations, 160–64, 173, 183
wisdom of the crowd, 108–9
Woodworth, Michael, 174
work, workplace, 7–8, 13, 46–47, 142
    assigning authority in, 159–60
    bosses in, 138, 154–55, 167, 171
    damages caused by bad behavior in, 62, 79, 81, 137, 145–46
    employee departures due to, 46, 133, 137, 150

fears about firing, 145–46
overseeing "bad apple"
employees, 162–63, 175
questions asked by, 125
rules and, 157
choosing leaders in, 193–95
culture of, 129, 194
curiosity and interaction in, 125
home problems caused by, 81
job candidates, 91, 95, 100, 193, 194

risks in leaving, 150
rules in, 156–58
teams in, 71, 125, 193
therapy and, 147
360-degree reviews in, 171
toxic environments in, 78–82, 159, 183
Wright, Frank Lloyd, 38
Wuornos, Aileen, 6

Xunzi, 10